EXAMINATIONS
A Commentary

EXAMINATIONS
A Commentary

J. C. MATHEWS
Senior Lecturer, Department of Educational Research,
University of Lancaster

London
GEORGE ALLEN & UNWIN
Boston   Sydney

George Allen & Unwin (Publishers) Ltd,
40 Museum Street, London WC1A 1LU, UK

George Allen & Unwin (Publishers) Ltd,
Park Lane, Hemel Hempstead, Herts HP2 4TE, UK

Allen & Unwin, Inc.,
Fifty Cross Street, Winchester, Mass. 01890, USA

George Allen & Unwin Australia Pty Ltd,
8 Napier Street, North Sydney, NSW 2060, Australia

First published in 1985.

British Library Cataloguing in Publication Data

Mathews, J. C.
    Examinations: a commentary.
1. Educational tests and measurements
I. Title
371.2′62   LB3051
ISBN 0–04–370160–4
    0–04–370161–2 Pbk.

Library of Congress Cataloging in Publication Data

Mathews, J. C. (John Charles)
    Examinations: a commentary
Bibliography: p. 243
Includes index.
1. High schools—England—Examinations. 2. High schools—
Wales—Examinations. 3. Grading and marking (Students)—England.
4. Grading and marking (Students)—Wales. 5. School credits—England.
6. School credits—Wales. I. Title.
LB3060.26.M38   1985   371.2′6   84–28279
ISBN 0–04–370160–4 (alk. paper)
ISBN 0–04–370161–2 (pbk.: alk. paper)

Set in 10 on 11 point Goudy by V & M Graphics Ltd, Aylesbury, Bucks
and printed in Great Britain by Billing and Sons Ltd, London and Worcester

Contents

Introduction   page   1
1   Origins   4
2   Purposes   18
3   Who Is in Control?   36
4   What Do They Test?   52
5   Design and Production   67
6   The Examining Process   87
7   Techniques of Examining   102
8   Are They Fair? I Social Bias   120
9   Are They Fair? II Comparability   138
10 Standards   165
11 New Ventures: I Recording Personal Achievement   185
12 New Ventures: II Profiles, Graded Tests, Credit
        Accumulation   202
13 What of the Future?   221
Bibliography   243
Index   253

Introduction

On an historical scale examinations are a recent phenomenon, at least in their application to the mass of people. Perhaps not quite so inescapable as death, they form, none the less, part of the experience of most people in the developed countries and increasingly in the developing countries. Seen in their early days as a means of liberation from the inequities of advancement through privilege, patronage and wealth, they now appear to some as a distorting influence on education and careers. It could well be that the next decade will be a critical period for examinations. In some countries there are signs of a decline in their use; indeed, there are instances of outright rejection; in others their use and influence increase. Precipitate rejection of them could be as unwise as slavish reliance on them. In any event, a period of appraisal seems to be called for and this book is designed to contribute to it. This is not to say that the book offers readymade solutions – those of us who have spent many years in the public examination system know only too well that very few of its problems have a single, right solution. So the book is analytical and discursive, rather than prescriptive; at the same time, it points to alternative courses of action and their likely consequences.

I have tried to avoid too solemn an approach; but this is not to deny the importance or seriousness of the subject. Banesh Hofmann (1964, p. 103) puts the point succinctly: 'Testing is no game. It is in deadly earnest ... lives can be warped and careers ruined.' However, those who are engaged in the day-to-day business of examining could not, while retaining their mental balance, dwell excessively on the consequences of their actions. This applies to all professions which touch the lives of people: medical, legal and teaching itself. Nevertheless, it behoves the profession of examining, as all other professions, to give an account of itself, and this is one reason why much of the book takes the form of posing and analysing apparently simple questions such as 'are examinations fair?'

One of the difficulties, however, is that when posing such questions to a profession the answers come back in the language peculiar to that profession. Examining is no exception to this; so I have been at some pains to avoid as far as possible the jargon which the professionals use, or at least the more pretentious parts of it. But it is not possible to convey the concepts of a highly technical activity entirely in everyday language, and where technical terms necessarily arise I have done my best to explain them simply.

I hope that I have avoided bias. There is a danger after a long period of engagement in a profession of polarizing either to the position of unquestioning acceptance of the establishment or to that of an iconoclast. The intention is to provoke a balanced discussion among a variety of people who have an interest: from those who are concerned with determining policy and practice through those responsible for the administration to those at the receiving end, teachers, students and parents.

Many experienced teachers have engaged in examining as committee members and agents of the public examining boards and to them something of what I have written will be already familiar. However, I hope that I have touched sufficiently diverse and novel aspects of examining to provide something of interest to them all. My main concern, after many years as a teacher and in teacher education, has been the lack of provision of courses and supporting material designed to educate teachers in one of the dominating influences on the curriculum of our schools and colleges. This applies to both pre-service and in-service courses. It may be thought that anything so mundane and, to some, distasteful as examinations should occupy an insignificant part of teacher education compared with those elements of it which are more academically respectable. Those who wish to make the study of examinations academically respectable should find little difficulty in doing so; they can involve themselves and their students in highly conceptual and demanding work in its technical, psychological, political and sociological aspects. That is not my main intention; I have tried to set all the many aspects of examining into perspective without obscuring the main issues by too much academic gloss. For those who wish to pursue any aspect in greater detail and depth, I have provided notes and references.

Examinations span all levels of education and nearly all countries, and most of the crucial issues are common to them all. I have drawn where necessary from my work in further and higher education and from examinations in schools abroad. But it has been necessary to confine most of the substance of the text to public examinations in secondary schools in England and Wales. Secondary school examinations now fall within the experience of all teachers at some time, and I feel that those who now teach in further and higher education will find something of use in this book for their own examinations and that it will give them a better understanding of the examining processes through which their applicants have passed. Likewise I hope that my friends and colleagues with whom I have worked in Scotland, also elsewhere in Europe, in Africa, Asia and Australia, will understand the reasons for the geographical restriction and still find interest in what I have written.

I owe so much to those with whom I have worked over the past twenty years that I hardly know where to start my 'thank yous'. Professor Frank Halliwell was primarily responsible for persuading me to undertake the design and operation of the Nuffield chemistry examinations. I have enjoyed a most amicable and fruitful co-operation with the officials of many examination boards at home and overseas, but I must make special reference to the two which have had the most formative influence:

London University and, more recently, the Joint Matriculation Board. All of them have contributed to my admiration for the high standards of technical competence and administration which the officers of examination boards maintain.

Then there are all the teachers who have assisted me as examiners, those whom I met when running courses in examining and many generations of my postgraduate students, who by their research and force of argument helped me to forge a coherent view of examinations. Of these, I make special mention of just one: Dr John Leece, who worked as my research officer for several years, wrote an excellent PhD thesis and after a short period at Newcastle and in the Philippines was tragically drowned on his way to take up a post in Australia.

Finally, I must record my gratitude to four people, each of whom read and criticized parts of the book in draft form: Professor S. Tomlinson and Mr G. M. Forrest, Mr C. Vickerman and Mr R. J. Whittaker. Their help was invaluable, thorough, perceptive and balanced, and I have made many changes for the better in the light of their comments. There are some issues on which our opinions differ, at least in emphasis; for the final version I take sole responsibility.

Acknowledgement

The author and publisher thank the Nuffield Foundation and the Longman Group for permission to reproduce p. 670 of *Revised Nuffield Chemistry. Teachers' Guide II*, 1978.

1

Origins

> The social aims of the system of civil service examinations were to restrict nepotism and to draw into the Imperial service able young men from the villages (Price, 1977, p. xiii).

Opinion on examinations ranges from total opposition through resigned acceptance to a touching faith in them as a pillar supporting the educational system if not society itself. There are few fields of human experience so beset by prejudice, and we would do well to slough off these prejudices and apply some radical questions to our various systems of examination. Before doing so, it is appropriate to devote a few pages to their origins and the ideals from which they are spawned if only to see what went wrong – if indeed anything has gone wrong.

It has become almost commonplace to trace aspects of Western culture to origins in ancient China; competitive entry to a civil service through public examination is but one of them. But the quotation which heads this chapter is apt; it is echoed in the words of many nineteenth-century educators and politicians and found expression in the examinations of the Indian Civil Service, the British military and civil services, the Prussian *Abitur* and French *Baccalauréat* and elsewhere. The parallels with ancient China are close enough. The young men in nineteenth-century Britain may have come from the house of the squire or the mill-owner rather than from the village itself, but the same aim held: to select young men for public or professional service by means other than family connection or a full purse (Halsey *et al.*, 1980). (In passing let it be noted that this new agency for selection was for men only, as were its predecessors; young women did not have access to it. Times have changed, of course, and women now have equal access, in theory at least, to examinations. To what extent this access to the means of selection leads to equality in a subsequent career is another matter.)

Roach's claim (1971) that 'examinations were one of the great inventions of nineteenth century Englishmen' could be countered by the Chinese precedent. But the point of invention or reinvention is academic; the nineteenth century saw the advent of examinations as we know them, and the twentieth has seen their extension to most levels of formal education. However, our reference to Chinese origins requires no apology: there is something in Chinese culture, particularly in recent events, which sharpens and clarifies issues that in the West have tended to become complex and obscure.

Universities and Access to Political Power

Before the advent of the Indian Civil Service examinations, there came the reformation in degree examinations at the universities (Lawson and Silver, 1973) and an increased emphasis on rewards for academic merit – among which was advancement in political and public service. Both Roach (1971) and Montgomery (1965) convincingly identify an interesting link between the increase in academic competition at the universities and of academically qualified politicians during the nineteenth century;[1] and they point to the encouragement which these politicians gave to the use of examinations for access to many other walks of life since it was that vehicle which had carried them at least to the threshold of their own careers.

Access to political power has never rested solely on academic success, even in the nineteenth century, and has further declined since the days of 'that finely spun web that stretched from Balliol to the cabinet room' (Packenham, 1979). But there is still little evidence of widespread political support in Britain for the abolition of examinations as instruments of selection; although some politicians do venture discreet doubts about the need for an examination at the age of 16,[2] and examinations at 11 have greatly declined, largely through political action. This acceptance – indeed encouragement – of public examinations by those in political power may reflect the views of that considerable proportion of people who have gained career success initially by mounting an examination ladder. The higher level of achievement by the children of parents whose own careers have been established in this way is more likely to arise from parental pressure and encouragement than from the parental genes. Whichever it may be, the effect seems to have been the establishment of a strong reproductive drive in the examination system which in the main has defied attempts to reduce its potency.

The university examinations of the last century, intended as they were to produce a small elite in politics and public service, need not concern us at any great length. Our present-day problems lie less with the selection of the very few than with the sifting of the many. Nevertheless, there are some relevant points to be made on the relation between university examination systems and access to the professions in the nineteenth century.

The changes in the tests which led to degrees at our ancient universities are well documented and the details will not be recounted here. In particular, the work of Roach (1971) and Montgomery (1978) sets those changes in the perspective of educational, social and political changes of the time. Nevertheless, there were several underlying features which have been subsequently reflected in examinations at lower levels: the academic substance of those examinations, the acceptance of the principle of competition and advancement by merit, the idea – novel at the time – that a common written test could be applied to many students at the same time, and arising from the common test the increase in the written medium of examinations at the expense of the oral and the practical.

It would be wrong to assert that the *substance* of university examinations changed little during the nineteenth century – there undoubtedly was change; but their essential nature remained. They were tests of intellect. More than that, they were tests set in the framework of knowledge as perceived at the time. The divisions into which the academic world directed their specialist studies: subjects, disciplines, field of study, modes of thought, call them what you will, remained substantially the same despite some mutation into various subspecies and hybrids. The status of each rose or fell with the passage of time and some, such as theology, fell quite a long way; but despite this, and despite fragmentation and regrouping and increases in number, the framework within which the pursuits of the mind were expected to operate remained relatively untouched.

The universities were primarily concerned with things of the mind and in distinguishing men one from another in terms of their ability to use their minds in one or more of the areas of study. They were concerned with the ability to reason and to discuss, to write and to talk. They were not directly concerned with a subsequent effectiveness in the world outside the academic one; indeed, they would have disclaimed any such intention – some still do. The ancient universities, at least, may have claimed a more direct link with matters of the soul and hence with the world to come. That claim was in decline even before Darwin and subsequently has dwindled to a vestige. It is of interest to note, however, that the print of this once-dominant aspect of the ancient universities remains to be seen in the curricula and even the examinations in schools.

Technical and Professional Examinations

It should not be thought that the universities were the only bodies to be developing their curricula and examinations. Particularly in the first half of the nineteenth century the governing bodies of the professions, the Royal Institute of Civil Engineers, the General Medical Council, the Royal Institute of Chemistry, to name but a few, set up systems of examinations by which they controlled entry to the professions and the levels of competence required in order to do so. Dore (1976) makes the point that in those early years 'The standards of competence required by various professions gradually became more precisely defined – at first by the practitioners who established their own means of testing and certifying skills.' Significantly he goes on to say: 'But gradually public authorities took an ever increasing hand' (ibid., p. 15).

At about the same time, mainly through the Royal Society of Arts and later the City and Guilds of London Institute, vocational examinations came into being for those training for trades and crafts. Designed for the increasing number of skilled men demanded by expanding industry and commerce, they were linked on the one hand to the apprenticeship system with origins going back at least to the Middle Ages and to the more recently founded mechanics institutes of the nineteenth century. The shift from apprenticeships at the place of work to institutionalized training, although not total, was significant; it corresponds to the gradual trend to remove training and certification from the professional bodies to the universities and other institutions of higher education. Apprenticeship and learning on the job did not disappear, of course; but the division between theory and practice became more apparent: practice was what was done at work, theory was what went on in schools and other educational institutions.

The move of some of the training from the place of work to the mechanics institutes and their like was quickly followed by a similar move in the system of qualification. At first examinations and certification were conducted by each institution separately,[3] but there soon followed a trend towards more general systems to give a wider currency to the certification; the Union of Lancashire and Cheshire Institutes (1839) is an example. Later the Science and Art Department (1853), the Royal Society of Arts (1854) and, later still, the City and Guilds of London Institute (1878) started examinations in technical education, although with different objectives and emphases, and continued the trend towards a more general national system. It is worthy of note that the function of the examinations was not simply to issue certificates and prizes and to select young people for advancement in trade and industry; a primary function was to 'encourage systematic study and punctuality of attendance among the students at Mechanics Institutes' (Montgomery, 1965, p. 77) and, equally significant, certain of the higher professional classes were 'barred from sitting'.

The Science and Art Department used its examinations linked to prizes, awards and capitation grants to stimulate scientific and technical education in the mechanics institutes mainly for evening work, and in schools for daytime work. The dual function of selection of the most able, and the enforced encouragement of a scientific and technical trend in the curriculum, was as deliberate in this field of education as it was in general education at both secondary and elementary levels. Although the direct financial instrument of payment by results was virtually to disappear by the end of the century, this dual function of examinations remained, based on the assumption that they could fulfil equally well both the evaluation of students and the evaluation of educational institutions.

It is significant that in technical education in Britain the control of examinations was not unified; it lay within a complex of organization, professional, educational, commercial, industrial and political. Although central government through the Science and Art Department and the Board of Education exercised some influence and control, this control was indirect. This tradition has continued and, as we shall see in the next section, shows similarity with the parallel development of examinations for a more general education in schools.

It would be false to set up a dichotomy of academic university examinations on the one hand, and practical professional and craft examinations on the other. Of course, the academic tests of the universities were not without significance in selecting the most able for the various professions, and equally the professional and craft examinations had a strong academic element. A clear line between mental ability and practical effectiveness is not one which can be drawn exactly, if at all. Nevertheless, a distinction between the academic and the directly professional can be perceived; this division is still with us and remains a cause for concern. The Royal Society of Arts is certainly aware of the problem, devoting all three of its Cantor Lectures in 1979 to the theme 'Education for capability', and the shortcomings of academic examinations was a recurring variation on the theme. In the third lecture Burgess (1979, p. 157) says, 'In testing the efficacy of the education provided we shall need to test what it is a student can *do*, rather than what he knows'.

Tests of Merit

The effects of competitive examinations on access to positions of political and professional authority were, on an historical scale, rapid. By the end of the century patronage, although still present in less overt forms, had declined greatly and it seems likely that most people with real power in politics, the civil service and the professions had, at some time, submitted themselves to this new form of selection and owed their positions, at least in part, to success in examinations. There were significant exceptions: the members of the growing Labour and trade union movements, although they subsequently acquired an intellectual Bloomsbury coterie and their own institution of higher education at Nuffield College, Oxford, achieved positions of power by competition more directly related to their function in society. And it is doubtful whether those in authority in business and industry owed much to examinations despite the extraordinary growth of the public schools and the numbers of the sons of the middle classes who attended them.

Whether this new move towards a meritocratic system of selection to positions of authority was for the better is a matter of judgement. Undoubtedly it was received with great enthusiasm. The competitive spirit in institutions of education was widely acclaimed, although as we shall observe later there were some dissenters who foresaw disadvantages, other than the loss of patronage, in using learning and scholarship as an avenue to positions of power, status and wealth.

The early claims made for examinations were profuse but rested on frail evidence. Roach (1971) records an interesting correspondence between Queen Victoria and Gladstone during discussions about the use of competitive examinations for gaining access to civil service posts. The Queen wrote, 'a check ... would be necessary upon the admission of candidates to compete for employment, securing that they should be otherwise eligible, besides the display of knowledge which they may exhibit under examination'. (An early plea for positive discrimination!) To which Gladstone replied: 'Experience at the universities and public schools of this country has shown that in a large majority of cases the test of open examination is also an effectual test of character' (ibid., p. 31). Over a century later we are still making more or less the same assumptions, although with perhaps less Gladstonian certainty on the rights of the matter.

The Locals

Gladstone's assertion not only stood for universities, but also for schools. This, then, is an appropriate point to shift the emphasis to school examinations. Important and influential as they were, examinations in the universities and professional bodies touched but few of the educated populace. Seen in the long term, it is probably on young people under the age of 18 in schools and colleges that they have had the greatest effect. In the United Kingdom, at least, this application of examinations to the young is increasing rather than decreasing,[4] and some discussion of their introduction into schools and their subsequent development can illuminate the present state of affairs.

The inception of the Local Examinations of Oxford and Cambridge universities in the middle of the nineteenth century is well documented (Brereton, 1944; Montgomery, 1965, 1978; Roach, 1971) and only those points which touch on subsequent events and policies will be discussed here. The first point is that these two examinations, first conducted in 1858, marked the beginning of the application of examinations to schools by an external body. There were other, earlier examining bodies concerned with secondary education, the College of Preceptors, for example, but it is from the Oxford and Cambridge Locals that our present system of external examinations for schools can be most directly traced. This does not discredit the initiative of Durham University which started its own 'local' examination in the same year, nor the London University Matriculation which preceded the Oxford and Cambridge Locals. The latter, however, was different in function from the Local examinations and London University did not enter the field until it instituted its Junior and Higher School Certificates early in the twentieth century along with similar examining authorities such as the Joint Matriculation Board of the Northern Universities. From this follows a second point: the external bodies which had the most formative influence on school examinations were essentially *academic*, unlike the College of Preceptors and the Royal Society of Arts, both of which had a vocational base. The reasons for this will be discussed shortly; the point to be made here is that the dichotomy between academic and vocational or functional tests arose early and it was the former which predominated in schools.[5] The reasons for this are clear and not necessarily to be disparaged. They are to be sought in the motives which lay behind the involvement of Oxford and Cambridge universities in school affairs, motives which today are still discernible, some would say dominant, in the influence of universities in public examinations as applied to schools. Foremost among these, and in keeping with the spirit of the times, was the desire to improve the quality of education provided in the middle-class schools,[6] without direct intervention of an outside body, particularly the state. Here we have an early example of the deliberate use of examinations applied by an external body to individual pupils with the express intention of influencing the curriculum provision in schools. There was more to the motives than that, of course: there was also the wish to extend admission to university beyond the students in the small number of the 'great' public schools, thus adding to the other forces already in motion which were tending to break down the boundaries between the aristocratic and middle classes in society at large.

The wish of the universities to display a more popular image appears to have been genuine. It sprang from a desire to appear more egalitarian (by the standards of the time) on the one hand, and on the other to demonstrate to a wider section of the people the worthwhileness of academic studies as purveyed by the universities rather than more directly vocational studies or 'useful knowledge' as they were sometimes called. There can be no doubt of the influence of the universities on public examinations both in schools and for the various services of state. The success of the reforms within the universities themselves convinced several of their influential members that the same reforms could be equally beneficial elsewhere and a system of examinations for schools was one of them.

It will not be altogether surprising to those who know the two universities in question to learn that the discussions which preceded the introduction of the Locals were not so much concerned with the desirability of intervention in the affairs of schools, nor of the substance of the examinations themselves, as with the title of the award and the place of religious knowledge in the requirements (Roach, 1971). Indeed, so sure were the originators of their role that direct inspection of the schools was canvassed both as complementary to the examinations and as an alternative to them.[7]

It was also a characteristic of the times that the establishment of a system which was to have a profound and prolonged effect on schools nationally – and soon internationally – came to pass through the initiative and drive of a very small number of people, and not through government. This was typical of the Victorian cult of the individual entrepreneur in commerce and industry, and it had its reflections in education. In connection with the Locals the name of Frederick Temple was probably the most prominent. Those were times when such matters were executed with a sureness and boldness which is breathtaking to those who, in recent years, have been concerned with discussions on changes to school examinations.[8] Of course, it would be incorrect to suppose that the introduction of the Locals was entirely innovatory or the work of one man. Much experience of examining was already to hand in the work of the College of Preceptors and the Society of Arts and, more directly, in the work of the Exeter Committee.[9]

After an uncertain start, the external examining of pupils in middle-class (secondary) schools was well under way by the end of the century in the United Kingdom and subsequent events have increased it to such an extent that it appears to carry all opposition by its own momentum, to the dismay of those who wish to stop or at least reform it. But we do well to summarize and reconsider the motives of those who started it. They were threefold: to improve academic standards, to provide an objective system of selection and to 'bring forward able boys and girls from a lower social level' (Roach, 1971, p. 9); these are themes which will recur in this book. So quite openly the examinations were intended to be used to change the curriculum in schools, and to change society, as well as to provide certificates; a commitment to social and curriculum engineering which would be unthinkable in some countries today.

The Elementary Schools

Examinations in elementary schools embodied essential differences from those of the middle-class or secondary schools. For one thing, they were established directly by government, not delegated, and they were conducted by visiting inspectors appointed by the state rather than by the remote control of the Locals through the universities. The substance of the examinations (reading, writing and arithmetic) was much more restricted and the level of attainment was lower. But the elementary school examinations of the Revised Code of 1862 did have some things in common with the Locals and with technical and vocational examinations. They were intended to improve the standards of teaching, by bringing pressure to bear on both teachers and managers, and to improve the level of attendance and thus provide educational advancement for those who otherwise would have left with little or no schooling. It is difficult to find a good word for the Revised Code. The financial pressure which was its main source of motivation appears to have been much less acceptable than the more subtle academic pressure of the universities through the Locals. Yet the same principle applied to technical education has attracted much less attention (Montgomery, 1965).

Clearly there were limits to which the laws of the market could be applied to education, even in the nineteenth century, and a return now to anything like the Revised Code would be out of the question. But did no one, or no school, benefit from the application of those tests? Would not some children have remained illiterate, never to read a book, if the Revised Code had not come into force? Obviously there must be better means than tests and financial sanctions and rewards by which teachers and schools can be held to account and pupils encouraged to learn; but in the light of the present 'back to basics' movement we may be concerned more about the means of the Revised Code than its ends.

Darwinism

There were common driving-forces in the nineteenth century behind the growth of examinations at all levels. Perhaps the most significant was the great surge of competitive energy which marked much of that extraordinary century, which can be marked in so many areas of human activity – the political, commercial and imperial, even in competitive games. Reference to games is not as trivial as it may appear. The idea of selection through competition, with all its Darwin-like implications, permeated society or at least that part of society which had raised itself above the level of destitution. As Roach (1971, p. 16) says: 'The idea of competition was in accord with the spirit of the age.' The widely held opinion that competition, in whatever form, refined the character for the better provided the advocates of examinations with a strong argument.

While academic criteria through competitive examinations undoubtedly held pride of place for advancement of individuals from mid-century onwards, other criteria also applied. Honey (1977, p. 111) quotes the principal of Brasenose College, Oxford, as saying, 'anyone who had been in the Eton Eight or in the cricket eleven of any Public School was accepted as an undergraduate without any fuss as to a matriculation exam'. The eruption of athleticism in the mid-nineteenth century is discussed by Mangan (1981), who relates the extraordinary changes which took place in the leisuretime activities in the public schools, both old and new, within a short space of years. From rural pursuits which ranged from country rambles to the killing of nearly any creature which moved (including robins!) (ibid., pp. 18, 20), these schools moved deliberately to organized games – much to the relief, one imagines, of the local wildlife. It is worth mentioning in passing that many of the competitive games, which now occupy so much of the leisure pursuits of people throughout the world arose, or gained impetus, from the Victorian public schools. Not only were these games regularized into more or less their present form, they provided an alternative vehicle for competition and advancement to that of scholarship. The latter having already been made respectable by Dr Arnold, competition through games followed on closely. The parallels are close: not only were games included in the curriculum, they became compulsory and provided a non-academic system of selection for the 'glittering prizes' of university and career (Baldwin, 1983). There was, of course, a strong emphasis on playing the game rather than on the result (the process rather than the product curriculum!); but one suspects that the result was not as unimportant as contemporary writers would have us believe.

The dominance of the written, academic mode of competition has persisted until the present time. There are other forms of competition, of course, and these will be considered in turn; but, while on the subject of competitive physical activities, the search for status for physical education, at secondary and higher levels, through entry into the examination system should be noted (Madeley, 1979). In its heyday physical activity, certainly in the form of competitive games, needed no such prop to maintain its high status in the curriculum; now, it seems, some physical educators feel the need for academic respectability.

Mangan (1981) makes another important point when he remarks that the conditions of the mid-nineteenth century were not simply those of individual competition, but of the growth of collective responsibility. Just as the activities and natural competitiveness of professional people became regulated in the professional institutions which were established throughout the century, so did academic competition become regulated in examination institutions. So, finally, did physical pursuits and competition move from the anarchy of fisticuffs, bullying and poaching to established organizations which controlled and regulated the competition and awarded the prizes. This formalization of competition among the young, be it academic or physical, is important; because, once established and regulated, it becomes more than a little difficult to disestablish or reform it. The institutions necessary for its control show a powerful resistance to change.

Personal Qualities

Coupled with formalized tests of academic merit and tests of ability in games was another domain of testing, less formalized, but nevertheless overt, in the public and grammar schools of the period. It is difficult to put a name to it. The term 'affective', much in vogue, almost covers it, in the sense that it was concerned with attributes of personality and character such as enthusiasm, dedication, persistence and the development of a set of values. But in the nineteenth century is was rather more; those attributes which then attracted approval, and which now may not, included conformity, loyalty, leadership and service, together with those qualities which can be attributed to the 'Christian gentleman'.

There was another set of tests to which nineteenth-century youth were subjected and in which, with the exception of a vocal and literate minority, they acquiesced. This is what Mangan (1981) has called 'social Darwinism' – the selection of those most fitted to 'get things done' both at school and in later life. The criteria involved in the social Darwinism of the time were many and complex. 'Manliness' predominated, linked inevitably with prowess at games. But there was more to it than that; the ability to progress, or even survive, in the hard communal life of the Victorian school was taken to indicate the ability to 'get on' in the equally hard world of the entrepreneur, soldier, or district officer of the Victorian empire. This rather strange blend of individual ruggedness and thrust together with collective loyalty and conformity was subject to none of the standardized personality testing of modern times. None the less, the standards were there, and so were the tests and the rewards: 'A boy who, at nineteen, can rule a house at a public school, at fifty can rule a nation' (Taylor, 1912, quoted by Mangan, 1981, p. 148).

What was true of the public school was not necessarily so for the rest of society; but it was not confined to the small aristocratic group who attended the nine schools which were the subject of the Clarendon Commission (Honey, 1977). Even in the early nineteenth century higher education had not been entirely confined to the rich and aristocratic. There was a trickle from the grammar schools who, through endowed exhibitions and scholarships, found their way by merit to Oxford and Cambridge. The son of a Lancaster carpenter, subsequently Dr William Whewell, in 1812 won by examination an exhibition to Trinity College, Cambridge (worth £40 4s 9½d in the first year). Nor were young Whewell's competitive talents confined to the classics and mathematics; a prize-fighter said of him, 'What a man was lost to the ring when they made you a professor' (Humber, 1968, p. 30).[10] It is natural that those who clawed their way from poverty and obscurity to distinction should seek to extend that opportunity to others. Whewell, who as Master of Trinity College was a leader in university reform, was not alone in this.

The mushroom-like growth of the various kinds of public school in the latter part of the century ensured that the competitive spirit – academic, social and athletic – extended to greatly increased numbers of the middle classes. And it did not stop there. Honey (1977, p. 120) notes that the Endowed School Act 1869 'facilitated the extension of the public-school model to a larger number of old established but essentially local schools'. Nor was the competitive spirit confined to Britain; it found its way to various parts of the Empire, where traces still remain in some of the older foundations.[11]

Competitions for the Lower Orders

But what of the 'lower orders'? Academic competition of a sort was available, at least to some: the growth of examinations through the Royal Society of Arts and the City and Guilds of London Institute has already been noted, giving access to the more lowly paid jobs in industry and commerce. After 1862, there was a different kind of competition in the tests of literacy and numeracy by means of which the children of the poor could work their way through the standards of the elementary schools. Subsequently these tests gave access for a few, through competitive scholarships, to the grammar schools and the first rung of another tall, academic ladder to higher education and the professions.

There was competition too for the lower classes in non-academic fields. In earlier days the competitive action, which filled what little leisuretime they had, was as violent and bloodthirsty as that of their lords. This was so well into the nineteenth century. Bailey (1978, p. 8) quotes a visiting Frenchman who, on witnessing a game of 'football' in Derby in 1829, was moved to say, 'if Englishmen called this playing, it would be impossible to say what they would call fighting'. Cockfighting and pugilism, although encouraged and supported by the aristocracy, were essentially conducted by the working classes as were many other equally bloody competitive pursuits. And just as the competitive leisure activities at school of the aristocracy and middle classes became less bloodthirsty and more formalized, so did those of the working classes; Bailey notes the growth of organized pigeon-racing and the advent of brass band contests at Belle Vue in Manchester, to name but two. The fighting of English gamecocks gave way to showing them at the many agricultural shows, which multiplied during the century. The element of competition still was there; there were prizes and fame to be won. But although the general trend to ritualize and formalize what appears to be a natural violence in human nature was common throughout society, and manifesting itself in similar ways, there were significant differences between the rewards of these competitions at different levels of society. Whereas success in pigeon-racing or brass band competitions led to a little local fame, they could hardly aspire to the status and national rewards of the academicism and athleticism of the public schools of the middle class and aristocracy.

The social barriers in academic and non-academic competition were high. The working classes *could* gain access through academic competition to higher education; there are some notable examples, but they are rare. And access through athleticism and other forms of competition was just as difficult. Indeed, much effort was expended to exclude the working classes from the newly formalized games of the public schools and universities. The Amateur Athletic Club (1866) in its definition of 'amateur' specifically excluded the 'mechanic, artisan, and labourer' (ibid., p. 131). The sanctions were largely economic; lack of money and lack of leisuretime made it virtually impossible for the working classes to join with the rest of society in equal competition in academic or non-academic pursuits. This state of affairs became eroded with time, with the growth of professionalism and the introduction of the short Saturday (see ibid.), which marked the beginning of the modern weekend and more leisuretime for all. (Nowhere was this more swiftly marked than in the Football Association, in which payment to players and thus access for the working class came relatively early.) But for the most part the distinction between the classes in competitive games was as acute in competitive games as it was in academic competition:

> Physical education for working class children meant not games but drill ... Drill found its way into the school's curriculum and, unlike sport, qualified for a grant. (ibid., p. 130)

Persistent Problems

In the formative years of the examinations of the last century can be seen the infant shape and nearly all the characteristics of our present examination systems. The same elements are there, the same strengths and weaknesses. Of course, there have been changes in scale and scope, and sometimes in technique, but having read the arguments put for and against examinations in the nineteenth century, one listens to discussions in the fading years of the twentieth with a strong sense of *déjà vu*. It would be well, therefore, to end this chapter by picking out those elements of the history of examinations which continue in our present debates. Why do we have them? Who should be subjected to examinations? Where, when and how should examinations be applied? And there are some related questions still to be asked, now as they were 100 years ago. Are examinations fair? Could they work better? Should we have them at all? If not, are there any alternatives? These questions will be the concern of subsequent chapters, but before proceeding with them it is desirable to identify at least one feature of the growth of the early examination system which is particularly relevant to the present day. Chief among them is the early trend from the particular and the personal to the general and impersonal. This is not quite the same as a move from the subjective to the objective; rather it marks a move from idiosyncrasy to uniformity. At one end of the scale there is the promotion of an individual by a single patron or the viva voce examining of one student by one examiner; at the other there is the mass examination at some distance from a centre, started by the Oxford and Cambridge Locals and now continued in the CSE and GCE systems.

This polarization from individuality to generality lies at the heart of the problems which persist in examinations today. The need is to reconcile individual differences in students and their individual curricula with the demand for a common curriculum and some universal form of assessment which will have a common currency and general applicability. At one extreme there may be a danger of a self-centred idiosyncrasy, and at the other a form of intellectual cloning. This, of course, is essentially a political problem and it lies at the heart of formal education itself. But in examinations, in some respects microcosms of formal education, the issues are starker. If we can resolve them at the level of examinations, we may have gone some way to resolve them in education itself.

Notes: Chapter 1

1 Robert Lowe is frequently quoted as an example, although it is ironic that Macaulay, who had much to do with the growth of examinations, failed to get honours in the 1822 tripos: Roach, 1971, p. 13.

2 In his address to the Seventeenth Standing Conference of Regional Examinations Boards, Mr Christopher Price, MP, while broadly accepting that an examination at the age of 16 is 'part of the machinery and furniture of the English educational system and there is no way we will get rid of it', went on to say: 'if I was designing the system from scratch, I'd probably design it without a sixteen plus examination.'

3 Montgomery, 1965, pp. 74–5, makes an interesting point about the early influence of the Edinburgh Schools of Arts.

4 In 1979 88·3 per cent of school-leavers in England and Wales attempted a GCE or CSE examination: see DES, 1979.

5 Broadfoot, 1979, ch. 2, goes still further: 'a premium on the reproduction of knowledge, passivity of mind and a competitive even mercenary spirit.'

6 It is difficult to define the 'middle-class' schools of the nineteenth century precisely, particularly in view of the political and social connotations which the term now has. Secondary and grammar schools come closest to it, excluding the Great Public Schools.

7 It is worth while noting that the examining boards in the United Kingdom still give or withhold 'approval' of centres at which examinations can be taken and if need be to inspect them, although the criteria tend to be organizational rather than educational.

8 The wide ranging, almost ponderous consultation (1982–3) attached to the formulation of national criteria for the proposed single system of examining at 16 plus is a case in point. The problems of arriving at a consensus by this process have proved to be considerable, and any radical proposal difficult.

9 Roach, 1971, gives a revealing account of the Exeter examinations, which were a local initiative with much the same purposes and techniques as those subsequently adopted by the Oxford and Cambridge Local Examinations.

10 The *Dictionary of National Biography* has a slightly different version: 'What a man was lost when they made you a parson.' Humber, 1968, pp. 30–1, also records: 'Young Whewell, rich in mind and body, decided to conserve his slender purse ... and walked all the way from Westmorland to Trinity College.'

11 Roach, 1971, p. 145, notes: 'Examinations proved eminently suitable for export.' He records the first export to Trinidad in 1863, followed by a request from Prince Alfred College, Adelaide, South Australia, to be made a local centre in 1867.

2

Purposes

The desire to submit to public examination is endemic to English education. (Petch, 1953, p. 125)

No doubt Petch was concerned to make an eye-catching, tongue in cheek pronouncement, not to be taken too literally because there was a time when examinations had little or no part to play in education, and it is not inconceivable that such a state of affairs will come again. And examinations are certainly not endemic to English-speaking education alone, although the virus in its present form owes much to its English origins. Furthermore, the disease, if it is such, lies not in the 'desire' – that surely is uncommon – but in the *use* to which examinations are put, particularly their function as steps on the ladder to a career. Dore (1976, p. 31) points more directly to the 'disease' and its educational consequences: 'Schools are places where one gets certificates . . . passports to even better jobs.'

Examinations are fair game in the hunt for educational scapegoats; they appear to have few friends even within the educational profession itself. Even in an earlier, more receptive period they were not without their detractors: H. E. Armstrong, as long ago as 1895, wrote: 'Our system of examinations is farcical, if not fraudulent, in the majority of cases, as a means of encouraging the acquisition of useful knowledge' (see Van Praagh, 1973, p. 42). Yet they show such power of survival, indeed growth, that one is led to accept that they fulfil an essential function in the educational system, at least as we now know it. This is not to say that those who seek to reject that function have no argument; nor can it be denied that some of the effects of examinations may be harmful. The fact remains that they have spread almost unchecked and it is necessary to explore the reasons.

In Chapter 1 it was noted that the competitive nature of examinations at the time of their origin was in keeping with the competitive nature of the contemporary society. Perhaps education in general, through its examination system, reflects the value which society places on competition? But such a view leaves many questions unanswered. Why have examinations not only persisted, but thrived, in cultural climates which while still to some degree competitive, cannot be equated with the 'social Darwinism' of 100 or so years ago? Why have they crossed geographic boundaries, east to west and north to south, and flourished in countries with different cultural heritages? Why do they span the political poles of capitalism and communism? And, perhaps most important, why are they thought to be particularly applicable to the scholastic endeavours of the *young*, when professional and commercial competition is equally, if not more so, a feature of middle age?

It could be argued that to search for reasons is ineffective; rather we should accept the phenomenon of examinations and seek to improve or abolish them as we wish. But examinations do appear to have a deliberate function and, therefore, a purposeful basis; and, if we are to seek for alternatives, it is important that we identify these underlying purposes since alternatives must serve the same. These purposes seem to have changed little over the years and may be divided conveniently into those associated with students (a generic term to cover anyone of any age who is being educated and examined), and those associated with schools and other educational institutions.

Sorting Students

Most students engage in some form of self-assessment, whereby they judge their progress through the school. Such assessments they usually keep to themselves. Attempts have been made to make use of self-assessment in a more explicit and formal manner, but at present they can be described as at best experimental (see Chapter 11). For the most part it can be assumed that students are at the receiving end of assessment initiated by others not themselves. In this most students, of all ages, are acquiescent; they submit for reasons of self-advancement or because they are impelled, they have little choice but to comply with whatever system of assessment society imposes on them. So how can that imposition be justified?

Selection
There is a certain inevitability in the way any comment on examinations emphasizes their selective function. Historically this was so and there is little reason to think otherwise today. Of course, examinations are not always crudely competitive, in the sense that they have been instituted solely to allow those who come to the top to have access to the best prizes in employment or further education. They can be used diagnostically, so that those who do best in science and mathematics, for example, will be encouraged to continue to study science and mathematics. Call them diagnostic if we must to make it respectable, they are still selective; some doors may be opened but others are closed. And since examinations become progressively more specialized the higher one goes up the academic ladder, inevitably people are directed into different channels

with few crossing-points between them. People are eliminated stage by stage. Some reach their destined employment (always assuming that employment is available) early in the process; for others the process is prolonged until a tiny fraction remains to take whatever rewards await those who prove themselves best in the competition.

A powerful argument for the use of examinations as the main instrument for sorting students is that they are egalitarian: they are said to be the same for everyone whether they be socially advantaged or disadvantaged; it matters not whether the candidates come from the upper or lower classes, inner city comprehensive or independent boarding-school; the questions are the same, the marking is the same and the certificates are the same. There appears to be no danger of favouritism either to individuals or institutions. To the extent that they are available to all and that assessment is impersonal, examinations can be said to provide equality of *opportunity*. Equality of *outcome* is another matter – a point which will be taken up in Chapter 8.

Of course, examinations are not the only agents whereby people are allocated to their respective niches. Selection is conducted on the basis of other criteria, particularly competence in whatever work people find themselves in. Throughout adolescence, however, and for some well into their twenties, the process of sorting by examination predominates. Young people are distilled into many fractions and the fractionating column is the examination system. Some, of course, never even get into the column but remain, unexaminable, a residue left behind in the retort.

Cost Effectiveness

If the sorting and allocation of people is a predominant purpose of the examination system, it is necessary, first, to question its efficiency, and then to consider its side-effects particularly on education itself. If efficiency were to be judged solely on cost, there can be little doubt that examinations – provided they are limited in scope and commonly applied to large populations – are as cheap an instrument as modern society is likely to devise and that they could be made cheaper. (It is cheaper to allow examination in five subjects than it is in fifty; and it is cheaper to set the same examination for thousands of candidates than it is to set separate examinations for each school.) The financial turnover of the school examination boards is considerable, but it is tiny compared with the costs which would ensue from a multiplicity of examinations conducted separately by all the employing bodies or institutions of higher education. Industry, the professions and higher education know this well, and they are only too happy to devolve responsibility and use the examining boards as their agents with no direct cost to themselves. Indirectly, of course, everyone pays: the costs are met by the entrance fees paid on behalf of the candidates out of national and local taxes or, in a few cases, by parents.

If efficiency is to be judged not only on the cost of the selection instrument, but on its reliability, then strong claims can be made for the present examinations on this score also: the refinement of techniques over a century or more of examining has reached a stage where it is difficult to conceive any substantial technical advance leading to greater accuracy. The same could be said of the organization, management and process of the examination system. Certainly there are errors of measurement; a degree of unreliability is inevitable and its size, if generally known and acted upon, would go some way to undermine the naïve reliance some selecting authorities place in examination grades (JMB, 1983a). Even so it is by no means certain that alternative instruments could be devised which would do the job as reliably and cheaply.

Consistency in an instrument is all very well, but it is of small consolation if it is not measuring the right things. In this context the 'right things' means those qualities which will be required in whatever activity, be it employment or education, for which people are being selected. There is a basic assumption underlying the selective function of examinations: a strong relation between what people do in examinations and what they do later. That there is some relation there can be no doubt; in general people who do well in examinations are reasonably competent thereafter. Sufficiently competent, that is, for the selectors to go on using examinations after many years of trial. Williams (1978, p. 366), referring to the United States, writes: 'It is not really conceivable that employers in that country should consistently pay more to graduates simply because they like the look of them.' What qualities graduates as a body actually possess is matter for debate, but one skill they have in common is that of doing well in examinations.

It was not always so; in the early years the tendency was to design an examination for selection to a particular occupation or for entrance to a particular university or college. Whether the substance of the examination matched the substance of the subsequent employment or education was not always clear; nor was the predictive power of the examination necessarily strong. The fact remains that individual professions or institutions tended to set their own examinations and not to rely on a more generally applied national system; that came later. Where a profession was clearly defined, as in law or medicine, no doubt the substance and technique of the examination, particularly at the end of the period of training, bore some relation to the subsequent practice in which the candidate would engage. In these instances the examination could be considered, in part, to be a test of competence in the relevant profession. At the same time, there could be an element of restricted entry, so that only a prescribed number would be 'passed', regardless of the competence of those who failed. It follows that even when closely linked to a profession the examinations were competitive as well as being tests of competence.

The idea that examinations have *general* application for selection, no matter what the object of the selection, was not slow gaining a hold and it has grown ever since. This uncritical acceptance by selectors of a predictive function of school and university examinations is a little difficult to explain except in terms of economy or disinterest or even laziness. It is all very well for employers and university tutors to delegate the responsibility for initial selection; but in view of the limited array of skills and knowledge which can be assessed in large-scale examinations it carries many unproven assumptions.

Capability

The attributes thought to be desirable for the world of work: 'versatility, initiative, pride in workmanship, conscientiousness, and time keeping' (see Mansell, 1982), are in marked contrast with those tested in conventional examinations. Even for university entrance one reads such assertions as 'What counts is the candidate's willpower, self confidence, perseverance, and character as a whole' (Agazzi, 1967, p. 72). There is an ambivalence in the attitude of employers and higher educators to examinations as instruments of selection which must cause some irritation in schools. If they really want those attributes in their entrants, they are asking not only for different examinations but for different schools. Peterson cuts through a good deal of humbug when he writes,

> Employers will always make use of whatever assessment system the schools provide ... What employers need from a 16 year old school leaver is a character reference and an assurance that he or she is literate and numerate. (Peterson, 1982)

Of all the reasons for the existence of examinations their use as instruments of selection must surely dominate; if that collapsed, so would examinations. If Peterson is right, large-scale examining across the curriculum in schools is an extravagant anachronism. The problem of finding alternatives for the other purposes of examinations, motivation of teachers and students, guidance of students and formative influence on the curriculum, would remain; but none of these necessarily requires a nationwide examination system and certificates which hold a national currency. The authority to retain or relinquish a public examination system lies in the main with the users of its output. The removal of so substantial a prop may cause misgivings in secondary schools, but primary schools have demonstrated that they can survive the removal of the examination goal and the case of secondary schools is not essentially different.

The foregoing should not be seen as a criticism of school examinations alone; the competition does not end there. After leaving school, a young person who is not employed or unemployed faces still more examinations in places of further or higher education. There are some differences. The examinations are likely to concern fewer candidates. The candidates may be subjected to a greater element of assessment during their course rather than at the end, and their examiners may also be their tutors. The subjects of the examination are likely to be narrower than at school and, possibly, but not always, more directly linked to their subsequent careers. However, the motivation in the student is likely to be equally strongly directed by the examination requirements. As any teacher in higher education knows, it is much easier to get a piece of work from a student if it 'counts' towards the degree. Equally they are aware that the stress engendered in students by examinations does not decrease with age and that the distinction between stress sufficient to produce maximum motivation and performance and too much, which produces disaster, is fine indeed.

There was a time, so the story goes, when it was possible to have a happy life at university without taking a degree and yet leave with an enriched education and enhanced prospects for one's career thereafter. When this golden age vanished, if indeed it ever existed, is beyond living memory. The fact now is that life in higher education is as much constrained by competition and selection as it is at school; no student needs to be reminded of the consequences of getting a 'third' or a 'first'.

In such a system of selection there is bound to be waste: waste of those who would have succeeded in later life but have not the ability to pass examinations, and waste of those who have that ability but do not succeed in careers for which the examinations have qualified them. The degree of misfit would be difficult to estimate; it may be thought not to matter. This may be so in countries which are rich enough to tolerate the waste; not so in poor countries which cannot tolerate it. Yet it is in the developing countries where the pressure of selection by examination may be most severe. Hunger is a sharp thorn, whether it be in the boxing-ring or the examination-room.

Motivation
Agreement among educationists on effective ways to enhance learning is hard to find. Perhaps the motivation which arises from the achievement of realistic and meaningful goals finds more support than most. While it may be agreeable to think that those goals should be generated within the learners themselves, the hard fact of day-to-day schooling is that teachers seem to rely heavily on the externally prescribed goals of examination results as a prime motivator. Far from taking the opportunity to do without the stimulus of external examinations, which was provided by the recommendations of the Norwood Report (1943), teachers have contributed to their growth by using the Certificate of Secondary Education (CSE) to extend examinations to areas of the curriculum and types of student which had hitherto escaped them.

No doubt students' desire to succeed, or the fear of failure, provides a convenient motivation sufficient to make the job of teaching easier than it otherwise would be, particularly in those who are within two or three years of the statutory school-leaving age; and no one who has had experience of teaching that group would deny the teacher any motivating influence that can be justified. But to rely principally on motivation through examinations sets considerable limitations to the ends of formal education. It severely confines internally generated goals. Furthermore, it does not apply to all those areas of experience which although they may properly be part of the curriculum are not amenable to public examination, and may be relegated as a result. The consequences which might follow the removal of the examination motive from young adolescents clearly are feared by the teaching profession. This apprehensiveness should be sufficient to sound a note of warning to those who would abolish or radically change public examinations. Some writers, Dore, for example, seem prepared to face those consequences with equanimity: 'Teachers would not be able to coast along on the tide of their pupils' career ambitions. They would actually have to teach' (Dore, 1976, p. 60). Harsh words! But perhaps we do pay too much regard to teachers' fears in this matter? The prop of external examinations at the statutory leaving age has been removed from most Australian schools without any apparent disaster.

A rather more subtle aspect of motivation and achievement is that motivation experienced by the teachers themselves in the reflected achievement of their students. No one would deny to teachers the pleasure which they may experience in the examination results of their students if the results are better than expected or even, let it be admitted, better than their colleagues' students. Indeed, it is not unknown to hear teachers speak of 'my' results; and this may well be justified since it is quite possible that the determining factor may be the effort of the teacher rather than the students. It is a small, intangible harvest at the year-end, after much sowing and cultivating. Who would begrudge it to a profession which is not noted for tangible rewards?

The motivational purpose of examinations may be a powerful force in maintaining the momentum and reinforcing the teacher's control of classroom activities, but it begs a further question. What, in real terms, is achieved other than the satisfaction of successful competition for its own sake? Does the process result in the acquisition of a skill which is valued, like the ability to swim or sing or write a computer program, or does the achievement lie in the acquisition of a certificate with but slight regard for the nature of the performance which gave rise to it? In schools as we know them at present it must be admitted that the motivation lies in the winning of the certificate itself and the doors which it may open rather than the particular skills which have been acquired. In other words, from the student's point of view it is the competitive, selective functions of the examination which matter. It is seen as a stepping-stone rather than a stamp indicating competence.

Certificate Inflation

From the student's point of view, then, examinations lead to certificates which serve as a currency with which access to careers can be purchased. Unfortunately it has become evident since the beginning of this century, and especially in the last two decades, that certificates do not maintain a stable value. The decline in the value of certificates, and the associated demand for higher and higher qualifications as payment for access to careers, has led to a level of 'certificate inflation' which may undermine the education systems of nations just as surely as financial inflation can undermine their economic systems. To put it simply, in both cases it is a matter of too much money chasing too few goods. As Dore (1976, p. 60) says, 'it is, alas, far easier to expand the school system than it is to expand the modern sector economy and increase the number of job opportunities.' Dore was writing about education in general and not just about examinations, pointing to the consequences of the overproduction of certificated people, particularly in developing countries.

One of the consequences of certificate inflation is increased stress for students and, to some extent, teachers. In time of full employment this is perhaps less noticeable, but in times of recession and increasing unemployment the consequences may be dramatic. No one who has taught through the 1960s and 1970s, and into the 1980s, can fail to be aware of the increased drive and application to study for examinations which has come about as the economy has gone into recession. This was not entirely unwelcome in many educational establishments. It is ironic, however, that the attempts to contain and diminish economic inflation by control of expenditure has led directly to an increase in certificate inflation. There comes a point when some certificates are simply not worth having because, as currency for access to employment, they have become the halfpennies of education. At that point there is a reaction in the academically less able students and the motivating factor of competitive examination loses its effect. If at the same time the examination goal has come to dominate the curriculum, there is nothing left in schooling for those whose certification prospects are small. The prospect, then, for schools and teachers is bleak indeed.

Those who oppose the use, or at least the excessive use, of examination certificates as means of allocating young people to a place in society paint a sombre picture not only of the pressure on students and the curriculum, but of the unfairness to certain groups of students who because of an inappropriate social or family background find themselves severely handicapped at the very start of the long hurdle race. This may well be so (see Chapter 8), but for the present it seems that society is prepared to continue to accept this dominant competitive function as the main reason for continuing with public examinations. Examinations began as an instrument of social mobility and so they will continue, albeit in a fairly crude way, as long as selectors find them reasonably effective at least as – in Williams's (1978) phrase – 'a first filter'.

The misplacement of students and the rough justice of examinations is a price society may be prepared to bear at least until acceptable alternatives arise. The adverse effects on the curriculum of schools, however, may be more significant. Since the strong trend during the twentieth century has been for employers and professions to rely on *pre*-qualification rather than qualification on the job, the burden of assessment for suitability for various employment has been thrown increasingly on educational establishments. It follows that the formative effects of examinations on the curriculum have deepened. This brings us to the second purpose of examinations: to serve as a formative influence on the curriculum.

Influencing the Curriculum

The purposes of the founding fathers of examinations included the assessment of schools and colleges as well as the assessment of students. Their intention of using examinations to change the curriculum and improve the quality of teaching appears, at first sight, out of keeping with present attitudes – among which 'the curriculum must come first' has become a pious cliché. Yet despite reiteration of that principle, the stance on the relation between examinations and curriculum is still ambivalent even in those countries which have sought deliberately to decrease the influence of examinations on the work of schools and colleges. A more realistic view is expressed by Bruce:

> The principle that examinations should follow the curriculum may be more inviolate than the Treaty of Utrecht but it could bear critical reappraisal ... Is there really nothing to be said for an examination which dictates the curriculum? (Bruce, 1969, p. 24)

Curriculum and examinations do influence each other, but the notion that the relation is so simple that either can be preconceived and then used to determine the other is naïve. The situation is far too complex to allow so simple a process. It might apply if the curriculum were considered to be no more than a list of topics in a syllabus. But the curriculum is multi-dimensional, involving not only subject-matter, but the balance between subjects, teaching and learning processes, and the abilities and qualities engendered in students. It would be speculative to assume that the curriculum could be controlled by prescribing the examination, and it is equally so to think that any prescribed curriculum could be effectively examined. The real point at issue is not which comes first, but what, if any, is to be the system of control of teachers and teaching and whether examinations have any part to play in it.

The assumption in the nineteenth century, still present although not quite so openly expressed today, was that market forces would act on the curriculum if a competitive system was allowed to operate on the attainment of students; the currency of that market being examination certificates and similar awards. That such a market can be effective is beyond doubt; the changes in formal education in the nineteenth and early twentieth century were as revolutionary as the Industrial Revolution itself, and examinations played no small part in bringing them about.[1]

Whether the effects were entirely as the promoters of examinations anticipated is less certain. The first complaints about the adverse effect of examinations on teaching and learning were heard in the early days, before the mass compulsion to take examinations took effect. Simon writes:

> Thus at Oxford, a new examination statute came into force in 1802 making possible a voluntary public examination for a 'class' ... The effect of this development, however, was that the student's education became more narrow than before, since he was likely to concentrate only on examined subjects. (Simon, 1974, p. 86)

But this complaint was untypical; on the whole the increasing diversity of the curriculum and the increasing diversity of examinations have gone hand in hand, although which is the causal factor is not easily determined. Indeed, such is the range and complexity of the subjects offered by schools and examination boards that a more frequently heard suggestion at present is for a return to a prescribed set of core subjects and even to the grouped certificate which attempts to ensure a balanced curriculum of essential areas of knowledge (Goacher, 1984).

The constraining effect of examinations lies not so much in the number of examined subjects which are available, but in the limitation they impose on the kinds of activity *within* subjects to those activities which can effectively be assessed in large-scale examinations. In the main these are activities of the *mind*, manifesting themselves in written or otherwise inscribed material. These points will be taken up in more detail in Chapter 7 in a review of the techniques and media of communication used in examinations. In general, it can be said that examinations have encouraged a concentration on mental processes, closely akin to the traditional categories of academic disciplines, and have contributed to an erosion of other attributes which could be fostered in institutions of education. Who can honestly claim that the social, moral, artistic and physical qualities of students can be adequately assessed in examinations as we know them? And what of the ability to manage, negotiate, or co-operate, and so on, which a person may expect to develop in his education as an asset for later life? It is inconceivable that these attributes can be cultivated through the medium of examinations. In Chapter 1 instances of these other kinds of activity were mentioned – athleticism and the self-governing house system of the public schools, for example – but the forces which introduced and maintained them did not include the requirements of formal examinations.

Intentions and Outcomes

There can be little doubt that examinations have been, and still are, effective instruments in determining the subjects of the curriculum and thereby the way in which knowledge is subdivided and organized and esteemed within educational institutions. But their effectiveness in determining or even encouraging particular styles of teaching and learning is much less certain. Perhaps the best-known instance of such an attempt in recent years was in the curriculum development of science subjects in the 1960s, initiated by science teachers and funded by the Nuffield Foundation. Waring (1979), in a powerful analysis of the origins and development of the Nuffield O-level chemistry projects, displays the mismatch between ideals and outcomes, including the inability of a public examination to reflect all the desired teaching and learning processes, particularly what has come to be called the 'guided discovery' approach. The will to do so was certainly there – but despite this and the introduction of new techniques of examining, some important aims of the project, affective, pedagogical, social and practical, could not be supported in the examination: 'Because of these omissions, pupils were being assessed on a limited range of the intended outcomes, a range that was essentially cognitive' (ibid., p. 157).

Other examples of this gap between the ideals of curriculum design and the realities of large-scale public examinations would not be difficult to find. This engenders some scepticism when one regards attempts to establish control of the curriculum of educational institutions through a control of examinations. No doubt a draconian measure, for example, the compulsory inclusion of religious education in an examination certificate for school-leavers, would bring about change in the curriculum of schools; but its effect on the way in which religious education is taught, and on the attitudes of teachers and students, could well be totally at variance with the ideals of those who conceived it.

It would be too hasty a judgement, however, to ascribe to examinations the sole responsibility for the gap between curriculum intentions and the realities of the curriculum in practice. Even without the mediating function of examinations this gap will exist. Becher and Maclure (1978, p. 18) make the point: 'Under no education system can the professional relationship between teacher and child be wholly constrained by a predetermined set of propositions laid down in advance by an outside authority.' This will be so regardless of the nature of the outside authority, be it central government, an inspectorate, an examining board, or even a teacher-dominated development group such as in the Nuffield science teaching projects. Teachers and their pupils necessarily adapt what is desirable to what is possible; survival in the classroom demands such adaptation and no system of examination or inspection will prevent it. Nevertheless, even if the limitations of examinations as instruments for prescribing the curriculum are recognized, their function in this respect should not be underestimated; and the nineteenth-century advocates of this approach have their modern counterparts. In this regard Bruce (1969) has already been quoted; Wyatt (1973, p. 1) writes: 'an examination has among its various functions that of an instrument of policy.' And Novosiltseva (1980, p. 1) says, 'while school facilities differ, they should all provide a stock of knowledge, which will be uniform in respect of both range and content, and this should be facilitated by the new requirements for examinations'.

These references are not made with any sense of deprecation; it is healthy that acknowledgement of the formative function of examinations should be made openly rather than deny that they have any such function. And it is worthy of note that this acknowledgement can come from such widely disparate sources as the Oxford and Cambridge Schools Examination Board and the USSR Academy of Pedagogical Sciences. The form of words of the Novosiltseva abstract is particularly interesting since it emphasizes uniformity and 'stock of knowledge'. If it is a matter of importance that a uniform, common base of subjects should be applied nationally, then a uniform and common examination syllabus would be effective indeed. What is more, it could well be done in such a way as to liberate rather than constrain educational institutions in their endeavours to develop their curricula to include personal and social development and all the other aspects of education which may be regarded as non-examinable. It will be argued in Chapter 13 that freedom in the curriculum is a finite quantity and it may be advantageous to restrict it in one area of the curriculum, the common element, in order to liberate it in another, the personal element.

Much of the argument against examinations, particularly their use as determinants of the curriculum, hinges on the concept of autonomy of teachers and the institutions within which they work. But to see this issue in absolute terms of autonomy or non-autonomy is nonsense both as a concept and as a reality; it has to be a matter of degree. There may be a bias to one or the other, and this can shift with changes of political or cultural climate, but to speak of abolition of examinations on the one hand, or control of the curriculum through them on the other, is to obscure the essential question. That question, which is to recur throughout this book, is to what extent should the curriculum and assessment of our educational institutions be general to the nation, and to what extent should it be specific to individual institutions or teachers or students. The issue will not be resolved by resource to clichés: 'teacher control', 'child-centred' and 'the curriculum must determine the examinations' may be convenient planks in political platforms, but their operational meanings require closer attention.

It would be rash to assert that the relation between schools and examination boards is one of perfect harmony. A 'them and us' attitude may still be perceived, although not nearly so strong as in the past. Schools and boards have arrived at a *modus operandi* which makes it possible for each to accept, if not always applaud, the actions of the other. They have achieved a marriage of convenience, if not of the heart. It could be argued that the examination boards, properly constituted, provide the most effective vehicle by which the teaching profession collectively can influence what is taught in our schools.

This state of mutual predictability between the schools and examining boards is essential to the effective operation of the system of public examinations. The worst thing that can happen is an unexpected change in the curriculum of schools or an unexpected departure in examinations from the published regulations and syllabuses. Small annual changes, suitably advertised, can be assimilated. Even the larger changes engendered by the curriculum development projects of recent years can be digested, given sufficient notice – although some boards have only just managed to cope with the changes and even then with some dilution of the essential spirit of the projects. Examining boards claim that they are reflective rather than prescriptive, that they follow curriculum development rather than initiate it. In the middle years of this century this claim was probably justified, although the cross-representation between the two parties is such that it would be difficult to determine whence change actually arose. Recently, however, examining boards have taken a more realistic view of their responsibility for what goes on in schools. Certainly the discussion and internal papers of the subject committees and the examination councils of examination boards are now as likely to be concerned with curriculum as strictly examination matters; it would be wrong to suppose that examination boards are unaware of their wider social and educational responsibilities. In the main they are aware and do care. It is the bounds of what it is possible to do within the limits of large-scale examinations coupled with the limits of what the schools want them to do which constrains them.

At the time of writing work on the common system of examining at 16 plus (GCSE) is being conducted by the examination boards, which are producing criteria and guidelines not only for the conduct of examinations, but also for the subjects of the curriculum. The latter essentially prescribe what is to be taught, for what objectives and, indirectly, by what processes; in short, they prescribe the curriculum or at least that part of it which is to be publicly examined.[2] Whatever the changes to schools and the examining authority which may come about, it is likely that once established they will settle to the same predictable relationship; but at least the curriculum responsibilities of the examination boards are now openly recognized. There are dangers in this somewhat incestuous relationship. The rewards go to those who do well in what schools consider important, and if what schools consider important is what examination boards require and can cope with, the cycle is complete and self-perpetuating.

From the point of view of schools and examining authorities this may be a reasonably happy state of affairs; for the students who have entry to a wider society, and for those who have to receive them into a great variety of occupations, it may be less so. The point has already been made that a dual system of schools and examinations tends to produce young people with various levels of scholastic attainment rather than with the sort of capabilities necessary for subsequent living. Perhaps that is as it should be; maybe schooling and examinations should be more concerned with abstractions than the realities of life be it work or leisure? But it is unreasonable to hold to both points in the argument. If our schools are primarily concerned with academic matters and those qualities which can be conveniently examined on a large scale, it is asking a lot of the general public to accept that they are equally effective in educating for a fuller life thereafter.

The World to Come

From the student's point of view the close relationship between curriculum and examination may not be of much concern. The route to reward for attainment and certificates for advancement is clear: for their subsequent well-being it is necessary to succeed in examinations and the relevance or otherwise of what they are doing may not weigh heavily with them – the competition is what matters rather than the curriculum. This is not to suggest that there is a total divorce between the curriculum and its attendant examinations on the one hand, and life thereafter on the other.[3] For some careers the connection with, for example, science and mathematics may be close. And in fairness to the school examination system it might be said that the requirements of those who rule the world to come are by no means clear and unified. Nowhere is this more apparent than in careers in technologies for which there is a considerable divergence of opinion as to what constitutes an appropriate school curriculum and for that matter what constitutes technology itself. There are those who argue for a strong element of technology in the curriculum either as a separate entity or as an essential part of many of the traditional subjects; and there are those who argue for an education in the so-called basic or supporting subjects, leaving the education in technology itself until later.

For those who seek a place for technology in the school curriculum, the prospect of using the examination system to provide an entry by force is tempting. Even if they are correct in supposing that the status of technology could be enhanced by entry into the curriculum, they may be misguided in supposing that examinations will effect it. So firmly is the idea established that one of the main effects of examinations is to determine the curriculum that its limitations and consequences are overlooked. One of the difficulties lies in the claims which are made for technology or, more particularly, the necessary characteristics of a technologist: co-operation, creativity, solving real problems, decision-making, imagination and the 'coordinated effort of mind, of heart, and of hand'[4] are phrases which come to mind. This might well be so and technology no doubt is the cross-disciplinary, ecletric activity which it claims to be. But anyone who thinks that these qualities are best encouraged by instituting a formal public examination has greatly exaggerated notions of what examinations can achieve in this respect. The desirable qualities are concerned not so much with assimilating and using a defined body of knowledge as with the *process* of solving real problems. Examinations as currently practised do a reasonable job in assessing the former; they are of much less use in the latter. Indeed, the attempt to set up a public examination for technology in schools, within the examination resources and techniques available, could engender a distorted view of technology and do it a disservice.

The demand for the inclusion of technology in the examination system tends to come from some of the engineering profession. It is interesting that other productive fields of human endeavour which could make equal claim to the characteristics of technology have little, if any, place in school examinations; they include: agriculture, medicine, teaching, marketing and the communications industry. One or two of these may lack status, but none of them at present lacks recruits.

The foregoing discussion should not be read as a defence of the school curriculum and its examinations as they now stand. Its main purpose is to indicate that although examinations have proved effective in changing or maintaining the curriculum in the past they cannot be relied upon to maintain more than a core of academic subjects within the curriculum and that this is likely to fall well short of the full expectations which society has of its schools. The maintenance of this core within the curriculum and within the subjects themselves could be more effective than it is at present; if that is what is required, then examinations *could* serve as the main controlling instrument.

The problem then arises of how to prevent a disproportionate concentration on the examined part of the curriculum to the detriment of the rest. It could be argued that the present wide spread of examined subjects does at least keep some of them in the curriculum albeit in a less than satisfactory form.[5] Possible solutions to this will be discussed in Chapter 13. Meanwhile it is encouraging to see that the problem is receiving consideration at many levels including the House of Commons (1981), a Select Committee of which wrote: 'We wish to stress here that it should not be assumed that all parts of the curriculum are appropriate for formal assessment.' In such statements it is possible to perceive the beginnings of a more realistic appraisal of what schooling and examining can be expected to do. The idea that both can be used to attain all the main ends of education in its fullest sense is being exposed for what it is: a convenient pretence to excuse the failure of society to achieve those ends by other means. Examinations can replicate but a small part of what goes on in schools, and schools can replicate but a small part of what goes on in society at large. It really is unfair for society to impose loads on them beyond their capacity to bear and then to use them as scapegoats when their inadequacies are revealed.

Self-Justification

The formalization of examinations in the nineteenth century brought about the creation of institutions to administer them. These examination authorities, as they may generally be called, show many of the characteristics of those other public and private institutions on which the organization and functioning of society is thought to depend. One of the characteristics of such bodies is that they develop an internal cohesion, a common purpose and a stability hardened with age, which engenders some resistance to change and an outright resistance to dissolution. The survival of the species and the instinct of the preservation of their organizational genes is strong. It can adapt to some extent to maintain an equilibrium between all the forces which play on it and the various functions it is required to fulfil, but it is unlikely to co-operate in its own extinction.

Examination boards operate at a very high level of integrity, impartiality and efficiency. The harmonious relationship of a part-time governing body of unpaid professional people responsible for policy, with a full-time secretariat responsible for running the organization, typifies many of our institutions at their best. The two parties co-operate to provide a system of examining which is very complex and – to the uninitiated – arcane. The system also engenders some degree of brand loyalty and a healthy competition between boards.

This corporate will is necessary and laudable in any efficient organization; but it carries with it the concomitant danger of self-justification. It is not so much that financial investment is great or that careers are at risk, although neither can be entirely overlooked; the danger lies in the stance that the very existence of the examining organizations is sufficient reason for the continuance of examinations themselves. This problem is not imaginary. The difficulties confronting those who seek to introduce a single system of school examining in England are only partly technical; they stem equally from loyalties to existing examination boards and the sense of identity which membership of a successful organization bestows. It has to be said that of all the legitimate purposes which could be attributed to examinations the continued existence of examining boards cannot be included among them.

In this chapter three main reasons have been advanced for the use of examinations: to motivate students and teachers, to provide an instrument of selection and equality of opportunity, and to exercise some control over the curriculum. There are others; one in particular, the use of examinations as a diagnostic aid in curriculum development (Kelly, 1971), will be considered in more detail in Chapter 12. But is there an overriding, unpublished reason? Could it be that examinations are part of a hidden curriculum, that is, part of a more general conspiracy to use the educational system to maintain a particular social system? It is well established that particular social groups tend to take particular examination subjects, as is the different performances of various social classes. Nor can it be denied that the examination system, particularly that in schools, has its origins in a move to improve and expand education for the growing number of middle-class children and to provide those children with an apparently objective method of gaining access to desirable careers. Broadfoot puts this point nicely:

> On the one hand, it is possible to see the institution of various kinds of educational assessment as crucial steps in the fight against nepotism and inefficiency and in opening up social mobility to a quite unprecedented extent. On the other hand, it is important to recognise the role of assessment in limiting such mobility and even more crucially, in legitimating what is still an education system strongly biased in favour of traditional privilege. (Broadfoot, 1979, p. 26)

It is an unwarranted jump, however, from establishing that various social groups perform differently in examinations to proclaiming a theory of conspiracy of a privileged elite against a deprived majority. This is not to maintain that these differences are unimportant or that the trends could lead to undesirable social consequences. But it really is rather hard on examinations and examining authorities to advance an unsubstantiated theory that they are deliberately at fault for many social ills and injustices, particularly when one reads some of the largely untried alternatives which have been proposed or surveys the examination systems of some countries which proclaim that they have a more egalitarian social system than others. Illich (1971, p. 77) wrote, 'Only hindsight will allow us to discover if the Great Cultural Revolution will turn out to be the first successful attempt at deschooling the institutions of society'. We now have that hindsight, and it reveals how near to disaster the deschooling and de-examining revolution brought that country.

That examinations are instruments for social and educational control is difficult to deny. It follows that they have a political purpose. This purpose may be implicit rather than explicit and the effects are difficult to determine. But whether the examination system be changed or maintained, there remains an even more fundamental question: *who controls it?*

Notes: Chapter 2

1 Perkin, 1969, draws an analogy between the principles of the entrepreneurial ideal and competitive education through examinations: see particularly pp. 221–59.
2 It is somewhat ironic to note that the Schools Council is now disbanded and its dual function divided between two committees, one for examinations and one for the curriculum.
3 The phrase 'world to come' is not used facetiously; in better times it was called 'world of work', as in DES, 1977a, p. 15.
4 The Confederation of Design and Technology Associations (n.d.), *Statement of Principles Concerning Education in Craft, Design and Technology*. A fuller account of the nature of technology and its place in the school curriculum is to be found in DES, 1977a, pp. 30–5.
5 A long-standing example of this problem is the use of practical examinations in science subjects. For years it was claimed that these examinations, despite their obvious shortcomings, were necessary if only to maintain an element of practical work in the science curriculum and to ensure that the authorities provided equipment and materials.

3
Who Is in Control?

If examinations are instruments for social and curriculum engineering, it is important to identify who controls them. This is not easy; examination systems are complex and they lie within complex educational and social systems. To assert that examinations are under the control of the teachers, the universities, or the government is much too simple. Not that teachers, universities, government and other bodies exercise no influence; they do, but it operates on different parts of the examination system, to different degrees, and in different ways.

The concern over the control of examinations has grown in recent years, possibly because examinations are now applied in some form to most students at the statutory school-leaving age. This coupled with the belief, possibly misguided, that control of examinations brings with it control of the curriculum seems to put excessive power over educational policy into the hands of those with authority over the examination system. Three kinds of question need to be asked: which groups have a legitimate interest? How can that interest be so organized as to be effective? What aspects of examinations and the curriculum are the proper concern of each?

The approach to these questions will be in terms of organized groups rather than individuals. This is not to overlook the influence of individuals; what is often taken to be a corporate policy may be that of a single person or a small number of people persuasive or powerful enough to carry a group with them. But this is not the place to analyse the inner workings of democratic institutions; it is necessary to assume that the policy which emanates from a group represents the will of that group.

It will simplify the analysis somewhat if the kinds of body (in the sense of organized groups) are reduced to four: governmental, educational, administrative and the remainder which I have called the 'market-place'. These bodies are not discrete: there are educators in government and politicians in education; there are administrators in education and teachers in administration; and the same can be said of industrialists, trade unionists and parents. A group with noticeable lack of influence (except in a few colleges and universities) are the students themselves; their views are usually filtered through the mouths of others.

Control by Government

A function of government is to exercise control over society. The only question to concern us here is whether examinations come within its province, and if so, how and to what extent. In this chapter I am concerned mainly with *central* government, while recognizing that local government may have a considerable, though different, influence.

The degree to which government participates, either directly or indirectly, in public examining depends on the more general climate of political opinion. In the early days when public examinations were being developed in England, the functions of government were much fewer than they are now. The direct intervention of government in the affairs of individuals and institutions was likely to engender a hostile response. This was particularly noticeable in educational provision, much being left to those bodies with a traditional interest, the churches in primary education, the professions in vocational education and private individuals or endowments in secondary education; the universities, of course, were virtually autonomous in higher education. But from the middle of the nineteenth century onwards the direct intervention of central government became more apparent, mainly through the growth of the inspection of schools and regulations for school examinations.

Although nineteenth-century governments were reluctant to exercise authority over established institutions, they were not slow to intervene in some of the new or rapidly changing institutions. This was particularly so in the provision of new or reorganized elementary schools after 1870, in which the intervention was direct and positive. And in preparation for this there was an even earlier example of government direction of the examination of candidates for the teaching profession. This direction[1] was not just through statements of general policy, but by means of very specific requirements of performance:

> Candidates will also be required ... To write from dictation sums in the first four rules of arithmetic, simple and compound; to work them correctly, and to know the table of weights and measures ... In schools connected with the Church of England they will be required to repeat the Catechism, and to show that they understand its meaning. (Maclure, 1975, p. 53)

Such statements give the lie to the belief that behavioural objectives are inventions of the twentieth century.

The now infamous Revised Code of 1862 required equally behavioural objectives for the examinations on which grants depended. A 'scholar' in standard VI should be able to read 'A short paragraph in a newspaper, or other modern narrative' (ibid., p. 80). When one considers the type of prose used in the newspapers and literature of the period, this was no easy attainment. In arithmetic a 'scholar' in standard I should be able to 'Form on black-board or slate, from dictation figures up to 20; name at sight figures up to 20; add and subtract figures up to 10, orally, from examples on black-board' (loc. cit.). Performance criteria at this level of exactness have not been the subject of government-controlled assessment in England and Wales from those times until the advent of the Assessment of Performance Unit (APU) over 100 years later. The performance criteria which have been formulated by the APU are, of course, different in substance and scope from those of the Revised Code. It would be difficult indeed for a government-sponsored agency to specify short paragraphs in a newspaper with all the attendant value judgements of political bias and literary style. And mathematics has changed somewhat since 1862. But the performance criteria are not different in kind:

the recognition of a right angle
the estimation of the size of angles with reasonable accuracy
the use of a protractor to measure angles accurately
the use of a protractor to construct an angle. (APU, 1982, p. 2)

It could be argued that the purposes of APU testing and Revised Code testing were essentially different, although both were set up by government. Overtly the APU is to identify standards of performance in schools in general, not in particular schools or individuals. Presumably some action is contemplated, but it is not prescribed in advance. On the other hand, the Revised Code testing was directly linked with the allocation of funds to particular schools and the consequences were immediate. Despite this, both the APU and the Revised Code have three fundamental characteristics in common: they are not primarily intended to put individual children into an order of merit for selection purposes; they specify in advance those skills which children at various ages could be expected to display; and they are intended to exercise some degree of centralized control over the curriculum of schools. Both are examples of the use of tests by central government to ensure that certain educational objectives are nationally attained. It would not be wise to push this analogy too far.

The Revised Code was linked with inspection of schools and the allocation of grants, whereas the APU is not. Despite the fears and prejudices of some individuals and schools to the contrary, the policy of the APU is of little direct threat to them. As an instrument for controlling or even monitoring the real curriculum, that is, what goes on in classrooms, the APU is but a feeble thing compared with the Revised Code which, whatever may be said about it, was very effective while it lasted. If government is really determined to exercise some operational control of the curriculum, it may have to shoot with both barrels: inspection *and* testing.

In secondary education in England and Wales government put the testing weapon into the hands of other bodies: the Secondary Schools Examination Council (1917), the Schools Council (1964) and, even further from direct control, the school examination boards. The 1911 Report of the Consultative Committee of the Board of Education, from which stems the present system of school examinations in England, linked a decentralized examination system with a strengthened Inspectorate.[2] Subsequent years, however, showed that in effect it was the examinations which were strengthened as agents for prescribing the curriculum rather than the Inspectorate. With a declining prescriptive function of the Inspectorate and with a very remote control of examinations, government in England found by the mid-1970s that it had virtually lost whatever influence it had over the curriculum of secondary schools at the operational level. Government could control funds and, to some extent, the general organization of schools; for example, the move towards comprehensive schools and away from selective schools. The effects of that move on the *curriculum* of these schools – which in the long run is what matters to pupils and parents – was left in the main to headteachers.

Subsequent attempts by government to regain some control of the secondary school curriculum through assessment are now becoming apparent through the proposed common system of examining at 16 plus (GCSE). Central government has taken the power to accept or reject the criteria which denote both the substance of the subjects of examination and the various levels of performance in each. This could amount to the use of some aspects of the Revised Code and the Regulations for Secondary Schools, the one specifying levels of performance, the other the substance of the curriculum.

The links of control from government to actual examinations are complex and their articulation is not easy to perceive. Government itself cannot hope to retain in its own hands all the threads which operate the examination system (Becher *et al.*, 1981). The power of government lies in setting up bodies to advise, inspect and administer. It is through the terms of reference and the constitution of these bodies that control is exercised. Thus the composition of the 1911 Consultative Committee and the subsequent Secondary Schools Examinations Council effectively established the organization and substance of the curriculum of secondary schools in England for some fifty years. Petch (1953) gives an account of the formative years at the beginning of this century through the eyes of the secretary of one of the newly constituted examination boards (Joint Matriculation Board). The impression given is one of consolidation, rationalization, and the preservation of a traditional curriculum, particularly through the 'grouping' structure of the school certificate, rather than of radical innovation in the curriculum through the medium of examinations. This policy must reflect a consensus of those chosen to serve on the policy-making bodies. In as much as government controls the composition of those bodies it can to some extent control examinations.

Government can set down the rules of the examination game and to some extent specify the way in which it is to be organized, but it does not actually manage it or play it. At the operational end the actual work from devising syllabuses, examination papers and mark schemes to marking papers and determining grades is mostly done by teachers. Whether they are from the schools, colleges, or universities, teachers will set what *they* think is appropriate to the students in their institutions and award marks for what *they* think is worthy. The system could not work otherwise, if only because there is no other body of people in sufficient numbers and with sufficient experience and skill to operate it. And unless the criteria for syllabuses and grades are formulated at an unprecedented level of detail, they will find a great deal of room for interpretation of whatever general criteria are applied from above.

Is government, then, powerless to influence events at the level of the schoolroom and examination room? At the operational level yes, but government can change the rules and managers – and could, if it wished, declare the game illegal. The last point is not facetious; sending off (abolition) could be an attractive final solution. If the game is to continue, however, government needs to think carefully about the level at which it can effectively determine policy and the degree to which it can control practice. In this respect the relation between government and public examinations has some similarity to that between government and nationalized industries and services such as national health services. Government can determine the kind of organization, the level of finance and, to some extent, higher management, but what actually happens in the wards and examination rooms has to be left to the practitioners; although a distinction has to be made between practitioners working as individuals and their corporate organizations working on their behalf. Whether what the practitioners do is actually what the patients or students would like them to do is another matter.

The position of the Inspectorate is an interesting one, particularly in a country where it is independent of the government, at least notionally. It would be idle to suppose that the Inspectorate will have no influence on those national criteria which will determine the nature of school examinations. They alone form a body which can exercise a reasonably consistent policy on curriculum matters independent of governmental and professional policy. The extent to which government will be willing to devolve judgement on national examination criteria to the Inspectorate is a crucial issue, giving rise as it does to a whole array of questions on the proper function of the Inspectorate and, perhaps most important, on the process of appointment to the Inspectorate and its relation to government.

An interesting question is not so much how and to what degree government can control public examinations, but how does it arrive at policies in the first place? Examining is a skilled trade; the intrusion of the novice or the incompetent can be calamitous and such events are seized on avidly by the national communications media, particularly in the 'silly season' when there is little else to report. Government, as a set of individuals, is no more knowledgeable about the science and art of examining than it is about the science and art of medicine; yet it forms opinions and policy on both. This is a matter which would be difficult to research. Much depends on inside knowledge of the operation of government, rather like that of C. P. Snow's pursuit of the same question in the scientific field. Much depends on the individuals in power and on the individuals and organizations who have their ear. It is not difficult to detect, behind government pronouncements on curriculum and examination affairs, the views of one or more of a small number of educationists. There are academics who have the ear of politicians; and if their views coincide with the general social policy, they will have influence. This is not just a matter of listening to academic opinion or reading the outcomes of educational research. The politically committed are adept at giving prominence to those parts of research which confirm their prejudices. From the array of educational research findings it is possible to make out a case for nearly anything, from a strict academic meritocracy to open access to Oxford and Cambridge universities.

Of course, government could let go all control of examinations, as it could of medicine, and leave it to a self-financing scheme run by the practitioners. However, it seems not to be in the nature of modern government to deny itself a view on any social or academic matter. This, however, is not a matter for pessimism. Provided that public and professional opinion prevents government from doing anything too silly, a generally acceptable system of examinations is likely to remain or at least go into a steady, controlled decline. Revolutionary change or even abolition are possible – but with the recent cautionary example of China in mind, even the most militant opponents may opt for the evolutionary extinction of the examination dinosaur.

Control by Teachers

We use the term 'teachers' in a general sense to include all those who are directly active in what goes on in educational institutions. In the context of this book I refer mainly to schoolteachers; but it is necessary to include other groups such as teachers in higher and further education, inspectors, advisers, curriculum developers and researchers. In some ways it is invidious to place teachers as one factor among equals in this matter. The most important arts of teaching include those of questioning, examining, diagnosing and guiding. But when it comes to the *control* of public examining to serve a more general social function, teachers have not always been regarded as equals.

Even if teachers as a body were not included in formal control and policy-making, as individuals at the operational level they do control what is examined and how it is examined. If most teachers will not or cannot effectively teach certain skills or subjects or parts of subjects, there is little point in other bodies imposing examinations on those areas. And teachers can undermine, if they so wish, the best laid plans of the enthusiasts for curriculum and examination reform. One did not have to read many scripts in the examinations of some of the new science curricula in the 1960s and 1970s to realize that despite the best intentions and carefully contrived objectives of the curriculum developers and examination designers, some teachers were teaching as they had always taught and students were learning as they had always learned. Furthermore, as far as accumulating marks in the examination was concerned, they were not experiencing any disadvantage; indeed, in some areas they may have profited from their traditional approach. This is simply another way of reinforcing an earlier point that external control, and externally imposed innovation, may have little or no effect if they do carry the support (or at least the acquiescence) and the competence of most teachers who are affected by it. It is the outcome which matters, not the intention, and teachers and their students alone control that.

The direct influence by teachers on the *outcomes* of examinations, be they scripts, objective tests, projects, or orals, is self-evident. Nearly all who have marked scripts must have felt that they were marking the teachers as much as the candidates. Even at the higher levels of education the effect of good and bad teachers is bound to be noticed in the examination output of their students. In the sense that they dominate the setting and marking of examinations, and the preparation of candidates for them, teachers clearly have a strong hold on the operational end of the system.

Strangely, however, the argument about the control of examinations by teachers rests not so much on the setting and marking and preparation of candidates as on formal representation of teachers on policy-making bodies. The demand for such representation, and increasing recognition of it in examining authorities, has grown in recent years. But mere representation leaves unanswered questions: who are the representatives, how are they appointed and what should be their function?

One of the more imaginative attempts to widen this representation on a policy-making body was the establishment of the Schools Council for the Curriculum and Examinations for England and Wales. (Strictly speaking, the Schools Council's function was advisory; it formulated policies on examinations but these policies had to be submitted for approval to the secretaries of state; so ultimate power for initiating changes in the general policy for public examinations rested with government.) The Council consisted of seventy-five members representing no fewer than thirty-four different bodies plus ten co-opted members. Ten of the bodies represented were teachers' organizations, and teachers accounted for a majority of membership. Many other organizations, such as the Trades Union Congress, the Confederation of British Industry, the Examining Boards (jointly) and the National Confederation of Parent–Teacher Associations, had but one representative. It could have been foreseen that such a large number of members of widely different interests would be an unwieldy instrument for determining or guiding national policy on curriculum and examinations. In the event, despite subsequent reorganization, it proved to be so.

As an organization for initiating development and research in curriculum and examinations and for providing a forum for debate at national level between wide-ranging interests the Schools Council gained the admiration of much of the rest of the world. During the 1960s and 1970s there flowed from Schools Council sponsorship so remarkable a number[3] of imaginative projects that few schools and teachers could have remained unaffected by them either directly or indirectly. But as an instrument for forging a national *policy* on curriculum and examinations the Schools Council proved ineffective, even on what might appear to be a fairly clear issue such as the curriculum and examinations for the 16–18 year-olds. This is seen by many as a virtue rather than a fault. Caston, a former joint secretary of the Schools Council, strongly advocates pluralism in these matters, 'the dispersal of power in education' (see Bell and Prescott, 1975). But for those who wish to see more cohesion and central control, a body so constituted is unlikely to provide it.

The recent tribulations of the Schools Council, leading finally to its demise, testify to the difficulty of keeping policy-making and politics apart. Of course, to be included in the machinery of policy-making bestows power, and politics is concerned with power. The point is that simply to count teachers' heads in the various committees of examining authorities is an uncertain criterion for establishing the degree of teacher control of examinations. A majority of teachers on all policy-making bodies from governing councils downwards may be a worthy principle from a political point of view, but the benefits which may accrue depend on who the teachers are and whom they represent. In his review of the work of the Schools Council Nisbet writes:

> To whom are the teacher representatives accountable? Their immediate accountability is to the union or association which nominates them ... To this extent the health of the Schools Council is linked with the vitality of democracy in the teachers' associations. (Bell and Prescott, 1975, pp. 69–70)

It should not be taken as axiomatic that a majority of teachers on all policy-making bodies necessarily leads to what is educationally best in the examination system or indeed to what most teachers want.

Petch (1953, p. 35) records that the Bryce Commission 'noted a general though not universal feeling that school teachers should be included on examining boards'.[4] The Joint Matriculation Board made an enlightened response, by 1903 standards, in giving its three co-opted places to three teachers, the headmasters of Manchester Grammar School, the Liverpool Institute and Leeds Grammar School. In 1907, even more enlightened, they co-opted the headmistress of Manchester High School for Girls. This could be called a process of *invitation*. Headmasters and headmistresses no doubt have the best interests of education at heart, but the decisions made by them, and those with whom they sat, depended on their values and prejudices *as individuals*. If the individuals had been different, then, so would the decisions – as would have been the examinations and curricula of secondary schools for many years afterwards.

What kind of teachers should the teacher-representatives be? Must they have a full teaching timetable or could headteachers, who may do little actual teaching, qualify? Much emphasis is placed on the *practising* teacher – but should someone with long and varied teaching experience be immediately ineligible on becoming a headteacher or adviser or lecturer? These are sensitive questions and subject to many extraneous factors including that of availability. The one great disadvantage under which teachers with full timetables labour is that their working-week is inflexible making attendance at meetings difficult and irritating to colleagues. In contrast, the other categories mentioned above may work equally hard and long but under a more flexible system which allows greater opportunity for outside work. This is an intractable problem and no readymade solutions will be offered here.

Surely, it will be claimed, if the democratic process of *election* is used, the dangers of unrepresentative, selective co-option would be avoided. If only it were that easy! The franchise could be established clearly, but what of the constituencies? Should the division be by all schools equally; if so, should it be by size of school, or type of school, or by number of examination entries? Or should it be by teaching subject? If the former operates, then subjects may be misrepresented; if the latter, schools may be misrepresented. This is not an attack on democratic election, as such; it is pointing out that the process is complex and can in the end lead to manipulation and unequal representation and that simply to reiterate the principle is not to solve the problem.

In addition to invitation and election, there is a third method, by *nomination*: nomination by universities, education authorities, teachers' organizations, or any other body thought to have a right to representation. The body concerned is simply asked to produce a fixed number of individuals to sit on the committees of the examining authority. Who they are and how they are appointed then ceases to be the business of the examination authority. There is little generalizable research on how such appointments are made in the field of education, and what such research would reveal is a matter for conjecture. But those who have had many years' experience of appointing and being appointed to serve on committees know very well how these things are usually contrived. The process of appointing a member of one committee to serve on another is a game played to a pattern if not a set of rules. The chairman in consultation with his secretary and possibly one or two members goes through the list of members, seeking someone who has the time, interest and knowledge (often in that order of priority) to undertake the work. It only remains to get support in open committee, which to any chairman worth his salt is not difficult, and invidious voting is usually avoided.

This may sound mildly cynical; indeed, it is difficult to experience much of this kind of work without becoming so. However, in a tolerant society, social systems, including public examinations, seem to operate quite well by these means of co-option, election and nomination. The general principle is that teachers appointed by one means or another should have a substantial, possibly a majority, representation on the bodies which administer public examinations. That battle has been won and need not be refought, but it is another matter when it comes to determining policy at higher levels where the general social good is at stake. At these levels it might be as well to consider the dangers inherent in control by a single group, even if that group is the profession that is most concerned. It should not be thought that placing majority control in the hands of teachers, leavened with a sprinkling of representatives from other walks of life, will necessarily lead to profound changes in the examination system. If such a body works by consensus, it will achieve a smooth operation and a bland product. Nor is the will of the majority likely to produce anything more innovatory. If the teachers are really representative of their colleagues, they will cover every range of opinion concerning examinations; and consensus, in the representation of all shades of opinion and the avoidance of undue disagreement, is death to significant change. Perhaps that is how things should be in public examinations. Certainly any sudden radical change leads to an outcry, not least from those teachers who actually have the task of preparing candidates. The idea that most teachers are revolutionaries does not bear scrutiny. The opportunity for revolutionary change which the Mode III system allows has not been fully grasped.[5]

To redress the balance, it must be acknowledged that the innovatory work of the nationally directed curriculum and examination projects has come very largely through the imaginative efforts of teachers. In more recent times the work on graded tests, credit accumulation and pupils' records of achievements (see Chapters 11 and 12) have also originated from individual teachers; but they come from a minority. The point is that majority control of high-level policy by teachers is as likely to inhibit change as it is to promote it if the majority is truly representative.

On the other hand, if a group albeit a minority is sufficiently determined and committed to a particular policy, it might be possible in some circumstances to manipulate all three methods, co-option, election and nomination, to attain control and bring about radical change even if that change were not in accord with the general will (I see no possibility of this at present). The 'general will' of society in the matter of examinations is not to be scoffed at. Most people may be ignorant of the detailed operation of examinations (that is the fault of the examination system as much as their own) but they do have views on the general principles and policy, and a notion of what is fair and equitable. Tapping these views, and allowing a degree of control to them, has been accorded little consideration in the past.

Control by the Market-Place

The general will of society at large is so vague a concept as to be of little help in a discussion such as this. Nevertheless, the control of policy on examinations should rest ultimately with all those who, either as individuals or as corporate institutions, work outside the educational and examination systems – in the market-place. Of course, it could be said that to give effect to the general wishes of society is a function of government; it would be a happy state of affairs if this were so. In reality the policy of government is more likely to be the policy of party, and the policy of party in this matter is likely to reflect that of a faction within the body of professional teachers and other educationists, perhaps modified by the civil service and Inspectorate. Party manifestos are usually a ragbag of policies within which the general public cannot pick and choose; one must take or reject the whole package and a policy on examinations is unlikely to get pride of place.

The token member of the Trades Union Congress, or the Confederation of British Industry, or an association of parents, sitting on an examining authority, no doubt goes some way to give the appearance that public examinations are not simply part of a closed system of education. To plant these individuals into the somewhat rarefied atmosphere of examining authorities is an unlikely means of bringing about change in policy. They are clay in the hands of the professionals who can produce scores of reasons for leaving things more or less as they are. This strategy of token representation may be no more than a device for rendering impotent those institutions which in wider society exercise great power. It will take a good deal more than token representation to break into the teacher–examiner alliance with any real authority.

The complaint may be less acute in those spheres of education which are more directly vocational. Although even here there are signs that such institutions as the Technical and Business Education Councils too readily accept traditional academic models of curriculum development and assessment. And higher education is certainly not above reproach. The examinations in universities are even more introverted than those of schools; their system of external examiners is not much more than taking in each other's washing. And in wider spheres still: to what extent can the general public influence the qualificatory examinations of those doctors and lawyers with whom they will ultimately deal directly as clients?

It seems that systems of examining tend to become closed, with their own self-generated ends dominant. And the longer they have been established, the more coherent becomes their organization and the thicker their defences against external threat. A certain amount of infiltration takes place, of course. The Nuffield and Schools Council curriculum projects were not without their effects on school examinations, and many individuals within the system cannot put aside their experiences as parents of candidates. More recently the Technical and Vocational Educational Initiative (TVEI) may be seen as an outflanking attack on the educational establishment. But by and large it cannot be claimed that examinations, particularly those for schools, are strongly influenced by institutions representing society in general.

This is not to say, however, that our school examinations system is inefficient. It is its very efficiency that deters attempts at change from outside and can thwart the most well intentioned of external bodies. Conceivably the public at large may prefer this state of affairs – to remain aloof, taking and using what examining authorities provide without attempting to exert a formative influence. On the other hand, if what examining boards provide becomes increasingly irrelevant to society, examinations will either atrophy or petrify into an expensive, non-functional ritual. Some would applaud either event; but public examinations have probably made a greater contribution to social mobility than any political theory, and to allow them to decline simply because mechanisms to allow access to public opinion barely exist could become a matter for regret.

The formal channels for public influence on public examinations may be ineffectual, but in fact a great deal of power lies in the hands of institutions outside the educational establishments – if they chose to exercise it. The real problem lies in the apathy of those institutions; it really is curious that while all parties concerned rarely lose an opportunity to abuse examinations, they remain content to delegate the responsibility for their initial selection procedures to external examination authorities. Consequently the examination industry continues to flourish. Becher *et al.* make the point:

in any service activity is only workable if it is acceptable to – i.e. is reasonably consistent with the values of – both practitioners and client. From the point of view of the latter, if an unacceptable policy is introduced in a free market, he or she will simply go elsewhere; in the context of public welfare provision, the natural response will be in terms of political protest. (Becher *et al.*, 1981, p. 152)

It seems that as far as examinations are concerned discontented clients – students, parents, employers and those in further education – either have nowhere else to go or are not sufficiently discontented to carry 'political protest' beyond the level of perennial grumbling.

Public examinations are largely monopolistic. At school level in England there is apparent choice between examining boards in GCE if not in CSE; and it is intended that choice will be available in the unified system of the two (GCSE). The choices, however, are different in detail rather than in kind. The truth of the matter is that a radical alternative to traditional examinations has yet to win general acceptance, although several are in the offing. In these circumstances it is not surprising that both practitioners and clients choose to ride on the publicly owned academic escalator rather than commit themselves to relatively untried, free-enterprise alternatives. Alternatives do exist (see Chapters 11 and 12), and if the parties with an interest choose not to use them, it can only be assumed that they lack the courage or at heart do not wish to abandon the traditional examinations.

Nevertheless, even those with a professional commitment to traditional examinations would admit to the limitations of examinations in revealing the qualities of students. Over the past 150 years examinations have evolved to a state of refinement beyond which substantial technical improvement is unlikely. In that case we must either do the best we can with the species which we have cultivated or look to others which will fulfil the same functions. But there has to be a market for them. Only society at large can provide that market, and if it will not accept the new, then we shall have to rest content with the old. If society wishes, a change in the examination system could be forced either by opting in an open market for alternatives or by electing a government which would legislate for the acceptance of them. This takes us full circle, to the direct intervention of government in the policy for determining appropriate means of providing for the people access to education and employment. The precedents are not encouraging.

Control by Examination Boards

Much of what has been written in this chapter so far concerns access to those bodies which formulate policy. Although the ultimate responsibility lies with government and indirectly with its advisory bodies, the dominant influence of the examining boards themselves in matters of policy should not be underestimated. There was a period leading up to 1964, in which a deliberate attempt was made to exclude the examination boards from the Secondary Schools Examination Council on the ground that their function was administrative not policy-making. This proved to be only temporary; the examination boards now have direct access to the Department of Education and Science (DES) and there can be little doubt of the power of their combined influence. Not only are the examination boards closer to the teaching profession and the school curriculum, they are armed with formidable technical experience which enables them to pronounce with a near-unassailable authority on the feasibility of proposals for policy changes.

It follows that in discussions on policy which aims to modify the existing system the voice of the examination boards carries much weight and can support or undermine government policy. If more radical proposals come from government, the examining boards might find the going rather harder. A move to abolish public examinations, for example, or at least replacement by a system which did not involve academic tests as we know them, could be countered only on social or political grounds, not technical ones. The examining boards would then find themselves fighting a different cause in which their technical weapons would not avail.

The policy in England and Wales has been to delegate the actual design and administration of examinations to a number of autonomous bodies. Most of the GCE boards stem from a university or group of universities. Historically this was how they originated and the university influence is still strong, particularly in their governing bodies in which general policy is determined. An exception to this is the Associated Examining Board which was sponsored by the City and Guilds of London Institute to meet the growing demand for examinations from those schools and colleges engaged in less traditional forms of secondary education after the Second World War.

The degree of autonomy of the GCE boards is high. Although legally they can issue certificates only with the approval of the Department of Education and Science, this is little more than a formality. They are required to follow whatever guidelines and regulations are laid down by government such as those which marked the transition from the School Certificate to the General Certificate of Education. They will also be required to follow whatever regulations are established for the General Certificate of Secondary Education. But their power to influence such changes of policy, and to resist any of which they disapprove, is considerable. The ultimate control of policy does rest with government, which could impose regulations; the boards would then be faced with the alternatives of accepting them or acting independently. The latter is not beyond the bounds of possibility. The GCE boards are not directly dependent on government finance, although it has to be acknowledged that most of their income comes from candidates' fees paid by local education authorities. It is just conceivable, therefore, that an examination board could decide to operate independently to serve the independent sector of secondary education. Government is unlikely to press unacceptable policies to such a point.

I appreciate that in so short a space my analysis has had to be greatly simplified and that it does some violence to a very complex situation. To expand a point made earlier I recognize the interaction and cross-representation between the various groups which have influence over the examination system. In particular, the examination boards cannot be regarded as totally independent bodies. They are part of the educational system and a glance at their constitutions[6] reveals the variety of educational experience represented on them. Nevertheless, the four bodies which I have identified are more than an analytical fabrication: to some degree the examination boards, the teachers, government and 'market-place' do act independently and bring to bear different, sometimes opposing, influences on public examinations. But this independence is very much tempered by the communication and co-operation between them. This cross-fertilization, however, should not blind us to the fact that at times the interests and policies of the four bodies do not coincide and that tensions between them do exist.

Where, then, does control of the examination system lie, even more pertinent, where *should* it lie? It is tempting to conclude that the source of control cannot be identified. That is not to say that examinations are out of control; for so efficient and well managed a machine that cannot be so. The answer must lie in the 'dispersal of power in education' referred to above. The co-operation and tension between the various bodies seems to have generated a pluralism of control which works quite effectively, even harmoniously; and therein lies its strength. This being so, perhaps we should leave well alone and pursue the question no further.

Notes: Chapter 3

1   Minutes of the Committee of Council on Education, 21 December 1846, Regulations Respecting the Education of Pupil Teachers and Stipendiary Monitors; quoted in Maclure, 1975, p. 53.

2   The Report of the Consultative Committee of the Board of Education on Examinations in Secondary Schools; quoted in Maclure, 1975: 'Examinations which are conducted by external examining bodies and of which the primary objective is an educational one, should be brought into intimate connection with inspection, the existing system of inspection being modified and developed to meet the new needs' (p. 166).

3   Trenaman reports 172 curriculum projects funded by the Council between 1964 and 1978: see Trenaman Report, 1981.

4   Petch, 1953, provides detailed evidence for this growth of teachers' representation on school examination boards, the Joint Matriculation Board in particular, during the first half of this century. The report of the Bryce Commission (1895) culminated in the Balfour Education Act 1902, establishing the responsibility of the state for secondary education and its inspection. Significantly, however, it recommended that examinations at secondary level should remain the responsibility of the education profession, not the state.

5 Even MacIntosh, who has long championed teacher involvement in the examining system, expresses disappointment in the amount of innovation which has resulted from the opportunity for school-based assessment through Mode III: see MacIntosh and Smith, 1974; Lello, 1979, p. 15.
6 The constitutions of the various boards are readily available; for example, JMB, 1983b.

4

What Do They Test?

No matter who controls examinations, and for what purposes, the immediate object of an examination is to assess some attributes of students; it is an instrument of measurement. An analysis of these attributes is not the simple matter which it might appear. The first complicating factor is time: are we concerned with what students can do at the particular moment at which they sit the examination, or what they have done in the past, or what they may be able to do in the future? Then there is the need to distinguish between the actual performance, what is actually set down on a script, and an *assumed* characteristic which gives rise to the performance such as the ability to remember or evaluate. There is also the need to distinguish between *particular* qualities within a narrowly prescribed area such as geography or physics, and *general* qualities, which are displayed in examinations as a whole. Finally, there is the need to distinguish between those qualities which examiners intend to test, the *objectives*, and those which are actually displayed, the *outcomes*. It might be useful to start with the last point, the distinction between objectives and outcomes.

Objectives or Outcomes?

In the design of an examination, setting out the objectives is a relatively easy matter and there is no lack of examples, although rather surprisingly the present custom of prescribing objectives in a formal way is comparatively recent in public examinations. It is now common practice in most school, technical and business examinations, while it has yet to gain a strong foothold in university examinations. Apart from the Revised Code (see p. 37), requirements in the past have been expressed in terms of statements about subject-matter to be covered rather than intrinsic qualities of the student which were to be displayed.

Present practice is to express the performance required of students not only in terms of subject-matter, but in terms of generalized abilities, usually mental ones. The latter have gained impetus through the publication of general models for describing cognitive processes, those of Bloom (1956) and Gagné (1970) probably being the best known and most widely used. Bloom's work, in particular, has been used almost universally; and although in recent years it increasingly has been subjected to criticism, its influence is still discernible in public examinations around the world.

The attractions of these models, in which examination objectives are set out in a hierarchy of generalized behaviours, are many. They are simple, neat and apparently logical, and they can be applied – although sometimes at the expense of considerable distortion – to most of the subjects in the curriculum. Their particular appeal to anyone who has worked internationally in examinations is that they provide a lingua franca spanning most countries, serving as a vehicle of communication and as a starting-point for training examiners, and also for comparative work. It is as a tool for analysis that Bloom's *Taxonomy of Educational Objectives* is most useful. As a means of exposing that most examinations, at least before the 1960s, depended largely on tests of memory, the taxonomy served education well and gave impetus to the move to design examinations which would test the higher abilities of comprehension, application, and so on, in a more systematic way.

The danger of undue reliance on Bloom's work, or any model of intellectual processes for that matter, is that however effective it is as an analytical tool, it is a good deal less effective as a basis for the design of curricula and their related examinations. The very title *Educational Objectives* is pretentious; the work sprang from an analysis of *examination outcomes* and there may be a world of difference between objectives and what students actually learn. Furthermore, we may make unjustified assumptions in deducing certain kinds of thought processes and kinds of learning from an analysis of examination questions and answers. It may be possible to analyse the task of writing an essay into several subtasks; for example, reproducing facts, logical ordering of facts, communicating clearly and grammatically, and so on. But the step from identifying the task and subtasks to a generalized model of cognitive processes is a large one indeed. At the same time, it is of interest to note that attempts to redesign examinations in the 1960s gave rise to specifications of objectives which often corresponded closely to some of the various levels of the Bloom taxonomy, even though at least on one occasion the author was ignorant of the work of Bloom.[1] This in itself indicates that the categories into which Bloom has analysed educational objectives have *some* universal validity.

Much has been made of the point that teachers find it difficult to reach agreement on the classification of examination questions into a prescribed pattern such as that of Bloom. This may be so when teachers first make the attempt; but those who have run courses and workshops for teachers on examination analysis and design find that this arises partly because teachers are unfamiliar with Bloom's work, and partly because they have never before given any serious thought to the levels of intellectual ability which an examination question demands of their students. Both conditions can be overcome with practice if the area of the curriculum examined is closely defined. It *is* possible to consider a particular educational outcome and classify it – if not entirely, at least mainly in one of the Bloom categories. Some outcomes are principally concerned with the intellect (cognitive), others with attitudes and values (affective) and others with physical behaviour (motor).[2] While acknowledging that no one outcome of education can lie entirely in one of those three domains, it is often self-evident that it is mainly concerned with one of them rather than the others. Similarly, at the finer levels it is possible to say, for example, that a particular examination question demands mainly the ability to remember rather than any of the higher cognitive abilities. This point is important because it returns us to what many consider to be the main function of the taxonomies: to reveal the limitations not only of examinations, but of formal education in general, and to point to what they do not cover as well as what they do.

Examinations as we know them originated mainly from the universities, and universities are concerned mainly with intellectual activities. So it was and so it has remained, even though actual control of examinations by universities has diminished. Perhaps this is as it should be. Bruner (1966) makes a compelling case for the importance of 'the will to learn' (by implication learning intellectual skills) as a pre-eminent human characteristic. He argues that since the human species has ceased to evolve by natural processes, it can only progress through learning processes which must be largely contrived and are not fortuitous: 'Human ... evolution [has] become Lamarkian and reversible rather than Darwinian and irreversible' (ibid., p. 113). If this is so, then both the curriculum and examinations rightly concentrate on the cognitive domain; and it barely needs the Bloom taxonomies to demonstrate that such is the case in most of our examinations. Whether the intellectual qualities which are engendered by examinations are those which Bruner had in mind, and whether the intensive cramming which precedes them encourages the will to learn, are issues which may be disputed. But the matter cannot rest here; there are other, more mundane, reasons for the emphasis on cognitive abilities. It has already been pointed out that the nature of examinations rests in part with their academic origins; it also rests with the techniques of assessment which they employ. Examinations as we know them could never have attained their present scale if they had not used common written papers and required written answers submitted by a large number of candidates at precisely the same time. More than that, the techniques of mass examining, and standardized marking and reporting, limited the demands made on students still further: in most cases to the tasks of writing, leavened to some extent with calculating and to an even lesser extent with some drawing. No one could seriously claim that these tasks, important though they are, represent the whole of education let alone human activity in general. President Kenneth Kaunda writes from a country much troubled by the 'diploma disease' and academic examinations:

> What about those other skills such as depth of judgement, a sense of perspective, and a compassionate understanding of human motivation. Some people say that such qualities are the hard won fruits of experience alone. I would be the last to deny the importance of learning lessons of experience, but I do insist that the foundations of these human skills can be laid in an education system which never loses the truth that it is a *person* and not just a brain that is being trained. (Kaunda, 1973, p. 26)

The implication is that schools should be concerned with much wider human attributes than purely intellectual ones. Few would disagree, but the President would be the first to acknowledge, having experienced an examination-dominated schooling himself, that examinations as we know them cannot be expected to reflect that breadth of education.

These limitations were recognized early at the start of the examination era and they persist. The proponents of examinations defended their position (and still do) mainly on two grounds. The first is that there is no better basis on which to assess the young, and secondly, that there are many underlying qualities which are necessary in order to succeed in the admittedly limited skills demanded in an examination. Roach (1971, p. 29) quotes Dean Hawes of Hereford as saying: 'Examinations are a test of commonsense and character as well as book learning. To do well in them demands perseverance and self denial which strengthens the character.' The argument is confident, though the evidence is slender. Since tests specific to commonsense, character, perseverance and self-denial are not readily to hand, it is convenient to assume that tests of a limited range of academic skills perform the same function. It might be more prudent to assume that examinations test no more than that which is manifested in the scripts. This returns us to the main theme of this chapter, what *do* examinations test, and what abilities *do* students display in their examination performance? Let us set aside fanciful claims for what we would *like* them to test.

Specification and Outcomes

For the present it would be as well to confine the discussion to examinations in which students respond in some written form, including comparatively recent forms of examining, namely, objective tests, structured questions, projects, and so on, in addition to the more familiar essay. Assessment through oral examinations or by direct observation of students at work may provide opportunities for extending the range of assessed performance; a fuller consideration of them will be found in Chapter 7.

It is now common practice to state what an examination is intended to test in the form of a specification which sets out, usually with quantitative weightings for each part, the various abilities which the student will be required to display, together with the subject-matter to which those abilities are to be applied. Such specifications are conveniently displayed in the form of two-dimensional grids.[3] One axis of the grid records the weighting given to each ability and the other the weight given to each section of subject-matter.

In general, these attempts to specify, in quantitative terms, what examiners seek to assess have been welcomed. They at least indicate that some thought has been given to what is to be assessed rather than assuming that it is self-evident; and they have had the effect of moving the emphasis from subject-matter alone to the attributes of the students themselves. They also provide a link with the objectives of the curriculum which are usually expressed in the same kind of terms. Furthermore, the specifications expose examination boards to the possibility of rigorous investigation into the feasibility of their intentions and into the gap between outcomes and objectives. The prescription of *intentions* in the form of quantitative specifications is laudable and many examination boards have accepted the need to publish them. On the other hand, there is a natural reluctance to give the same degree of publicity to the *outcomes* of examinations in the form of analysis of the papers, the mark schemes and the scripts.

It is to the credit of many examination authorities that they have allowed research on the outcomes of some of their examinations. In doing so they put themselves in a position similar to football referees or cricket and tennis umpires exposed to the television replay in slow motion; and sometimes the findings can be equally embarrassing. It is not the purpose of this book to describe the methodology of this type of research, but there are some difficulties to which attention should be drawn.

It is comparatively easy to allocate a particular question and its corresponding mark schemes and answers to a defined area of subject-matter and any competent teacher could do so. The problems lie more in the general attributes of students: skills, abilities, qualities, call them what you will. The first difficulty is in determining whether these attributes exist at all as separate entities. Are there such things as the ability to recall, to comprehend, formulate hypotheses, critically appraise, use patterns, apply logic, evaluate, and so on, which students have, or have not, at their command? It would be a happy state of affairs if we had an answer to that question which could gain general acceptance. But the state of theories of learning and cognitive development is one of confusion, if not outright disagreement. Even the much used (and misused) theories of Piaget, perennially quoted in countless essays by student teachers, are now thought to be much more limited in their application than has been believed (Brown and Desforges, 1977). Nevertheless, it may be that practising teachers, at a purely pragmatic level, find it convenient to classify various kinds of student performance into discrete categories. Certainly much of the work of Bloom was based on that assumption, and up to a point it is justified. But this pragmatic approach is not without its difficulties. Even if teachers were able to agree in their classification of certain performances which students display in their examination scripts, it does not follow that these can be translated in absolute terms to intrinsic attributes inherently possessed by students. And it is by no means certain that teachers can agree until they have been trained and hence preconditioned to one particular model of the intellect.

There is yet another difficulty. Even if we had agreement on a general classification of abilities and even if teachers could infallibly recognize them, do examination questions allow students to manifest those abilities in their answers. It is all very well to claim that an essay question *allows* a student to exhibit the ability to critically analyse and evaluate; indeed, it may, but it is no easy task for a reader of the essay to detect it, although it may well be easier to detect the lack of it. It is difficult enough if one knows the student or can probe more deeply in a subsequent viva voce examination – but in mass examining it is well-nigh impossible. A question which is novel to one candidate, requiring skills of interpretation, comprehension and application to an unfamiliar situation, may be no more than an exercise in recall on the part of another who has been prepared differently and may even have rehearsed answers provided by the teacher. As Rowntree (1977, p. 175) has written, 'If we need to know what the student is, or even knows, we must look beyond what he does'.

This discussion on the limitations of the specification of examination questions, and the classification of kinds of student response, are not directed against attempts to make examiners more accountable for what they do. Accountability of teachers, including examiners, is a policy which has gained momentum in recent years and there are plenty willing to pursue it and indeed relish it. It does, however, call into question the apparent exactness of examination specifications bestowed by the allocation of numbers; and while allowing that some specification is better than none, it does open up the possibility that these seemingly precise statements are spurious. Nevertheless, the fact that examination boards are prepared to set out specifications does allow a more general review of what examinations are at least *intended* to test, even if some uncertainty remains as to whether they actually do so. It also provides an indication of the relative importance in the minds of the examiners of the various kinds of performance, which in turn allows comparison with the objectives of a curriculum and an estimate of the face validity of the examination.

'Mere Recall'

Perhaps the most common charge laid against examinations is that in the main they test 'mere recall'. Analyses of many different examination papers give weight to the view that a good memory, coupled with the ability to transfer to paper what is remembered, can be the main source of success. I am not aware of any research into the ways by which students prepare for examinations, but it would be surprising if such research did not reveal that committing material to memory did not form the greater part of preparation at all levels, including degree work, and in most subjects. It would be difficult to account for the success of 'crammers' in any other way.

The effect of decades of these kinds of examination, and the tradition of cramming, has been to bring good memory into disrepute as a desirable attribute to be encouraged in students. The curriculum projects of the 1960s and 1970s certainly played down the importance of memory, and this was reflected in both the published aims of the curriculum designers and the specifications of the examiners. In those times it would have been rash for any examiner to specify even as much as 50 per cent of the questions to test recall, or in Bloomian terms 'knowledge', except possibly in an examination designed for students who were not in the higher ability groups.

The reaction against recall is not surprising. It may in some instances be justified, but is it altogether wise? The almost obligatory preface 'mere' has served to reduce the term to a cliché and to lower the status of memory as something rather beneath the higher skills of the more able students: 'One can always look up facts in books.' This is fallacious. If one is writing an essay or a book, it may be so; but most people do not spend their lives writing essays or books. Recall of past experience is the mainspring of all our activities and frequently it has to be immediate and cannot wait on a visit to the library. Even academics – arch-proponents of the 'higher skills' – would admit that in seminar and debate and negotiation the most formidable are those who can recall pertinent facts at will. And anyone who thinks that the less able are better at memorizing than doing other things has never taught the lower streams.

An attempt to restore memory to its proper place (and to eradicate the 'mere') is not necessarily a reactionary move; nor does it inevitably sanction a return to the memorization of useless information, and it certainly does not obviate the need for the higher skills. In the event it is unlikely that harm has been done by the shift towards the higher skills in the examination specifications. For one thing, all of those questions which are classified in the higher levels require a basis of recalled information if they are to be answered. Even those questions which provide necessary information, or allow the use of books of data, still cannot be answered successfully without a good deal of memorized information; so the actual weight attached to it may well be a good deal greater than some of the specifications indicate.

So much emphasis has been placed in recent years on the so-called higher skills, and on such qualities as creativity and problem-solving, that the attributes of an informed person have tended to be forgotten, at least among educationists and examiners. Anyone who has marked examination scripts will be well aware of spurious attempts to set out original arguments, sometimes on matters of great social importance, on the basis of very little evidence or information of any kind. To encourage ill-informed, unsubstantiated comment on all manner of important issues does a disservice to both education and examinations. It is somewhat ironic that, at the same time, some of the most popular television and radio programmes have taken the form of competitions[4] which have been mainly tests of memory, sometimes of conspicuously useless information. Plainly in the public mind tests of intellect are tests of the ability to recall, sometimes under stressful situations. I hasten to disclaim any intention to set these up as models of assessment for public examinations; clearly the nature of the information, the context in which it is obtained and the use to which it is put are more important than the virtue of a good memory for its own sake. This brings us to the content or subject-matter on which examinations are based.

Subjects

So far the discussion has been directed towards general abilities of students unrelated to the material to which those abilities are applied. Much of the work on the classification of student performance has deliberately attempted to be generally applicable to all learning, regardless of *what* is learned. Bloom (1956) sought to identify kinds of student 'behaviours', which could be considered independently from the substance of those behaviours. The strength of this approach was that it appeared to make the classification of behaviours universally applicable. The weakness lies in the assumption that an examination specification should make those general abilities the determining factor rather than the subject-matter to which they are applied.

The idea that examinations could be content-free; that they could be devised without reference to what the students had actually studied; and that they could be specified solely in terms of conceptualized categories of students' behaviours, was exposed as an impossibility as soon as examiners tried to devise the actual tests.[5] In fairness to Bloom and his colleagues it has to be said that they never assumed that a test could be content-free. Whatever the impression that may have been given in the Taxonomies, it was subsequently corrected. In 1971, for example, he writes:

Think critically about what? Here the content area must be specified. Critical thinking skills may differ from discipline to discipline; but more important, unless the content area is also specified, planning, selecting materials, and determining methods of presentation become impossible. (Bloom *et al.*, 1971, p. 23)

Highly generalized tests such as those purporting to test spatial ability or linguistic ability may get nearer to being content-free than the more familiar forms of examination; but even in them previous learning cannot be entirely eliminated as a factor in test performance. The tendency to generalize the learning process, and the skills acquired through it, was not confined to the educational taxonomists and psychologists. Pring (1975, p. 116) points to the move in the 1970s towards the '"undifferentiated" curriculum, the concentration on the "learning" process rather than the subject matter, and an interdisciplinary approach'. He refers to the influential educational lobby which gained sponsorship for projects of curriculum development in which integration was the dominant principle. Pring's critical analysis of what he calls the new orthodoxy, and its ill-defined assumptions is worthy of study. He refers to the 'unargued and highly questionable assumption that a subject-based curriculum is irrelevant to the needs of pupils' (ibid., p. 130). Of course, this does not necessarily make a case for subject-based examinations, but the same arguments can be ranged against those examinations or schemes of assessment which claim to be subject-free.

In part, the emphasis on general categories of student performance, which has dominated examination design in recent years, may be a reaction against the previous practice of specifying examinations solely in terms of subject-matter. The move has gained impetus from the radical questions which are being asked about the nature of the subject-matter of the curriculum, the categories into which it has been divided, and their relative status. But no matter how the various kinds of student attributes are defined and classified and how the various kinds of subject-matter of the curriculum are defined and classified, some statement about both is necessary for the design of examinations if we are to avoid the nonsense of assuming that, for example, analysis in chemistry is the same as analysis of the visual arts or of a passage from Shakespeare.

'Recognized' Subjects

The replacement of the School Certificate (SC) by the General Certificate of Education (GCE) in England and Wales marked a significant change in attitude towards the subject-matter of examinations and, indirectly, towards the school curriculum. From the inception of school examinations in the Oxford and Cambridge Locals until the introduction of the GCE, there was formal recognition that some subjects were more important than others. The acceptance of these recognized subjects was forced on the schools by means of the regulations which governed the award of certificates. Oxford University made the first move in 1857, establishing a Delegacy

> to conduct examinations of non-members of the university in religious knowledge, English, history, languages, mathematics, physical science and other subjects forming part of the liberal education of youth. (Roach, 1971, p. 72)

Over the next 100 years there were modifications to this list. Religious knowledge, so important a requirement to Oxford and Cambridge universities, declined. Subsequently the regulations governing the award of the School Certificate, established in 1918, enforced a particular pattern of subjects on the examinations and the secondary school curriculum by introducing the 'grouped certificate'. The establishment of the School Certificate and the events leading up to it are well documented by Petch:

> Subjects were to be in three groups (i) English subjects, (ii) languages, (iii) sciences and mathematics; to gain a certificate a candidate must pass in each of the three. A fourth group of subjects (Music, Drawing, Manual Work and Housecraft) need not be offered; indeed doubt was expressed whether the subjects could be adequately examined in the present state of their development. (Petch, 1953, p. 68)

The influence of this examination requirement on the curriculum of secondary schools was dominant.

Petch also records the slow erosion of the grouped certificate and the struggle for recognition of the group four subjects. This erosion was part of movements towards equality (whatever that might mean) of all subjects in the school curriculum, which culminated in the GCE and later in the Certificate of Secondary Education (CSE). Both of these examinations were single-subject not grouped; that is, a certificate could be obtained in any number of subjects of any kind provided that they were recognized by the examining authority.

The introduction of the single-subject examination allowed all subjects normally to be found in the school curriculum to be examined and recorded on a certificate. More than that, it encouraged the invention of new subjects, hence their proliferation in the handbooks of the examination boards in the 1960s and 1970s. Formally this appeared to give equal status to all the subdivisions of the school curriculum; but in effect the hierarchical status of subjects was maintained to a significant degree by the requirements of the market-place, that is, the entrance requirements of employers, further and higher education tutors, and the ingrained attitudes of parents and teachers. At the time of writing, a strong lobby has arisen for the reintroduction, if not of a grouped certificate at least a core of essential subjects which should be awarded special status in the curriculum and hence in the corresponding public examination (Joseph, 1984a).

The changes over the years in regulations concerning the subject-matter of examinations reveal two strands of thought. One is the use of examinations to regulate the subject-matter of the curriculum; the other is the system of values which accords greater importance to some parts of the curriculum than others, at least for the purpose of certification and qualification for subsequent employment and education. While there have been changes in emphasis in both, these two elements remain part of the attitude of educationists and society in general to the nature of knowledge and its relation to education and examinations. And it does seem that organizational change, as demonstrated by the introduction of the GCE and CSE, does little to diminish the effect of the values of the market-place.

In an analysis of these two dominant strands of thought it is difficult to disentangle logical attitudes from traditional. It should not be forgotten that in their early days public examinations were seen as a liberating force, both educationally and socially, eroding if not breaking the narrow, traditional classical curriculum at secondary level and replacing it by a broad, liberal curriculum. To this effect examinations have proved a powerful weapon; it has taken over 100 years but finally the classical curriculum has become a vestige still lamented by a few (Headmasters' Conference, 1982), to be replaced, first, by the pattern reflected by the grouped certificate, and later by the infinite variety offered in the thick publications of approved syllabuses.

This increase in the variety of subject-matter may be seen as a move to allow the forces of the market, rather than the prescribed values of central authority, to operate on examinations and curricula. These forces may be in opposition; certainly the very first research publication of the Schools Council (1968) showed that teachers and parents had different views on curricular and examination priorities.

It is easy to detect an ambivalence in this matter. On the one hand, this open-ended, *Schmorgesbord* approach to the choice of subjects can be hailed as a means of increasing freedom of choice and furthering the autonomy of students and teachers, and on the other, it can be pointed out that it may result in further division between the more able students who continue to take the high-status subjects and the less able who take those of low status. While an overt recognition that some subjects are worth more than others has not yet returned to full strength, there is plenty of evidence that it still exists and is growing despite many ingenious attempts to put a different gloss on the issue. One of the recommendations of the first Keeves Report, *Education and Change in South Australia* (1981, section 11.1 (*d*)), is that the subjects of the new Year 12 Certificate should be classified into four groups 'according to their functions of either preparation for further study ... preparation for special tertiary courses, curriculum diversification, or to provide a sound general education'. Whether it will be possible to categorize the curriculum in this manner and still retain equal status for all four groups of subjects only time will tell.

Whether we like it or not, the fact has to be faced that the curriculum of most schools is organized on the basis of subjects; that there are differences in kind between the subjects; and that a subset of them, variously called academic or traditional, have a higher status than the others. This status may depend on the intrinsic nature of each subject and the unique and essential contribution which each makes to an understanding of the human condition and its environment, in as much as each should form a necessary part of the curriculum of every child. On the other hand, the status may arise from external forces which require a successful performance as a condition for entry to higher education and certain esteemed professions. Given this situation, it seems inevitable that the high-status subject-matter in public examinations will be restricted in the main to the traditional academic subjects.

The Search for Status

Even if it were shown that this difference in status between subjects is undesirable and inequitable, there are no easy solutions to the problem. One in particular that has been tried, although without great success, is the 'if you can't beat them, join them' approach. The outcome of this has been the establishment of school examinations in subjects outside the traditional academic ones: technology of one kind or another, physical education, various forms of the arts and domestic activities, for example. It has been rather painful to witness the great amount of effort which many people have expended in the attempt to achieve status for their subject by breaking into the exclusive ring of traditional examination subjects. One which has succeeded, at least in terms of numbers of candidates, is art; and it has carried with it several others which formed the 'group IV' subjects in the former School Certificate. Petch (1953, p. 91) refers to 'the all-embracing hospitality of Group IV, ranging from Art, through Music, Domestic Subjects and Commercial Subjects to Mechanical Sciences'. But even this modest success has been bought at a price. The technical constraints of mass examining, relying as it does mainly on written material centrally marked, do not favour some of the more practical – some would say more useful – areas of education. The attempt to fit them into public examinations inevitably is distorting and indeed may do them a disservice.

Perhaps a more realistic approach is that adopted by Keeves (1981), which is openly to recognize that the general perception of subjects is that they fall into different groups and hence have different functions. Whether these differences are real or apparent is immaterial to the present discussion, it is sufficient that most people regard them as such. If also we recognize that some are more examinable than others, it might be better to accept the fact and seek status for the less examinable elsewhere and by other means.

The Keeves type of solution brings with it other problems more far-reaching than the immediate educational ones. If in operation it is found that one type of child has advantage in one group of subjects, particularly if that is the group most likely to lead to higher education, the risk of social division and discontent increases. It is then only too easy to ascribe social and political motives to the formal distinction between groups of subjects. Young's comment on the apparently progressive projects of the Schools Council epitomizes this:

> [they] have, to a large extent, reflected an acceptance of the academic/nonacademic distinction as characterising two kinds of knowledge, suitable for two distinct groups of children and associated with fairly distinct occupational rewards. (Young, 1975, p. 41)

It is but a small step from this position to one in which the divisions within the curriculum and examinations can be associated with the divisions within society. The assumption that formal examinations are part of a deliberate strategy by those in power to maintain a class system may be prejudiced. Nevertheless, if it can be demonstrated that the way in which the subject-matter of examinations is structured and given status penalizes those who are already at a disadvantage, it behoves those who control and administer public examinations at least to consider *the consequences* of the system if not the underlying motives.

It follows that those who effectively determine the subjects and subject-matter of examinations, educators and employers alike, could well give some radical thought to the assumptions which underlie their requirements. Tradition alone will not do, and even recourse to arguments of basic skills and utility may be suspect. To rely on both at the same time could well be a nonsense since the concepts of utility and basic skills are changing year by year in a world of accelerating change. This point does not escape Keeves (1981, p. 102): 'It is also important to recognise that Australian society is in a stage of transition from, in the main, a manufacturing to a service society.'

Those subjects which continue to attract the greater proportion of examination candidates, language, history, mathematics and science,[6] are indeed the cornerstones of a liberal education; but we should not pretend that they occupy the greater part of the social and working life and thought of the mass of people, at least in the form in which they are presented in examinations. To attempt to establish that the subject-matter of examinations is sufficiently representative of the affairs of mankind is to stretch credibility too far. If, on the other hand, it can be established that they serve as the only practicable vehicle for reasonably valid and equitable assessment and selection, then we must make the best of what we have and try by other means to give proper esteem to the less examinable aspects of education and to the unexaminable, though worthy, characteristics of the young people who are subject to it; a point which is taken further in Chapter 13.

Notes: Chapter 4

1 I can vouch for the fact that although the specifications of the objectives of the Nuffield O-level chemistry examination corresponded to some of the Bloom levels of cognitive objectives, I was ignorant of Bloom's work at the time; see Waring, 1979.

2 Bloom, 1956, in *Handbook I* sets out a taxonomy in the cognitive domain. Subsequently *Handbook II* was published – see Krathwohl *et al.*, 1964 – which dealt with the affective domain. Later still the trilogy was completed by the work of Harrow, 1972, which dealt with mainly physical activities.

3 **Multiple-choice questions in Nuffield Chemistry examinations**

The fixed-response questions used in Paper 1 for either examination are intended to complement all other measures of ability used in the Nuffield Chemistry examinations. Multiple-choice questions are a simple means of ensuring an even assessment of the entire course. Thus, for some years, Paper 1 has been constructed according to a predetermined specification. A two-dimensional grid is used, setting abilities against activities encountered during the course. For this purpose, the abilities and activities considered are:

Abilities
1. Knowledge
2. Comprehension
3. Application
4. Analysis/evaluation

Activities
1. Composition and changes in materials
2. Practical techniques
3. Patterns in the behaviour of materials
4. Essential measurements
5. Concepts concerning the particulate and electrical nature of matter.
In addition, another two-dimensional grid is used which sets Topics against Abilities.

Figure A3.1 shows the Ability/Activity specification for the multiple-choice paper for Nuffield Chemistry. The figures show the desired weighting for a 70-item paper: the actual weighting is not shown.

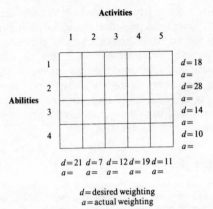

Figure A3.1 *Ability/Activity specification for the multiple-choice paper*

4   *Mastermind, Brain of Britain, Top of the Form*, and many others.
5   This was certainly so in the examinations which followed the Nuffield science projects. The O-level chemistry project was advertised as a 'sample' scheme, teachers being encouraged to devise their own schemes within the general framework of the Nuffield approach. It became immediately apparent that there were very few questions which did not make *some* assumptions about *what* the students had learned. This was a major factor in turning the sample scheme into *the* scheme in the eyes of the teachers.
6   The Annual Reports of the Joint Matriculation Board and others provide a concise and convenient summary of the numbers of candidates entering for each subject over a period of years.

5

Design and Production

The extent to which the examination boards influence the formulation of *policy* on examinations is an open question (see Chapter 3). However, when it comes to *production*, the responsibility clearly does rest with the boards, and it is the purpose of this chapter and Chapter 6 to outline and comment on the sequence of events from examination design through the various processes leading finally to the promulgation of results. Although examples will be drawn in the main from one examination board, the various stages and sequence of the production process are applicable to them all, although they may differ in detail.

The Basis for Design (What Every Examiner Should Know)

Conventional wisdom proclaims that the curriculum must come first; the curriculum, therefore, must be the basis for design. To put it another way, the designer of an examination should have as a starting-point a knowledge of all the main elements which have gone to make up the learning experiences of the candidates, which implies a knowledge not only of the subject-matter, but also the intended outcomes and methods of teaching.

The principle is, at face-value, unassailable; in the practice of large-scale examining it carries assumptions some of which hardly stand close scrutiny. It assumes that teachers are agreed on those essential elements of the curriculum; that examiners are in a position to know what they are; that there is sufficient common ground to produce a single examination which will be equally suitable for everyone; and that it is technically possible to transpose all the desirable aspects of the curriculum from the learning process to the examining process. In practice it is naïve to expect the design of an examination to reflect completely the actual, or even the ideal, curriculum. Nevertheless, whether it is explicit or implicit the basis for the design of an examination is essentially curricular.

Curriculum Validity

This is an appropriate point at which to introduce the concept of *curriculum validity*, which may be defined as *the degree to which the examination situation matches the learning situation*. The attainment of an acceptable level of curriculum validity assumes that the designers of the examination are in a position to know what goes on, or is intended to go on, in the classroom and thus reflect in the examination all the desirable qualities in the essential elements of good teaching and learning practice. It is logical to conclude that designer, examiner and teacher should be one and the same; indeed, this is one of the principles which underlie the movement towards school-based examining. That movement may be a step to greater curriculum validity but it raises other difficulties, which will be discussed later; claims that it is the answer to all the problems of examining should be regarded with some caution. In any event school-based examinations as we know them require validation of their design by an external board, so a judgement on the curricular basis still has to be made indirectly by someone other than the teacher. The discussion which follows, therefore, is concerned principally with the board-based examiners operating outside schools.

Since the basis is essentially curricular, it is apparent that those responsible for developing a design should be those with responsibility for and experience in the planning and operation of particular courses of study; not those who simply define aims, objectives and topics, but those who understand the constraints under which teachers and students will work. In practice this is usually so. An examination board puts the responsibility for design on to an appropriate subject committee. The committee may, in turn, appoint a development group to draw up a draft syllabus and examination design, usually with sample questions. These drafts are reviewed and possibly altered by the whole subject committee and then by the Examinations Council of the board which has the ultimate responsibility for approval or disapproval.

At all the stages experienced teachers have a determining influence, so that the final design is based on their judgements of their own teaching practice and what they conceive to be, or ought to be, the practice of their colleagues. This raises the fundamental issue of whether examination design is based on the curriculum as it *is* or as it *ought to be*. No matter how much it may be claimed that the design is a *reflection*, it is difficult to see how it can avoid a good measure of *prescription*.

Whether the design of an examination be prescriptive or descriptive, whether it is formulated by one teacher for his students alone or by a group of examiners for someone else's students, there remains a common set of questions which have to be considered as a basis for design:

(1)   What is taught?
(2)   How is it taught?
(3)   How is it learned?
(4)   What can the students be expected to do as a result of this experience?

There is a deceptive simplicity in such questions; and simple questions, as every examiner knows, are often the most difficult to answer. In practice those who design examinations acknowledge that they cannot get definitive answers to the four questions. They can only proceed by making assumptions about them: that what is taught is the subject-matter set out in the syllabus and that the manner in which it is taught, the activities in which the students engage, and the kinds of performance expected of them conform with their own experience or what they conceive to be common practice. Even with firsthand teaching experience, they cannot extrapolate with any certainty from this to cases in general. If they have no recent experience of the curriculum, the assumptions about general practice become even more abstract and consequently are less likely to have curriculum validity.[1] Firsthand experience of the curriculum is not the only criterion of competence for those responsible for designing an appropriate examination; but it is a necessary one. The gap between curriculum practice and examination practice is difficult enough to bridge in the most favourable circumstances: to attempt to design for the latter without experience of the former is to invite disaster.

Why, it may be asked, is it necessary to be aware of teaching styles and learning activities; would not a knowledge of the subject-matter and the desired outcomes suffice in the form of a subject-matter/student behaviour specification described in Chapter 4? But this is to take too narrow a view of both curriculum and examinations. The curriculum is inadequately defined simply by a list of topics and generalized student attributes; it concerns active processes between teacher and learner and no description of a curriculum can be complete without them. If, for example, students are encouraged in class to learn by actively solving problems or by being allowed to challenge and criticize preconceived values, their curriculum will be different in kind from one in which students passively receive predetermined methods of problem-solving and other people's values. Or if students are required to participate mainly in *conversation* in a second language, then their curriculum will be different from one in which they mainly *read* and *write* a second language. It is not necessary to make judgements between the various styles to recognize that they would require different styles of assessment if curriculum validity is to be sufficiently maintained in an examination.

Unfortunately even if examination designers are aware that a particular style of teaching and learning is in use, they cannot be certain that it is in *general* use, nor can they be certain of reflecting it in the examination. This is especially so in more active styles of learning, to which much prominence has been given in curriculum development projects in recent years. They may be summarized in statements such as: children should actively experience what it is like to work as a scientist/historian/artist, and so on. They find another expression in the so-called *process*-based curriculum. This trend had early expression in the Nuffield Science projects:

Pupils should gain an understanding that lasts throughout their lives of what it means to approach a problem scientifically ... science should be presented to pupils in a way in which *they* can conduct an enquiry into the nature of things as well as a body of information built up by the enquiries of other people. Pupils must approach their studies through experiments designed to awaken the spirit of investigation. (Nuffield Foundation, 1975, pp. 2–3)

Lest such an approach be written off as 'progressive', it should be mentioned that it is not new; it has been acknowledged as a precept, if not always a practice, in education for centuries, certainly since Comenius wrote: 'men ... must learn to know and investigate the things themselves and not the observations that people have made about the things' (Keatinge, 1896, p. 302).

Of course, a respectable ancestry does not in itself make a learning style respectable. Be that as it may, it has had a considerable following, even though it may be sometimes observed in intention rather than in practice. The point at issue is not whether this is a good or bad approach to teaching and learning, but whether it can be reflected in public examinations. In the Nuffield chemistry examinations at O level it was decided that it could not, so the direct assessment of practical work was excluded; a decision which tacitly admitted the limitations of the concept of curriculum validity in large-scale examining.

Elsewhere attempts to meet the point have usually taken the form of devolving a part of the examination from assessment by external examiners to internal assessment by teachers. The Nuffield A-level chemistry project allowed 15 per cent to internal assessment of which part involved marks for the process of investigation rather than for the product. The Schools Council Integrated Science Project allowed 20 per cent to internal assessment most of which was attached to aims related to what might loosely be called a 'scientific approach'. The Schools Council Geography 14–18 Project allowed an even greater (50 per cent) weighting to internal assessment with considerable emphasis on such attributes as 'persistence and initiative on the part of the student'.

Worthy though these attempts to reflect teaching and learning styles in examinations may be, their degree of success has yet to be established. It is all very well to set out assessment criteria which appear to allow a considerable weight to the process of learning rather than its product, and to devise moderating schemes which allow exchange of ideas and criteria between teachers who are engaged in assessing it; but one can be forgiven some doubts about how teachers actually arrive at these assessments. It is, of course, a particularly difficult area to research – like most other research which is concerned with classroom processes. However, despite the lack of evidence on how they are actually operated, the schemes of internal assessment referred to above do provide at least the *opportunity* for an assessment of the active participation of the student during the learning process in addition to an assessment of the final products at the end of it.

The principle that an examination design should start with a consideration of the curriculum is founded not only on the desirability of attaining high curriculum validity, but it also acknowledges that examinations have a formative as well as a reflective function. No matter how much one may wish the relationship to be entirely dominated by the curriculum, it is in practice cyclical. The examination may indeed reflect the curriculum, but it will also reinforce it; it is a relationship in which the beginning and end defy separation. This being so, it is doubly important that the design of an examination should at least not constrain desirable teaching and learning processes; even if it cannot actively encourage them, it should allow the possibility.

The application of these principles to examining on a large scale assumes general agreement and general practice of a particular style of teaching and learning. But rarely does such agreement exist; indeed, it could be argued that it should not exist. It may be that examinations have more than enough influence over the *content* of the curriculum without extending that influence to such personal characteristics as styles of teaching and learning. This puts examiners into a predicament which defies resolution. On the one hand, if they deliberately try to encourage a particular teaching/learning style, they will offend those who prefer another. On the other hand, if they try to remain neutral in this matter, they will be accused of designing solely in terms of the content of the curriculum. The problem is difficult enough when examining for like-minded devotees of a curriculum project, into which they enter of their own volition; the difficulty is compounded when an examination is required to encompass the whole nation.

It is this predicament which underlies many of the problems which have been encountered in the attempts to arrive at generally agreed criteria for a national system of examining at 16 plus in England and Wales. The greater and more diverse the population which is to be served, the more difficult it is to reach an agreed curriculum base for the examination. If that base is to be determined by consensus rather than by majority decision or government direction, it is likely to be in sufficiently general terms as to mean all things to all men.[2] Even so apparently a simple decision as whether to introduce oral work as a compulsory element in English language raises argument. This example is but one of many; a compulsory assessment of practical work in the sciences is another. The tendency to a tissue rejection of these foreign bodies should not be ascribed to mere reaction, nor to arguments of technical difficulty and cost (although both may be pertinent). There is the much more persuasive argument that the scope of such assessments, if they are to be feasible in large-scale examining, is so limited that they will be confined to a narrow range of activities with a correspondingly adverse effect on what is taught. The favoured solution to this problem at present is either to allow a small weight of external assessment to these unruly elements or to pass the responsibility for their assessment to the teachers in the school. If the former is adopted, the element in question is demoted to a position of relative unimportance. If the latter, a fresh set of problems arises: the difficulty of obtaining equivalence in practice, and in standard and acceptability, of the various schemes of assessment adopted by individual teachers.

To draw this argument together: it needs to be recognized that precision, commonality and fixed standards in examinations at national level can only be achieved at the expense of freedom in curriculum choice for schools, teachers and students, and will result in a narrowing of the curriculum base. Conversely, although it is easier to reflect the full range of curricular activities in small-scale assessment by teachers within individual schools and classrooms, there is an inevitable loss of equivalence both of the nature of student performance and the standard of that performance. In short, *commonality and individuality are in opposition*, a theme which will recur. The issue is perhaps not quite as stark as that presented above. There are possibilities for compromise, although the difficulty could also be resolved by a more clear-cut political act in favour of either standardized national tests in a small number of subjects or the abandonment of external examining altogether. The latter would be tantamount to political hand washing by passing the problem to the schools. But whatever happens, the designers of examinations at every level should first ask those four fundamental questions about the curriculum.

The Design

It is all very well to say that examination design should be based on the curriculum; but even if the designers do have a clear and complete view of the curriculum, it is by no means an easy matter to convert it to an effective design for an examination. A precise identification of the constituent parts or components, an appropriate and harmonious relationship between them and, at the same time, satisfaction for the many and varied (and highly critical) clients is the essence of good design. It is also a demand for perfection which the art and technology of examining is far from attaining. But 'say not the struggle nought availeth', examiners should strive to produce some sort of design not just a random assembly of bits.

The Components
To some extent this point has been covered in Chapter 4, in which were described specifications of generalized student skills and subject-matter. But an overall specification in those terms alone is insufficient as a

starting-point for the design of a complete examination; consideration has to be given to the nature of the component building-blocks from which the examination is to be constructed. The traditional unit for designing an examination has been the *question*, and until recent times the design has amounted to no more than requiring answers to a small number of these questions packaged within the traditional timespan of two or three hours, usually allowing various degrees of choice to the student. Of course, the questions were not always questions as such: they were often brief instructions to 'describe', 'give an account of', 'compare and contrast', 'analyse', 'discuss', and so on; sometimes attempts to give higher status to a question involved a qualification such as 'critically discuss'. This style continues, particularly in universities and colleges, and questions provide a quick easy unit for assembling an examination.

The nature of questions will be pursued more fully in Chapter 7; the point to be made here is that, in many school examinations, questions alone no longer serve as the basic unit for examination design. One of the outcomes of the surge in curriculum development in the past twenty years or so has been an increase in the complexity of the parts which go to make up an examination design. This has given rise not only to many different styles of questions, but to different ways of describing the main parts of an examination; these may be summarized as follows.

Division by subject-matter. This is the most familiar form of division, in which parts of an examination correspond to parts of the syllabus. For example,

> Three papers will be set: Paper I (European History), Paper II (British History) and Paper III (American History). Within each paper one alternative will be set on each of several periods. (JMB, 1982d, p. 45)

This type of division may also reflect a division among examiners themselves, they are allocated to sections in which they have their main expertise and are allowed separate mark schemes.

Such a division may or may not be allocated a particular timespan. If it constitutes a whole paper that is a part of the examination which has been separately timetabled, the period of time will be known in advance. If it forms a section of a paper, the time allocated rests with the candidate within, of course, the limits of the total timetabled period.

Division by question type. This type of division is also one of long standing, although more recent than the division by subject-matter. The most familiar is exemplified by several of the curriculum development projects of the 1960s and 1970s,[3] in which the examinations are in three parts: objective tests, structured questions and free response (more generally known as essay type).

The reasons for using more than one type of question in an examination may rest on both educational and technical grounds and are discussed more fully in Chapter 7. Once it is decided for whatever reason to use more than one type of question, it is common practice to allocate each main type to a separate part of the examination. This allows separate marking and, perhaps more important, allows the candidates to answer in one form throughout rather than having to switch from one form to another in successive questions.

Division by mode. This is a division in which the responsibility for assessment is separated, usually between examiners external to the school and examiners within the school, or some combination of the two. The justification for this may be either to allow internal assessment of those attributes which cannot be assessed by external agency or assessment of the same attributes by both external and internal agencies, a form of duplicate marking. For either reason, this kind of division is increasingly used and it is the one which usually gives rise to most argument since the external v. internal polarization is perhaps the most fundamental in all discussion on examinations, raising as it does the crucial issues of *who* should control them, and if there is to be dual control, who should predominate and what should be the relation between them. The division of an examination between externally assessed and internally assessed components has been a feature of many examinations for some time now both in schools and in further and higher education. The tendency has been to attach a greater weight to the external component; there are plenty of examples of internal components accounting for 10–40 per cent of the total, but the use of 50 per cent or more is unusual.[4]

Division by time. The division of an examination into parts may be for no reason other than to allow it to be taken in convenient periods of time. The upper and lower limits are governed by such considerations as the maximum time which a student could be expected to work without undue fatigue and the minimum time which can be effectively organized within an examination timetable; three hours to one hour seems to be the usual range. These periods of time may be related to particular styles of question: the shorter period for an objective test, for example, and the longer period for writing essays or doing a practical examination. They may, on the other hand, be no more than a device for dividing the whole examination into parts, with no particular set of educational or assessment objectives attached to any of these parts, simply to allow convenient timetabling. (The problem of the timetabling of public examinations is not to be underestimated. It may seem a trivial matter among apparently more weighty ones, but it is a very complex operation and not one which can allow an infinite variety of periods of time.)

Most of the foregoing assumes the traditional practice of conducting examinations at the end of a course of study, often called 'terminal assessment'. But there is a growing practice of examining *during* a course, particularly for an internally assessed component. This has been given various names of which 'continuous assessment' is the most common; 'concurrent assessment' is perhaps more suitable and less misleading. Justification for the inclusion of a concurrent element in the design of an examination may be made on various grounds: it allows more frequent assessment and enhances reliability; it allows subject-matter and skills to be covered more fully; and it allows a modular system of course design in which a part of the course is completed and assessed as a unit which is at least partly independent of others.

The idea of a modular curriculum, together with a modular system of assessment, in which units and credits are completed and accumulated to provide finally a single award has yet to find general acceptance at school level, where terminal assessment is still the norm. Although the CSE and GCE certificates are accumulative in the sense that students may add to their tally of subjects over a period of time, attainment in each subject is normally assessed at the end of its course and, in practice, most students attempt the certificate only once. Even in higher education the tradition of attaining all the parts of a degree within a short period at the end of three or four years dies hard, although the credit accumulation system of the degrees of the Open University has gone some way to undermining it.

Whether greater and more lasting attainment results from the accumulation of modular assessments over a whole course than from terminal assessment is more a matter of opinion and preference than of proof. The organizational constraints alone place in doubt the feasibility of a large-scale application of this system at school level and they have tended to deter the designers of school examinations who may have wished to divide their examinations sequentially over time to correspond to the completion of parts of the course of study. Because of this, the idea is sufficiently novel for it to be discussed further in Chapter 12, in which alternatives to the conventional terminal examination are considered.

Division by difficulty. Difficulty is a carelessly used concept. The only form of examining in which it is used with any precision is in objective testing, in which the difficulty of a question can be expressed as the proportion of candidates who got it wrong. (Usually the statistic produced in objective tests is the *facility index* which reflects the proportion of candidates who gave the *correct* answer.[5]) But poor performance may arise from factors other than inherent characteristics of the question itself: insufficient or inappropriate learning, bad teaching, severe marking, and so on. For the purpose of this section, however, we may take it that the difficulty of a question in the eyes of an examiner stems from some inherent feature of the question, so that, even if all the other factors are equal, the question will produce fewer good answers than will questions thought to be easier.

In other words, examiners, either from experience or as in the case of objective tests, by pre-testing, can prespecify some questions as being more difficult than others. The outcome of the examination may prove them wrong, of course, but that is beside the point at the moment.

It follows that it is possible to divide the examination at the design stage into parts according to a perceived level of difficulty. At present this kind of division is rare in examinations at any level because each examination system has tended to be restricted to a fairly narrow band of the range of general ability, so that a reasonable level of performance can be obtained by most of the candidates on most of the questions. But if the ability range of the candidates is extended as in the proposals for a common examination at 16 plus (GCSE) in England and Wales (DES, 1982), the situation may arise in which many of the questions are beyond the reach of a considerable proportion of candidates. If these questions are included, the candidates of lower ability may well score zero; if they are excluded, the more able candidates may be denied the opportunity of displaying their full ability. In these circumstances an examiner may decide to group the questions in such a way as to put all the difficult questions into one part of the paper which would be attempted only by the more able candidates. This device is commonly known as the 'differentiated paper' and is being advocated for use in many subjects in the GCSE. (*Differentiated* is a misleading term; most examination components are differentiated from one another in some way. The term has come to be used only for examinations in which the components are differentiated using the criterion of difficulty. It has been the purpose of this section to identify other criteria for distinguishing between components.)

Operational experience of the use of differentiated papers is slight. Tattersall (1983) reviews the experience in England and Wales and identifies three forms of examination in which the components are deliberately designed to be at different levels of difficulty, as given below.

Category A consists of one paper taken by all candidates, and two or more papers at different levels of difficulty, from which a candidate must chose one. A common syllabus applies to all candidates.[6]

Category B consists of a series of overlapping papers the combinations of which relate to the perceived ability or aspirations of the students. Tattersall describes a scheme in which four examination papers are available to test for three levels of ability:

(1)   level of ability A (lowest) candidates take papers 1 and 2;
(2)   level of ability B candidates take papers 2 and 3;
(3)   level of ability C (highest) candidates take papers 3 and 4.

The four papers are linked to levels of the syllabus each building on the former. Thus, paper 2 includes the content and abilities required in paper 1. Paper 3 includes the syllabuses for papers 1 and 2, and paper 4 subsumes all of the syllabuses. It follows that this design has some similarities to graded testing (see Chapter 12).

Category C is in the form of a basic examination (which may comprise more than one paper) and an optional examination (usually only one paper) available for the more able candidates. Usually the highest grades are not available to candidates who take only the basic paper(s). The main difference between this and category A is that entry to the second extension paper is entirely at the discretion of the students and their teachers, and that there is usually some extension of syllabuses involved in it.

The criterion of difficulty has, in theory, much to recommend it for dividing an examination into component parts. Where it is necessary to examine over a wide ability range, it appears to allow the design of an examination in which there is at least a part which is within the competence of the least able, while allowing other parts suitable for the most able, thus discrimination may be achieved over a wide range of ability. The review of feasibility studies undertaken by Tattersall, however, suggests that differentiated papers, of whatever category, may have limited use.

It is significant that most of the feasibility studies have been in mathematics, in which it is probably easier to predict levels of difficulty than in any other subject. Furthermore, there are statistical problems in equating the performance of those who take the more difficult papers with those who do not. And teachers have the unenviable task of advising students on which papers to take to match their perceived ability. This brings us to the question of choice.

Choice

Choice, whether it be between different components of an examination or between questions within that component, has long been a feature in the design of many examinations. On the face of it, it appears to allow individual freedom in the choice of whatever aspects of a subject may be of most interest to the candidate. The appearance is that freedom of choice within an examination encourages curricular freedom for schools, teachers and students; the reality is rather different. Far from encouraging breadth in the curriculum, choice within an examination can have the effect of narrowing the curriculum for individual students. Four questions need to be asked: who chooses, when, on what basis and between which parts of the examination?

Choice between Questions
Almost everyone who has ever taken an examination at any level will have experienced the requirement to choose, say, four questions out of eight. The choice appears to rest entirely with the candidate; but at school level,

at least, the choice may be pre-empted by instructions or guidance from the teacher. These instructions may be based on the parts of the syllabus subject-matter which the teacher has been able to cover in the classroom. Some syllabuses contain so much material that it may not be possible for all of it to be taught; furthermore, it may not be possible for all of it to be represented in the examination. The actual freedom of choice open to the candidate is then considerably narrowed. This situation is represented in Figure 5.1, where the large circle A represents the whole syllabus; the smaller circle B represents the part of the syllabus the teacher has been able to teach; and the other smaller circle C represents that part of the syllabus included in the examination. It follows that the freedom of choice of the student is effectively confined to the shaded part of the diagram. Worse still, the student may not have learned or revised all that has been taught. If he is lucky, all that he has learned rests within the shaded part; but it may not, and if he is really out of luck, it may rest entirely in the unshaded part of B.

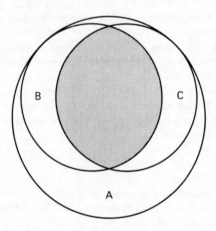

Figure 5.1

An apparently simple choice becomes increasingly more complex. In desperation the candidate may, as a last resort or for his last question, choose from the unshaded part of C; that is a question on subject-matter which has been neither taught nor learned. Those readers who have been examiners may well have experienced answers on subject-matter within A but outside B *and* C, that is, within the syllabus but on subject-matter which has not been taught and to a question which has not been set; and answers on subject-matter entirely outside the A circle are not unknown.

To compound the problem still further, when choice of this type is available candidates do not all take the same examination. There are seventy combinations of four questions out of eight; so there exists the possibility of that number of examinations which, at least in part and sometimes totally, are different from one another. If the intrinsic difficulty of the questions varies, or if they demand different skills or if the standard of marking varies, the problem of equating performance across all those combinations is formidable (Nuttall and Willmott, 1972).

There is some evidence that the kind of question chosen is related to the ability of the candidate. In chemistry, for example, the least able candidates tend to go for the more general, discursive questions, while the more able tend to choose questions of the problem-solving or mathematical type. So choice is not necessarily by subject-matter alone but on the candidate's *perception* of the difficulty of the question. This perception, however, may be based on slender evidence and on a very hurried reading of questions which may reveal unforeseen difficulties when the answer is actually composed. These decisions have to be made during the examination with all its attendant stress and pressure of time, none of which is conducive to considered judgements.

In short, choice of question within an examination design may be superficially a gesture towards freedom in the curriculum. In practice it can be narrowing, capricious and a temptation to indulge in the often unrewarding vice of question-spotting.

Choice between Components

Where choice is to be made between various main components of a school examination, whether it be based on subject-matter or mode or difficulty, it usually rests with the teacher rather than the student. Even in higher and further education there is usually little room for a student to choose topics outside those which are formally taught. In other words, what is studied and assessed and how it is assessed rests in the hands of teachers rather than students.

Essentially these are curricular choices rather than assessment choices. They are made well in advance, sometimes two years or more, before the formal examination. It is at that earlier point that a teacher will decide, for example, which period of history or which option in physics will be studied and examined; which students will be entered for a school-based or an external examination; and which students will take the difficult or easy components of a differentiated examination. The critical choice and the one which causes most controversy is the last one. Pre-selection by teachers of primary school pupils suitable for entry and special teaching for the 11+ examination has effectively determined the subsequent education and careers of children in England and Wales for many years past. A similar choice at 13+ of those who should enter for the Certificate of Secondary Education or the General Certificate of Education has similar effects. These are choices *between* examinations. But choice *within* an examination can be equally critical. A decision not to enter a student for the more difficult combinations within a differentiated examination (an important issue in the GCSE) may exclude the possibility of attaining higher grades and all that they might lead to.

No Choice

The tendency in recent years has been towards more freedom of choice in the design of both curricula and their attendant examinations. Within subjects the number of options of subject-matter, modes of assessment and kinds of questions has multiplied. As the number of variables increased the possibility of finding equivalence between the many combinations has decreased. The emphasis on pupil-centred education has led to the individualization of curricula and consequently of assessment. Extrapolated, this could lead to every student studying an individually designed curriculum and hence taking an individually designed examination. Comparability of performance then becomes impossible.

The extreme situation may be considered desirable, provided that the consequences of totally individualized examinations are accepted. This is not likely in the immediate future and one of the main concerns of the designer of an examination at present is to reach a compromise between what is common to all candidates and what is particular to groups or individual candidates. This has led to moves towards a core-plus-options structure in the design of examinations in many subjects; a move which at the time of writing has official sanction for the proposed GCSE. Under the heading 'Subject specific criteria', a recent White Paper states:

> The definition of subject titles is intended not to impose uniformity but to establish an agreed core of subject matter and learning objectives for a syllabus with a given title. The object is to reduce unnecessary variety without preventing examining groups from offering syllabuses with some distinctive characteristics. (DES, 1982, p. 10)

In other words, the requirement is for a portion of the subject-matter of an examination in a particular subject to be common to all candidates – although not necessarily requiring the same papers – the remainder being in the form of options over which choice by candidate or teacher can be exercised. The common material, furthermore, is to be of such a kind as to identify the main characteristics of the subject area. The nature of the options would be more open: different periods and books in English, applications of science in different industries and technologies, different art forms, different musical skills, and so on.

The increasing popularity of the core-plus-options structure stems from a desire to reconcile the demand for a common core curriculum, together with a common element of basic skills and knowledge within each subject in that curriculum, and the desire of individual teachers and students to retain some freedom of choice within the curriculum. The point of balance between the two is a matter of judgement. A more contentious issue arises, however, in the relations between the options and between each option and the common element.

The problem is twofold. An option and the common element – if similar in content and demand – may reinforce each other; that is, performance is enhanced in both because they have a good deal of teaching in common. If this occurs in some options but not in others, the reinforced options may attract a disproportionate number of candidates. The second problem lies in the attempt to establish comparability between options in terms of their difficulty. Teachers and students have an eye for the soft option, and although their perception may be wrong and their reaction to it misguided, comparability becomes difficult if less able candidates select soft options. There are also organizational and financial problems which multiply as the variety of choice multiplies, increasing the complexity of the examination and increasing the cost per candidate particularly for those options which are undersubscribed.

There is no doubt that the simplest and cheapest way of constructing an examination is to require all the candidates to take the same papers and the same questions, and to allow no choice whatsoever. The degree of choice, and the resulting complexity of examinations, is a reflection of choice and complexity in the curriculum despite the assertion that in practice it is examinations which determine the curriculum. Increased complexity and freedom of choice is bound to result in increased cost and decreased comparability, whether it be in curriculum or motor cars. It is small wonder that in time of financial stringency there is growing pressure for simplification and conformity.

Writing the Questions

Who Writes Them?
The function of chief examiners is to give effect to the examination design; they may not have had a leading part in the design, although there are instances in which they have done both. Traditionally each examination question has been written by one person, usually a chief examiner, working alone. Up to a point this is still the case – even multiple-choice items, instructions for a practical test and schedules for a viva voce examination are conceived in the first instance by an individual. In the more conventional examinations one person may still be responsible for writing all the questions or at least the majority, although they are usually subject to a subsequent reviewing procedure which is outlined below.

When the questions are fairly simple, it is possible for one experienced examiner with a fertile mind to produce acceptable questions over many years while maintaining at least a semblance of originality in each one of them. But with objective test questions and structured questions (see

Chapter 7), the task of writing is much more complex and demanding. It was largely the introduction of these questions which in recent years has given rise to the practice of *team* writing. In the production of a test of, say, fifty objective test questions or ten structured questions each member of a team of writers might be given a quota of questions to a prescribed specification, the total probably exceeding three or four times the final number required. All the questions are then reviewed, revised, or rejected, again by a small group rather than by an individual, until they are sufficient in number and type to meet the specification of that part of the examination.

The practice of team writing has been generally welcomed. It spreads the load of work which has increased greatly as examinations have increased in complexity; and it decreases subjectivity and stereotyping which are dangers when only one person is involved. But perhaps the most telling argument for team writing is that it brings more people, usually teachers, to bear at the *creative* end of examining. Many thousands of teachers are used in the marking process, but this is tedious and mentally unrewarding even if there is a modest financial reward. If the examining process is to be brought closer to that of teaching and learning, then how better to do so than to use as many teachers as possible by bringing their collective experience to bear on the setting of questions as well as marking answers?

The advent of team writing, however, does not diminish the responsibility and status of chief examiners; both may well be enhanced. It is still the chief examiners who must face the scrutiny of the draft papers. They may write fewer questions than in the past, but they have the more difficult task of guiding and co-ordinating the work of the writers. It is small wonder, therefore, that examining boards submit their chief examiners to a rigorous evaluation before appointment and during their period of duty. This period may be for quite a number of years – five could be taken as a norm – but the appointments are usually reviewed annually. It is common but not universal practice for chief examiners to be appointed from the ranks of long-serving examiners. This helps to ensure the appointment of those who have been tried by the system in action and have had the opportunity to display the necessary qualities. A likely consequence of this, however, is a high level of conservation in the production of examinations. True, the more innovatory members of a team might push a chief examiner into new directions; but it would not be unfair to say that a chief examiner's main function is to maintain the essential elements of the structure and continuity of standards of the examination, working within the brief imposed by those responsible for the general design.

How Are They Written?
There has been a general belief that writing examination questions is an

easy matter. Caleb Cotton's remark[7] will find an echo in minds of many who have questioned the competence of the questioners: 'Examinations are formidable even to the best prepared, for the greatest fool can ask more than the wisest man can answer.' No doubt it *is* easy simply to ask candidates to 'give an account of', 'discuss', 'describe the preparation of ...', 'compare and contrast', 'translate', or 'calculate' with little or no thought as to what might be the answer. This is rarely the case: if the substance of the demand is a familiar element in the syllabus and if the question in similar form has been asked previously, then it is only too easy to anticipate a particular and limited answer because it will have been given in a largely similar form in previous examinations. But to write questions which genuinely test the ability of students to apply themselves to unfamiliar situations, to analyse with precision, to evaluate consistently, and to construct with imagination and skill requires a good deal more thought and skill on the part of the examiner. Above all it requires an insight into good practice in the classroom and experience of how a good teacher asks questions and a good student answers them.

These skills come to the fore particularly when constructing objective test and structured questions. Objective test questions may be criticized on many grounds, particularly when they comprise the sole form of examining, and bad examples of them are only too easy to find. But at their best they are written by someone who knows not only the correct response, but also the most likely sources of error and misunderstanding which emerge when the problem arises in the teaching situation. Even more is it the case in good structured questions, in which the candidates are presented with interesting but unfamiliar material and then have their understanding probed by a series of related questions, structured so that the most able can answer them all and the least able at least some. That, in a sentence, comes as near as possible to a definition both of good teaching and good examining.

Ability as a teacher is insufficient in itself to produce good writers of questions. There are technical skills to be learned and errors to be avoided. This has long been recognized and one of the more beneficial outcomes of the innovations in school examinations which began in the 1960s were the workshops set up to instruct and, more important, to give practice to teachers recruited as writers of questions. This practice has grown and is now almost worldwide in school examinations, even penetrating some institutions of higher education.

How Are They Assembled?
It is normal practice in school examinations to put the final responsibility for the assembly and approval of the papers in their final form into the hands of a committee (sometimes called the preparatory committee) the composition of which is of paramount importance for the production of a valid examination. Its members collectively should be qualified to criticize

and propose changes to draft material on educational, subject and assessment grounds. This they have the power to do, from the smallest detail of accuracy of the subject-matter to the overall curriculum balance. A day of scrutiny of an active preparatory committee can be a painful experience for a chief examiner. In advance of the meeting the draft papers will have been scrutinized by a special member of the committee, the reviser. The reviser is usually a teacher in the subject area, but not one who prepares candidates for the particular examination board. His function is to read the draft papers 'to ensure that the papers comply with the requirements of the syllabus and that they are a fair and reasonable test for the candidates at the level concerned' (JMB, 1983b, p. 52).

The reviser's report is available to the committee and the chief examiner. The members of the committee will also have reported on the drafts, and the chief examiner will have seen and responded to their reports before the meeting. The discussions at the meeting of the preparatory committee are directed towards obtaining a consensus agreement on whatever changes have been suggested – not always an easy matter. Subsequently the reviser has the responsibility of confirming that the decisions of the committee have been properly reflected in the final form of the examination.

To say that the process of scrutiny and revision is rigorous is an understatement; it is rare for an error or inappropriate question to slip through the various processes of refinement, although to the embarrass-ment of all concerned it happens occasionally. It has to be said, however, that the whole process has a bias towards conservation not innovation. The function of all the people involved is to ensure that the final form of the examination paper is in accordance with present practice and that it will meet the expectations of the teachers whom the members of the committee represent. The changes tend to be ones of detail or relatively small shifts of balance. It would be wrong to look to chief examiners and preparatory committees for radical change; that comes, if it comes at all, much earlier in the design stage. This is not to belittle the skill and experience of those concerned in production. They have refined examinations of this type to a level of excellence on which it would be difficult to improve. What is more, it must be remembered that the majority are practising teachers and their material rewards as examiners do not match the very great responsibility which they carry.

The Timescale

The complexity of the design and production of a public examination for schools would surprise most members of the general public and indeed some members of the teaching profession. It can also be very time-consuming both in the amount of work which has to be put into it and the period between conception and publication. Even when a syllabus and examination design is well established it may take up to two years to produce each annual examination in its operational form. If an examination is to be offered in a new area, the interval between the first suggestion and the first operational examination may be of the order of five years. And if a whole new system of examinations is to be introduced, the period of gestation may be anything up to twenty years.[8]

Those whose experience of examination production is limited to writing and marking internal, end-of-year school examinations may be forgiven for wondering why the timescale in public examinations is similar to that for producing a new aircraft and greater than for new motor cars. It arises not so much from technical considerations as from the need to negotiate, consult, obtain approval and, of course, to give proper notice to those who have to take them. The introduction of a new technique, an objective test, or moderated internal assessment, for example, may require a period of trial in order to get it to an appropriate level of reliability. But it is true to say that no *radically* different technique has arisen in the past twenty years; such as they are will be surveyed in Chapter 7.

In the production of an internal examination a teacher is responsible only to himself, his students and such house rules as his institution cares to impose. A public examination body, encumbered with the need to attain at least regional and possibly national and international currency, is faced with a daunting array of requirements which have to be satisfied and people who have to be consulted; no part of the process just outlined can be neglected.

Notes: Chapter 5

1 The decision as to what period of absence from the classroom should disqualify a chief examiner from examining is a nice one; in my own case I decided that four years was sufficient.
2 The comments of the Secretary of State – see DES, 1982 – on the first submission of national criteria from the Joint Council of the GCE and CSE examination boards, and the subsequent correspondence between the two parties, highlights the difficulty of achieving a national consensus on curriculum and examination matters.
3 For example: Nuffield Chemistry (Revised), 1975, *Teachers' Guide I*, appendix 5.
4 The JMB A-level geography examination (1984) is fairly typical: 'Paper I Physical Geography three hours, 40 per cent (the natural environment). Paper II Human Geography three hours, 40 per cent. Practical Geography (assessed *either* by the teacher at the centre *or* by a practical examination of two and a half hours), 20 per cent'.
5 Most standard works on testing show how the facility index and other indices used in objective testing may be calculated: see Mathews, 1977, p. 23, 'Total number of candidates $(N) = 90$. Number of correct responses to Item $(R) = 63$. Facility of Item (F) $= \dfrac{R}{N} = \dfrac{63}{90} = 0.70$ or 70%'.
6 The longest-running example of the category A form is the Welsh Joint Examination Committee's 16+ mathematics examination. This examination was first run concurrently with an equivalent examination in which all candidates took common papers. The differentiated examination proved to be much more popular and the common examination has now been abandoned: see Tattersall, 1983.

7   Quoted in Schools Council, 1980b.
8   The proposals for a common examination at 16 plus in England and Wales by the amalgamation of the GCE and CSE into the General Certificate of Secondary Education (GCSE) were first published in 1971 by the Schools Council and discussed for some years before that. In 1984 the national criteria which essentially constitute a general basis for design were submitted to the secretary of state for approval. Approval has now been given – see Joseph, 1984b – although the details of syllabus and specification of examinations remain to be decided and published, and sufficient notice has to be given to schools to prepare their students for the first examination in 1988.

6

The Examining Process

The process of large-scale examining is very complex and cannot be described in detail here. Nevertheless, the magnitude of the operation and the meticulous care for detail at all stages of the production of the papers, requiring as it does organization and management of high quality, should not pass entirely unnoticed. In addition the printing and proof reading must be done speedily and in total secrecy. Government papers nowadays may be 'leaked' with no more than passing embarrassment; not so examination papers. It only needs one to go astray to raise the possibility of the production of a whole new examination, repeating all the processes outlined in Chapter 5 and in a greatly reduced time; such an event within a public examination board is much more than an embarrassment. Nevertheless, this varied and complex task is carried out year after year with relentless efficiency and the sealed envelopes marked 'not to be opened before ...' arrive at the examination centres.

Nor should the efficient organization and management in the schools and colleges which comprise the centres be forgotten. Long before the actual examination, entries have to be made, candidate by candidate, subject by subject, option by option, mode by mode and sometimes board by board. The number of these variables is great and in recent years has increased, so of course have the chances of making mistakes. It says much for the teaching profession that mistakes are rare; but the price of efficiency is the expenditure of much time and a high level of anxiety on the part of those who are given the responsibility for conducting the examinations. Mistakes do happen, of course, telephones do ring in the examining board offices at the time of an examination and the nightmare of entering a whole class of children for the wrong paper has for one teacher become a reality. Fortunately examination boards have their ways of dealing with these emergencies with astonishing speed and calm and fairness.

The difficulties in England and Wales are of our own making. If the examination boards were to unite, if the number of subjects were reduced greatly, if options within subjects were to be abolished and internal assessment by teachers abandoned, then a much simpler system less prone to error could be established. Such changes would affect not only the production and issuing of the papers, they would simplify and possibly increase the reliability of marking. There must come a point where the level of complexity brings about a decline in efficiency of administration, given a constant level of human and financial resources. Furthermore, it is not just the efficiency of the examination system which is at stake: the disruption which ensues during the examination season detracts from the principal function of a school which is to teach. For some age groups, virtually a whole term of teaching is lost, not counting the time spent in revision and examination rehearsals.

Regrettable though lost teaching-time is, it may be less cause for concern than the personal stress which is engendered in students by examinations. It seems that more research has been done into this unfortunate side-effect at the undergraduate rather than at school level. Ryle (1969, p. 100) points to several levels of psychiatric disorder which can arise before and during examinations, including: 'excessive sleepiness, which represents a kind of "frozen rabbit" opting out of horrid reality.' Ryle suggests as a remedy a range of assessments, such as coursework and projects, in addition to the traditional terminal examination, so that students can recoup poor performance in one part with better performance in another and so spread the load of anxiety. Since he wrote the use of these alternative methods has grown in higher education and in schools. However, an alternative system, as Ryle acknowledges, 'is likely to produce its own crop of casualties' (ibid., p. 103).

In some countries the problem may be even more severe, and reports have been heard of alarm at suicides among schoolchildren. It does not need empirical research to establish the incidence of examination stress; there can be few adults who have not experienced it themselves or witnessed it in their children and, with a growing population of examinees, the incidence must increase. It seems that apprehension is an inescapable reaction to sitting examinations for most people be they old or young. And while acknowledging that a low degree of stress may enhance performance, an excess of it is likely to detract from performance (Gaudry and Speilburger, 1971). The point at issue is not the incidence of stress, but its level; there must come a point for individuals, as for nations, when it is no longer to be tolerated.

Invigilation

The actual proceedings of an examination contain a strong element of ritual (Ryle, 1969, p. 100). There are regulations to be obeyed, rubrics to be followed, sometimes even a formality of dress. The candidates process at an appointed time to appointed places (spaced by regulation) before an almost priestlike group of invigilators. Instructions are then read in the approved form of words, papers issued and heads bowed in silence for up to three hours; the whole ceremony may begin and end with the sounding of bells. Like much ritual the purpose is serious and the experience awesome. No one laughs in an examination room; the forced, slightly hysterical, chatter and laughter to be heard from those who wait beforehand is silenced. It is difficult to see how the necessary regulations for examinations as we know them could be applied in circumstances other than these. Yet to both observer and participant the impression of unreality, of divorce from real education and living, is inescapable.

One of the main innovations which advanced the phenomenon of mass examinations in the last century was the use of a common written examination paper to be administered to all candidates at the same time in different localities. This took the place of face-to-face disputation and interrogation and inevitably increased the distance between examiner and examined. For the most part examinees have nothing more than pieces of paper with which to react; at school level they rarely meet their examiners. Examinations, necessary though they may be, are in the main contrived and unnatural experiences. Even in areas such as medicine, where a closer relation of examinations to reality is rightly thought to be necessary, attempts to face candidates with actual professional problems are not without their difficulties. (The views of Fleming, 1976, and others on both traditional and simulated clinical examinations make disconcerting reading.[1]) There must be similar situations in examinations for many other professions, including teaching, in which professional competence is a matter of prime importance. At the point of selection for further and higher education perhaps the artificiality of the selection experience matters less; the more cynical may claim that since they are merely moving from one vicarious experience to another, the instrument of passage can legitimately be of the same kind.

Marking

This is the point at which assessment and measurement takes place. The term 'measurement' can be justified by reference to the fact that it is at this part of the process that numbers are attached to the performance of candidates. That literal grades are sometimes used does not greatly deflect the point since they are simply an alternative way of placing the quality of work on a scale; in any event, literal grades and numerical marks are sometimes translated one into the other (often with great statistical impropriety), implying that there is an equivalence between them. Either way the assessment is given a quantitative aspect at this stage.

Measurement implies a standardized instrument of assessment and an operative who can consistently apply it. In some instances, such as the marking of an objective test, the operation is undertaken by a scanning machine and consistency can be safely assumed; but in others the operative is human and consistency cannot be assumed, although much is done to reduce inconsistencies to an acceptable level. The instrument or standard may range from a specification of the predetermined correct choice[2] in each item of an objective test to general criteria applied to the marking of essays. Between the two is the more commonly used *mark scheme*, in which required points in answers are set out (with possibly several equivalent alternatives) together with a score in the form of a number attached to each. Much less common is the system whereby scores are subtracted from a maximum for anticipated errors; in general, mark schemes are used to measure positive rather than negative outcomes.

Mark schemes, preprogrammed computer marking and even multiple marking[3] may give the appearance of something being measured at a high level of exactness. It would be wiser to assume that this impression is false – the sources of inexactness are many and may be classed in three groups:

(1)   uncertainty about the nature of the attributes of students which are to be examined and the units of measurement which can be attached to them;

(2)   uncertainty about the degree to which the questions and answers actually relate to those attributes even if their nature is identified;

(3)   inexactness in mark schemes, and variety of interpretation and application of the mark schemes by the markers.

In fairness it must be said that the examination boards recognize that the appearance of exactness given by a numerical score, such as 45 out of 100, is misleading. They do what they can to make marking precise, but most of their efforts are concentrated on the third source of error, that is, the variability between markers; and it is to this aspect, usually referred to as the *reliability* of an examination, that the present comments are directed.

Clearly it is important that teachers responsible for preparing students for examinations have some knowledge of how scripts are marked. While it is to be hoped that teachers do not entirely base their teaching on the expectations of examiners, it would be wrong to pretend that this is not a dominating factor in those courses which terminate in a public examination. It has been common practice for teachers to apply for work as assistant examiners, that is, markers, simply to find out the expectations of chief examiners. Published syllabuses, objectives and the examination papers themselves reveal a certain amount of what examiners are looking for, as do the examiners' reports which are subsequently published. But these cannot be as informative as firsthand experience of marking and attending the standardizing meetings. Access to mark schemes is difficult to attain; even requests from research workers are carefully considered before mark schemes are released. The reluctance of boards to publish mark schemes is defended on the grounds that no one scheme is definitive; each is specific to a particular question paper and a proper appreciation of them requires participation in the discussions between examiners before marking takes place. There can be little doubt that the publication of mark schemes immediately after an examination would lead to some difficult correspondence between the various parties.

Although understandable from the point of view of an examining board, it does seem a little hard on teachers that the particular schemes for allocating marks are withheld from them, unless they are willing to serve and are acceptable as assistant examiners. The boards are aware of the demand and have gone some way to satisfy it (without regularly publishing mark schemes) by publishing general information on marking, often including examples together with a justificatory commentary (JMB, 1982b, 1982c, 1983c; Oxford Local Examinations, 1978).

Standardization

Markers can make mistakes. These range from errors of judgement through disregard or misinterpretation of a part of a mark scheme to simple arithmetical errors in addition. The last are very likely to be picked up and remedied by the army of clerical scrutineers which descends on the scripts when they are returned to the examination boards. Some of the other errors may or may not be rectified, depending on whether or not scripts are seen by another examiner – and this usually applies only to a minority of them. Absolute precision in marking by human beings is unattainable; but provided that the quality control is sufficiently stringent the margin of error arising from examiners' mistakes can be kept within bounds. This state of affairs may be less acceptable to those who are exposed to the examination system and to its consequences than it is to those who apply it. The former may take some consolation from the fact that errors are as likely to lift a candidate's mark as to depress it.

Perhaps more important than mistakes, however, is the difference in the temperaments of examiners. In simple terms this may be described as a predisposition to either toughness or tenderness in awarding marks. This may vary not only from one examiner to another, but within an individual examiner, depending on the conditions under which he is examining – before or after work, for example, or before or after a meal or a drink, or any other factor which might affect his attitude or level of attention to the marking. This brings us to that part of the process called *standardization*.

The standardizing procedures have been refined over the years, and although they may vary in detail from board to board they do not differ in principle. The key people are again the chief examiners. It is their prime duty at this stage to ensure an acceptable degree of equivalence in the marking of the assistants. To put it another way: they are the repository of the standard, and it places on them great responsibility and volume of work, having regard to the large number of assistants and variations in both temperament and expertise.

A typical standardizing procedure would be as follows. As soon as all the examiners have had time to mark a sample of the scripts on the basis of a provisional mark scheme they attend a *standardizing meeting*; this is usually within a few days of the examination. At this meeting, under the chairmanship of the chief examiner, they agree any changes which may be necessary to the provisional mark scheme. It is at this point that discrepancies can be revealed between the responses which the examiners have anticipated and what the candidates, and indirectly their teachers, think are appropriate answers. It is an example of direct influence of the examined on the examiners; and in fairness to the latter it has to be said that they are usually ready to accept reasonable alternative answers and differences in interpretation of the questions. As a result, the mark scheme is usually expanded to allow for a greater variety of answers than had been anticipated. It is also at this point that the chief examiner may be confronted with ambiguities and occasionally errors in the questions. It can be somewhat embarrassing to find such faults despite the prolonged and rigorous period of scrutiny and revision of the papers. However, it does happen and is remedied as well as possible, the general principle being that candidates should not be penalized as a result of faults or ambiguities in the questions.

It is also normal practice at standardizing meetings, now that photocopying is readily available, for all examiners to mark copies of a common sample of scripts. This helps the chief examiner to identify variations in practice between his assistants and to further establish uniformity. Newly appointed assistant examiners may be required to submit a further sample of marked scripts to the chief examiner soon after the meeting.

Subsequently as the marked scripts are returned to the board further samples from the work of each assistant are selected and re-marked by the chief examiner who can then compare his scores, which are taken to be definitive, with those of his assistants. Should the discrepancies be such as to reveal that an assistant is substantially and unacceptably out of line, all his scripts may be allocated to another for re-marking. If the differences between the marks of the chief examiner and an assistant are significant, but not sufficiently large to call for re-marking, a statistical adjustment of that set of marks may take place. This adjustment requires considerable experience and care since the nature of the difference may be complex. For example, a particular examiner may be severe over all the candidates or only with the weakest or only with the most able. It follows that any adjustment must be sensitive to all the factors involved and all the evidence available. There must be some occasions when those concerned are somewhat sceptical of the efficacy of what they are doing.

It can be seen that much effort is expended in the attempt to ensure that the marking of all examiners is at an acceptable level of equivalence.[4] It is also apparent that the whole system depends ultimately on the judgement of one person, the chief examiner. He is 'the standard' and it is he who is also expected to detect, and to some degree quantify, deviations from it.

The sudden introduction of radical innovation such as the national curriculum projects creates a special problem because the necessary experience to establish a standard in that kind of curriculum development cannot be found immediately. In such cases it has been normal practice to run two chief examiners in harness, one representing the new and the other the established curriculum. In these circumstances a sufficient degree of agreement between the two may not be achieved easily since there may be fundamental differences in aims.[5]

Awarding

After all the standardizing and checking, events move rapidly towards the collation of marks and the final meetings at which the grades are awarded for each examination. In one respect the use of computers has eased the clerical load of this part of the process; in others it has become more complex. Statistical processes are now used to present a variety of interpretations of the raw marks the better to assist the judgements of the examiners. In addition, many examinations now consist of several different parts each of which may have to be statistically processed separately. This period has to be one of intense activity and meticulous organization, in which computer time is at a premium in order to have the required information available for the award meetings (Forrest and Vickerman, 1982, pp. 24–7).

Before the award meeting, chief examiners will have come to some provisional judgements about the level of performance of candidates compared with previous years, and the difficulty of their papers compared with previous years. In the light of these judgements they are likely to have established the approximate levels of marks which would form the borderlines between grades. These *provisional* views are communicated to the officers of the board before the overall examination statistics are available.

In summary, the following information is likely to be available for the chief examiners at the award meeting:

(1) The distribution of marks on each examiner-marked component of the examination. These are the marks after any adjustments have been made to correct departures of individual examiners from the standards established at the examiners' meeting.

(2) The distribution of marks on other examination components which are not marked by examiners. These would include objective test scores and the marks awarded for components which have been internally assessed by the schools; for example, practical and project work. In the case of an objective test an item analysis would also be provided (see Chapter 7).

(3)   The overall distribution of aggregate marks for all candidates after the marks for each component have been added together.

(4)   The equivalent statistics for the previous year, including the percentage of candidates awarded each grade. Statistics from other boards in the previous year, and reports of inter-board comparability studies, may also be available.

(5)   An estimate of the mark, or range of marks, on the aggregate distribution at which certain critical grade boundaries are likely to fall. This estimate is made by the board's staff on the basis of the chief examiner's provisional judgements and on the statistical evidence of previous years. On a seven-point scale these critical boundaries are likely to be: 1/2, 3/4 and 5/6, or on a literal scale, A/B, C/D and E/F. (Practice is not standard across examination boards.)

(6)   In some boards it is also likely that information is available which will help the examiners to compare awards in their particular subjects with awards in other subjects (see Chapter 9, p. 147).

The Discussion

It is difficult to convey the flavour of the discursive part of an award meeting to anyone who has not had the opportunity to attend. Those present are likely to include the chairman of the subject committee,[6] senior officers of the board (often the secretary or his deputy), officers with responsibilities for the examination in the subject, any member of the Examination Council who wishes to attend, the chief examiners responsible for each main component and the senior chief examiner. The early stages of the discussion take the form of talking round the examiners' general impressions of the papers and the candidates' performance. There are considerable limitations to these provisional judgements by impression. For one thing, the actual performances are not defined in anything approaching operational terms, that is, the actual tasks that the candidates should be able to do at various levels of competence. Another limiting factor is that it is not normally possible for an examiner to receive a representative sample of the work done.[7] And as mentioned above, in a complex examination structure it is rarely possible for any one examiner to have direct knowledge of performance in all parts of it. It would not be unfair to say that it is rare for anyone, even the senior chief examiner, to have a comprehensive knowledge of a representative sample of performance in all parts of the examination. In some parts, such as an internally assessed element, it is impossible for an external chief examiner to have any direct knowledge of the performance.

However, by dint of discussion and their experience of previous years a small group of chief examiners begins to arrive at a range of *aggregate* marks within which the principle grade boundaries may be established.

The next step is usually for the secretary, a senior officer of the board, to contribute some guidance particularly on the statistical implications of the tentative grade boundaries. This is likely to be of the sort: 'if we agree that the minimum aggregate mark for a grade C is x, then the percentage of candidates who will attain that grade or higher will be y.' It is at this point that comparisons with previous years and other subjects and, possibly, other boards will take place.

The Decision

The awarding group may now begin to move towards a firmer decision, although still provisional, on where the minimum aggregate mark for a particular grade, say grade C, should lie. The criteria on which they would defend this decision might be of the type: 'our view is that the examination as a whole, or one part of it in particular, was rather more demanding than last year, so we are prepared to accept a somewhat lower minimum mark this year for this grade.' Or, 'our view is that the quality of candidates sitting the examination this year is lower than previous years; we feel justified, therefore, in setting the minimum mark for this grade at such a point as to allow a smaller percentage of candidates to achieve it.'

In school examinations in England and Wales these decisions on awards are not made to correspond with predetermined fixed percentages of candidates allowed into each grade or to correspond with predetermined marks. In subjects where there is a large entry which is thought to be stable in quality from year to year there may be some general guidelines, such as given in Table 6.1. In practice this is not taken as a rigid set of norms. Even in the major well-established subjects variation will take place year by year and the final decisions rest with the chief examiners at the award meetings, not with a prescription such as the one given below.

Keeping in mind the various impressions of the standard, together with the statistical evidence and whatever guidelines may be available about the distribution of grades, the chief examiners reach a decision about the minimum mark required for each of the critical grades. The decision is a professional judgement reached by consensus among the chief examiners.

Table 6.1

Grade	Percentage of candidates in each grade	Cumulative percentage of candidates
A	10	10
B	15	25
C	10	35
D	15	50
E	20	70
F	30	100

Although the officers of the board may provide information and guidance, the decision is not theirs.

Once the critical grade margins have been agreed, the remaining margins are usually determined by a simple statistical procedure. For example, if the boundaries A/B and C/D have been fixed, the boundary between B and C may be determined as the halfway point between the lowest mark in grade A and the lowest mark in grade C.

Safeguards

The fixing of the margins for all the grade boundaries is not the end of the matter. There usually follows a borderline review, in which all of the available work of candidates who have fallen just below the minimum mark required for some of the key grades is reviewed in order to see if there is any evidence to warrant raising their grade. The selection of the scripts for this process rests with the discretion of the chief examiners, and the scripts which have been marked by the examiners who are seen as less reliable are normally singled out for this special review. The borderline review is primarily intended to *raise* marks if evidence can be found to justify it. Occasionally, but only for scripts marked by a particularly erratic examiner, marks may be lowered. In all cases these borderline changes are made from the evidence of performance of the candidates and not on purely statistical grounds. The process can be time-consuming and is entirely devoted to the prevention of injustice. There is also special consideration of candidates who have taken the examination under a disability.

The Criteria

Since the whole process ends with a series of decisions, which may profoundly affect the lives of those subjected to them, it is not unreasonable to ask for the basis on which they are made. In other words, what are the criteria on which the work of the candidates is allocated to particular grades? It is a simple question and it usually evokes an equally simple answer: that the basis for the decisions rests with the judgement of the awarding group. While there may be many hundreds of people concerned with the design, construction, administration and marking of an examination, the final decision rests with a very small number at the award meeting; it is they who must carry the standards from one year to the next, and it is upon this rock that mass public examinations are founded. There can be little doubt that an experienced chief examiner can, with years of experience and given a stable population and a stable form and specification for the examination, exercise a remarkably consistent judgement on the grading procedures within one board. In times past when examinations were simple and the number of candidates small and innovation negligible, chief examiners could claim with justification that they had a firm view of what constituted the standards and an equally firm control over their assistants' interpretation of those standards. Under such circumstances a single chief examiner, with a long tenure of office, provided the surest repository of professional standards. But times of rapid change in the form and substance of examinations and in the populations of candidates call to question this cornerstone of the system.

Doubts arise from several sources. There is the inability of examiners to describe what the standards are in terms of recognizable performance. Even when their attention is specifically drawn to the need for such descriptions the kind of statements which arise may be of the form,

> The grade C candidate has a reasonable command of physics 'language' and his/her application of laws in straightforward situations is good. Adequate understanding of written questions, tables and graphs is shown and he/she can recall enough knowledge to answer competently most of one question. The grade C candidate is generally able to select appropriate formulae and to substitute correct values accurately. In particular areas of the syllabus, however, depth of knowledge is lacking and a candidate tends to give partial answers, vague descriptions and incomplete definitions; only rarely will a grade C candidate produce a full high-quality answer to an extended question. (Forrest and Williams, 1983, p. 16)

This is a statement formulated after a long, expensive and rigorous research study, in which the participants were experienced examiners working under controlled conditions and with a direct instruction to specify grade-related performance. No doubt each had individual criteria by which they could recognize such attributes as 'reasonable command' and 'adequate understanding'. But these terms are relative and subjective; they carry no information about actual performance and can have little common meaning in communication between examiners, less still between examiners and those outside the educational and examination system who use the results. The example given above is not singled out for special criticism; on the contrary, much more effort and experience went into that exercise than is the norm in public examining. Many others make the same point. For example, in the recent work on the 16+ examination in England and Wales, the working party in history arrived at the following:

> The average response of a Grade 6 candidate would include demonstration of the ability:
> to recall and display a limited amount of accurate and relevant historical knowledge; to show an understanding of historical concepts supported by obvious examples; to identify and list differences and similarities; ... etc. (GCE and CSE Boards' Joint Council for 16+, 1982, p. 6)

These criteria are in the same category as the general objectives which now preface most examination syllabuses. As general statements of the outcomes of a course of study at various levels they have some function in the communication of results; but their relative and vague nature is evident. Even so, they carry more precision than many others as, for example, the following from the Certificate of Secondary Education examination:

> Grade 4 describes the standard of performance expected from a candidate of average ability in the subject who has applied himself to a course of study regarded by teachers of the subject as appropriate to his age, ability and aptitude. (Secondary Schools Examinations Council, 1963, p. 9)

The best that can be said about these statements of the criteria for awarding grades is that they serve as a façade behind which experienced examiners and awarding committees can exercise their common sense; on this assumption it is not my intention to be critical of them. The point is made elsewhere (Chapter 12) that the search for precision is not necessarily one to be pressed; it is much easier to be precise about the trivial than the profound, and no one would wish to make the substance of examination questions and answers any more trivial than they are already. It may well be that a chief examiner's 'feel' for the kinds of performance which constitute the standards is our last safeguard against what Tumin (1970) called 'psychometric trivialisation'; one has only to read the objective test items in Bloom's taxonomy to be made aware of that danger. In the final analysis all judgement is subjective, even when so-called objective tests are used, and those who search for more objective techniques and operationally defined criteria might be tempted by an apparent exactness which may well turn out to be spurious. There have been many warnings against the temptation to minimize examiners' judgements, none more forceful than that of Hofmann (1964) in what he calls 'the flight from subjectivity'.

Publication

Once the examiners have made their decisions, they can retire from the scene of action, but much remains to be done: further clerical checks, more computation and printouts and, finally, the consolidation of the results on to broadsheets for dispatch to each centre. Over the years the organization and management of this process have been refined until they are a model of efficiency. Errors occur, but they are rare and further clerical checks and marking are usually available should a centre suspect that an error has been made.

The critical moment when students learn their individual examination results must surely be a lasting memory for many. The apparent simplicity of the list of subjects and grades: English B, History C, French F, and so on, obscures the depth and complexity of meanings which it conveys to the recipient. To be present on these occasions, as many teachers are, is to witness high drama; the swift changes between elation and depression are more appropriate to the primary events in life than to this artificial trial to which we put most of our young. This culmination of the examination process can be every bit as nerve-wracking as its outset.

Stressful though it may be, the reporting of results to candidates and to their future educators and employers is a necessary part of the process, and although perhaps it could be done differently, its necessity is not in dispute. But that is not the end of the matter: the students and the direct users of the results are those who *need* to know, but there are many others who also *want* to know. The press wants to know because the public wants to know, local and central government wants to know; and they want to know not in order to make judgements about individual students, but for all manner of reasons ranging from the evaluation of schools, or departments within schools, to simple curiosity.

The publication of examination results for purposes other than those which concern individual candidates is a contentious matter which in many countries has overtones at the highest political level. At first sight there may seem to be no good reason for withholding the information; if one of the prime functions of educational institutions is to train their inmates for examinations, it would surely seem sensible to evaluate those institutions by the degree to which they are successful in doing so. This practice is now well established in England and Wales where not only are individual schools evaluated in this way, but also the education authorities in which they reside (see Chapter 8).

If only it were as simple as that! The dominant reliance on the single criterion of examination success in the evaluation of schools betrays some naïve assumptions and ambivalent attitudes on the part of society in general, and the users of examination results in particular. On the one hand, they would like to see schools inculcating those qualities which are thought necessary for a full personal development and for integration into a stable, productive society and they complain that a narrow academic curriculum and its complement of examinations does not enhance those qualities. On the other hand, they make inordinate use of the published examination results for the evaluation of both students and schools. The reasons for this ambivalence can lie only in an innate conservatism of attitudes to the curriculum of schools and a regrettable laziness in demanding a simple, easily comprehended scale of grades attached to subjects: a measure which can be applied to sort out students and schools with the minimum of effort. Burgess sums up the attitude of employers in particular:

What employers typically say is that they take the possession of a certificate or a degree as a very general indication of a level of capacity and application. They do not see it as indicating the acquisition of any information or skill that can be productively used. They all assert that it is they who have to educate and train the young person who comes to them. (Burgess, 1979, p. 144)

So we have a situation in which examination results serve as crude first sieves for employment and further education with scant regard for the skills they actually represent; a situation in which society at large uses examination results to judge the status of schools and, at the same time, in which schools complain that the pursuit of examination results constrains the pursuit of more worthwhile educational goals.

That distorted educational judgements can ensue from the misuse of examination results is evident. The immediate question, however, is whether these distortions should be fostered by allowing general publication of the results. In the present social climate in which an open accountability is demanded of every institution, particularly if it be supported by public funds, it would appear difficult to oppose general publication. Something could be done, however, to regulate the form which publications take. It would seem proper, for example, to prevent the general publication of the results of named individuals unless permission were given. It seems odd that to publish the fact that one person is less hard-working than another could be libellous; yet to publish the fact that one person is much less successful at examinations, and by implication less intelligent, is regularly done without so much as a by-your-leave. Certainly this is true of the local press and, in certain cases, of the national press as well.

In the publication of examination results for whole schools it is difficult to envisage a form which would not be misleading. The actual number of passes in various grades in various subjects would take no note of the size of the school. The percentage of the school population would be little better since schools differ in their policy of examination entry; some enter all who wish to be entered, others only those who, in the view of the school, have a reasonable chance of success. But most misleading of all is the lack of information which the raw results would give about the kind of population within the school, whether it comprises the most able or the least able or various mixtures of ability. It all points to a very cautious interpretation and use of published totals of examination successes by schools. But the demand for information of every conceivable sort is characteristic of our times and appears to be insatiable. The day cannot be far off perhaps when all examination results of all educational institutions will be immediately available for television display through Prestel or Ceefax or some such system; and once the raw data becomes available, the interpretation of it will be in the hands of those who seek to confirm their prejudices.

Notes: Chapter 6

1 The authors give an amusing, although basically serious, criticism of the clinical examinations, which at the time of writing are regarded as an essential hurdle in graduate and postgraduate qualifications in medicine. Among other points, they say, 'the most chronic patients like to constitute themselves as assistant examiners in which role some of them have become quite skilled': Fleming, 1976, p. 1.

2 This is usually called the 'key'. Thus if A is the correct response from five, A–E, A is the key for that item (question).

3 Multiple-impression marking involves the award of marks or grades by two or more markers on the same piece of work using very general criteria.

4 It is common practice in examining boards for chief examiners after each examination to rate each assistant examiner for competence. If assistants do not maintain an acceptable level of competence, they are not re-employed.

5 I hasten to record that on the two occasions when I have had the experience of sharing responsibility with a fellow chief examiner the relations have been entirely amicable and fruitful.

6 In some boards, particularly the CSE, other members of the subject committee may also be present.

7 It is normal practice for an examiner to be allocated all the scripts from a small number of centres. Although the centres may be selected at random, it does not follow that the candidates in those centres are representative of the whole population of the examination.

7

Techniques of Examining

This chapter is concerned with the mechanics of examining, the ways and means of questioning, answering and marking. Its object is to clarify and comment on the identification and classification of techniques rather than to provide a guide on how to set and mark questions and answers. Nor will it deal with such matters as concurrent, continuous and terminal assessment, which are to do with timing rather than technique.

The literature on examination techniques shows some terminological confusion. Many terms which are used to denote types of question refer not to questions, but to types of answer: essay questions, short-answer questions and calculation questions, for example. Others refer to the form of marking rather than to the type of question: objective questions, fixed-response questions, free-response questions, and so on. It is helpful, therefore, to distinguish four main elements in any technique of examining: the types of question, the types of answer, the methods of marking and the media of communication. The four elements are not totally distinct; one depends on another: the form of marking depends partly on the form of answer which, in turn, depends partly on the form of question. However, it is helpful in an analysis of techniques to consider each separately, with the exception of answers and marking which are so closely related that they are best considered together. Although it might appear to be logical to start with types of question, it is types of answers and marking which will be considered first since it is in this area that most confusion arises.

Answers and Marking

In order to place answers in an examination into various categories a criterion for classification is required. Several are at hand, some more useful than others. The most appropriate will be that which is most generally applicable and most useful.

Length of answer has served as such a criterion (although usually to define types of question): long essays, short essays, short answers, one-word answers, yes/no answers, and so on. It is difficult to maintain, however, that these characteristics of length or number of words, or time taken in answering, have much fundamental importance in meeting the purposes of examinations. Furthermore, they may be misleading if used as the prime consideration in deciding upon a technique. If the main purpose of an examination is to write at length and at speed, or conversely to respond briefly and abruptly no matter how complex the issue, then length and time of answer may be a prime consideration. If not, the length should be given less prominence when classifying types of answer.

Another way of classifying answers is to allocate them to various student attributes which are said to be demonstrated in them, particularly intellectual attributes. The problem here is the lack of evidence of which student attributes are actually being displayed: are they powers of memory or application or evaluation or manipulative skill or attributes of personality? Who can tell? It may be that examiners, with practice, can reach a reasonable level of agreement between themselves; but to extrapolate from what a candidate writes down – or says or does – to more abstract cognitive or affective characteristics involves many assumptions which are not easily sustained. Even if two candidates give identical answers to the same question, one might have arrived at it largely by memory while for the other the question may have demanded the ability to apply general principles to unfamiliar material.

I suggest that the most important criterion for classifying answers is *to what degree is the candidate free to respond as he wishes and gain credit for doing so?* (adapted from Schools Council, 1973, p. 35). Or to look at it from the examiner's point of view: *to what degree does the mark scheme predetermine acceptable responses?* The degree to which candidates must acquiesce to preconceived 'right' answers if they are to be given credit is fundamental not just to examinations, but to the whole of formal education. The issue is raised whenever there is discussion about the extent to which educational processes and products must be common to all and the extent to which diverse and even opposing views will be allowed.

The concept of freedom of response is not simply a matter of freedom to choose between questions. If all answers to all questions are to be either right or wrong, then there is still no room for variety of answers or presentation of arguments and points of view which may differ from – and even be in conflict with – those of the examiner. And it should not be thought that the principle can be applied only to the traditionally more discursive subjects. It can be applied, although possibly with less emphasis, to those subjects such as the sciences which are generally considered to be more exact. Certainly if science curricula and examinations are to be widened to allow a consideration of the more disputatious social and environmental aspects of science, it is difficult to see how an examiner can fail to allow considerable diversity of view in the answers to some questions.

By what means can answers be classified in this way? Certainly not by an analysis of the demands made in the question itself. Examiners may ask candidates to 'discuss' and 'evaluate'; it does not follow that credit will subsequently be given to real discussion or evaluation, particularly if it happens to diverge from the examiner's predetermined view of what is appropriate. Nor does an analysis of the answers necessarily provide the evidence for classifying them according to this criterion; the candidate may well have engaged in genuine discussion and got very little by way of marks for his pains. The only relevant data on which a classification can be based is the *way in which the answer is marked*. This is why answers and marking have been joined in the title of this section.

The refinements of marking and the gradations of predetermination of acceptable answers are infinite. It is useful to consider them in three general categories which then allows a classification into three kinds of acceptable answers, as follows.

Fixed Response

As the term implies, no degree of freedom is allowed in the answer; candidates either answer exactly as the examiner has predetermined or they gain no mark. (They may even be penalized with a negative mark in some examinations where 'guessing' is to be discouraged.) The obvious example which comes to mind is the so-called objective test question in all its manifestations: multiple choice, completion, multiple completion, matching pairs, true–false, and so on. Whatever their form, these questions allow answers which only can be right or wrong in the sense that they gain or do not gain a mark. The differences between the many kinds are slight compared with their fundamental, common characteristic that they all prescribe a fixed response: 'if a student wishes to be successful in an objective test he must think as the examiner thinks; there is no room for divergence' (Mathews, 1977, p. 2). Herein lies the so-called objectivity of objective tests. In the sense of uniformity of judgement and total consistency in marking, no matter who the candidate is, these questions can be called objective. So totally predetermined are the acceptable responses that a candidate's answers, which usually consist of pencil marks on an answer card, can be scored by passing them through an electronic scanner with virtually no possibility of error, something which cannot be claimed for human marking.

This is not the place to dwell at length on the pros and cons of objective tests; examples and expositions abound of their virtues and vices. But this much should be said: their objectivity begins and ends with the consistency and rigidity of scoring. This in turn allows the calculation of stable, statistical characteristics of the individual questions and the tests as a whole, particularly to demonstrate how difficult or easy they are and how well they discriminate between the candidates (item analysis). The substance of the question, the nature of the responses from which a choice must be made and, above all, the decision as to what is deemed to be *the* correct response are determined by *people* not machine. In that light, objective questions are as subjective as any other questions.

This should not be taken to be a totally adverse criticism of objective tests and the marking of answers by machine. In circumstances where answers can be generally agreed they are useful in providing an assessment which can cover a lot of subject-matter in a short space of time, with high consistency and predictability of measurement. There are various explanations for the recent growth of objective tests in school examinations, not all of them strictly educational. In the minds of some administrators they offered a cheap alternative to the slow, expensive and sometimes unreliable human marker, an advantage which proved something of an illusion for small populations of candidates since writing good objective tests relies heavily on a human resource which is even harder to find than good markers. Of course, the cost per candidate decreases as the number of candidates increases. It is small wonder, therefore, that many countries, particularly the poor ones, have resorted to the use of objective tests on a large scale, especially for tests in which the whole school population is subjected to a selection procedure before continuing with their education. The thought must arise that the choice is made from expediency rather than the conviction that the tests reflect what is best in schooling.

But there are some good educational reasons for using objective tests for at least a part of an examination. They allow those who find writing difficult to display some attainment which might otherwise have remained hidden. They reflect a common classroom situation in which a teacher may have to offer a choice of responses when an open-ended question has elicited nothing; in this way objective tests can make a contribution to curriculum validity. And they do allow a rigorous analysis of the incidence of right and wrong choices, thus revealing strengths and weaknesses in the teaching and the examination itself (see Chapter 12). But the very fact that they can be used in this way reinforces their dominant characteristics: convergent thinking and conformity.

Free Response

Of course, no response to an examination question is entirely free and open-ended; candidates cannot expect to be allowed to answer in any way they wish. Since the object of marking is to attach a mark or a grade to an answer, examiners must have some criteria for awarding them. It follows that no matter how open-ended a question may be or how strongly it may invite candidates to respond imaginatively and subjectively, the writer of the question must have had *some* qualities in mind which he hoped to see displayed in the answer. The level of generality of the criteria for marking is the determining factor. The more specific the criteria, the more the examiners are committing themselves and the candidates to a predetermined model answer; the more general the criteria, the greater the degree of freedom allowed to the candidate in the answer.

The principle appears simple and obvious; the practice, however, is beset with many problems. It is all very well to invite diverse answers, and even to promise to give some regard to perverse answers provided that they show originality and imagination; but examining, at least as far as the general public is concerned, is supposed to be an exact science; and exactness declines greatly in these permissive circumstances. It is possible, of course, to give an appearance of exactness to a rough judgement by attaching a number to it. Establishments of higher education have been known to mark essays on a percentage scale, producing a mark of 55, for example, which may *appear* to be different from one of 56 but is, nevertheless, spurious. It may be possible for an examiner to sort essays into a small number of categories – on a five-point scale, for instance – with reasonable consistency; but it is not reasonable to expect very fine discrimination when scripts are being marked by impression using general criteria.

There are other safeguards. Standardizing trials, described in Chapter 6, increase reliability within a group of examiners, although some will always tend to toughness or tenderness. The safeguard most frequently applied is to mark each answer at least twice with different examiners, neither being aware of what mark the other has given. The final mark is calculated as the average or sum of the two. This works quite well, although it is expensive and it does tend to bunch the marks near to the mean. It is not a sure safeguard against an inequitable mark, however. If by chance a piece of work is marked by two examiners who *both* tend to toughness or tenderness, an error may be aggravated.

This is not the place to delve into the details of these techniques for marking answers of this kind; the problems are now well known. (Heywood, 1977; Sheridan, 1974). But space has to be found for a comment on the *bogus* free response. This refers to questions in which examiners appear to ask for free and divergent responses, while they really intend no such thing. This is why the marking criteria are essential if questions of this kind are to be properly classified. It is all very well to ask candidates to 'discuss', 'comment on', 'evaluate', 'criticize', and so on, but the request is dishonest if the examiner then proceeds to mark the responses by means of a detailed, inflexible mark scheme in which the points to be rewarded or penalized have been predetermined. If the demand for consistency and reliability of marking outweighs all others, there is inevitable pressure on examiners to drift in the direction of the detailed mark scheme with limited flexibility. That might be acceptable, provided that both teachers and candidates are told which game they are playing.

Intermediate
This is not a very satisfactory term to denote the most familiar method of allocating marks to answers, and covers others such as mark schemes, marking schedules and model answers. While not exactly prescribing what constitutes a wrong or right answer, the intention is to use a

predetermined, detailed scheme for allocating a mark or marks to each point which is anticipated in acceptable answers. Thus the level of freedom of response by the candidate and freedom of judgement by the examiner, outlined in the previous section, is much reduced. At the same time, a degree of human judgement is allowed after the event, which is not possible in the electronic marking of responses to objective tests.

Judgement operates at two points in the marking procedure. When the writer of a question drafts his mark scheme, he does so in terms of those points in answers to which marks are to be awarded, together with acceptable variations. He may not write it out as a model answer; nevertheless, the whole schedule of points to be rewarded constitutes such a model. He is not omniscient, however, so it is inevitable that candidates in their answers will present alternatives which have not occurred to the question-writer. It is necessary, therefore, to modify the marking scheme, usually to enlarge it. This is done at the standardizing meeting, described in Chapter 6.

The second point at which modification may be made to the mark scheme is when the bulk of the scripts are subsequently read and marked by the individual examiners. It is at this point that the human marker can still exercise his judgement (which a machine cannot) to meet variations in answers which have not been foreseen in the final version of the mark scheme. This tradition of allowing subjective judgement to the examiner, even when the points for reward can be largely predetermined, is strong in the traditions of British examinations. It is not surprising, therefore, that objective tests in school examinations although they have been strongly in vogue in recent years, rarely constitute as much as one-half of the total assessment. Such freedom is bought at a price, of course; and no one with examination experience would claim total exactness for the most detailed and refined of mark schemes, even in the so-called exact subjects like mathematics and science.

But how does the candidate know what the examiner is looking for in the various parts of the model answer? In the traditional, brief 'describe this' or 'discuss that' question it is often impossible to tell what things the examiner considers to be more important than others. How often have we heard candidates coming out of examination rooms complaining, 'I did not know what he [the examiner] wanted'. That is a pity and betrays a lack of effective communication. If an examiner has already decided what should constitute the various parts of an acceptable answer and the weight to be attached to each, why keep the candidate in ignorance? Of course, if the examiner is more concerned with the answer as a whole, then such information is irrelevant since it should be marked as a whole by the general criteria explained in the preceding section. Again there is no good reason for letting candidates think that they are being judged by one system when the examiner is actually going to use another.

It was this wish to give to the candidate more understanding of an examiner's intentions which, in part, gave rise to the now popular *structured question*.[1] There are limitations and disadvantages to structured questions, of course. They do not give opportunity for imaginative writing at length as do the free-response questions; nor can they match the exactness of marking of the objective or fixed-response questions. In this they suffer the defects of lying somewhere between the two in an intermediate form. They do, however, have several useful characteristics.

On the matter of marking, the structure of the mark scheme matches the structure of the set of questions, thus making the examiner's requirements more clearly apparent to the candidate. In addition, the weighting attached to each question in the set is made known to the candidate, because it is customary to specify the mark attached to each on the question paper itself. Candidates are given further guidance on how much to write by leaving an appropriate space on the question paper itself and on which the answer is written.

Other features commend themselves. It is common practice to provide a good deal of information in the stem (introduction) to each set of questions to which candidates can apply their knowledge rather than simply recall. It reflects the practice, common to all good teachers, of taking a complex situation or problem and breaking it down into its related parts, so that even the least able in a class can make a contribution. Thus the set of questions is so arranged as to allow the weaker students to get at least some of the early ones right and not to suffer the feeling of total failure to which the problem as an unstructured whole may have given rise. It follows that such questions may be particularly useful in examining a population of candidates of wide ability range since the gradation of difficulty should allow the least able to score some marks, while only the most able should score all marks.

This brief summary of the characteristics of structured questions indicates that they can be expected to make a considerable contribution to the curriculum validity of an examination. They do not reflect all of good teaching practice, but they do reflect an important part of it, the art of structuring a complex problem in such a way as to lead, by skilful questioning, *all* students to *some* understanding of it (Mathews, 1974).

It requires a great deal of skill and practice to design good structured questions. The corollary to the preceding paragraph is that the best people to write them are good teachers. This can be taken further: I would claim that the skills necessary for writing structured questions should be part of the training of every teacher. Not only does it provide practice in the art of structuring and questioning, it demands the ability to anticipate in the marking scheme those responses which the students are likely to make in the answers to them. Nothing could be closer to good classroom practice.

Questions

The point has been made already that many so-called questions are really instructions, and that they are often in such vague terms as to be misinterpreted by both examiner and candidate. If a useful distinction is to be made between various kinds of question, something more educationally significant than the imprecise verb of instruction is required. Furthermore, the criterion for classification of questions should be independent of the kind of answer which they demand. One which usefully makes a distinction between questions and, at the same time, indicates trends in the art of writing them is *the degree to which a question provides material on which candidates are required to work* (Schools Council, 1973).

Information Demanding

At one end of the scale are questions of the type: 'discuss the moral implications of nuclear deterrents.' Questions like these provide no material or information of any sort which candidates can use in their responses. The question briefly raises a single issue and leaves the rest to the candidate. They are easy to write since they tell the candidate nothing; they give no data which may be useful, nor do they indicate the criteria by which the answers will be judged. They make hardly any demands of the question-writer, which perhaps explains why they have been so widely used. It may be proper to ask such questions, of course, provided that the examiner intends them to be as open-ended as they appear and provided that the candidate reasonably can be expected to have acquired sufficient information and powers of judgement to advance a satisfactory answer. Regrettably there must be many instances in which neither of these conditions is met.

The brief, information-less question is not likely to disappear entirely from school examinations (and certainly not from the examinations in higher education), but the doubt remains that they have dominated for reasons of convenience for the examiners: they are so easy to write and so difficult to answer and mark – unless examiners are content with the ill-informed, pre-learned and often trivial answers which they encourage. And to what extent can it possibly be claimed that they reflect good practice in the classroom, or that they anticipate the type of situation candidates will subsequently have to face when their formal education is over and they work or seek work? Real learning and real life does not often take the form of writing a few hundred words on a topic presented at a moment's notice. The usual point made in their favour is that these questions demand the ability to marshal information in such a way as to make a reasoned argument. Such an attribute is one highly to be prized in later life; but how often, for most people, is it required in such a form and in such circumstances?

Information Providing

At the other end of the scale there is increasing use of questions which have contained within them, or as a supplement to them, material which the candidates are required to use. Structured- response questions usually give material in the stem, which serves both as a source of information and as a focus for the set of questions which follows. The nature of the material varies widely depending on the topic: tabulated data, maps, photographs and passages of prose or poetry; all are to be found in questions now in use.

The provision of material, often quite complex, in the stem of a question is a conscious attempt to bring the examination nearer to the process of teaching and learning, particularly if the material is unfamiliar. The idea, then, is that the candidate will be required to *use* information and to rely less on the unaided recall of information, descriptions and discussions previously rehearsed. If the material is especially complex, it can be structured by asking a set of related simpler questions just as a skilled teacher would do in class. It is not necessary to restrict this style of questioning to structured questions, however; the question stem could equally well be followed by a set of multiple-choice questions or even an open-ended question involving a free response.

Most of the questions of this type used in school examinations have provided the necessary material within the question itself (the stem). This has disadvantages. There is the matter of size, for example: if a great deal of material is put into the stem of each question, the paper becomes very bulky and may provide too much to read and assimilate in the short period of three hours or less of a normal examination. In this event candidates, particularly those slow to read and assimilate, may be hindered rather than helped. On the other hand, if the amount of material is reduced too much, there may be insufficient to be useful. For these reasons there are quite severe limits to the use of material in the question itself as a simulation of real problems within the context of formal examinations.

If, however, the idea is extended to the presentation of material in forms which do not constitute a part of the actual question, the scope can be considerably enlarged. Isolated instances have arisen in school examinations: there is the use of a book of data in the Nuffield A-level chemistry examination, and the use of second-language dictionaries is perhaps the longest-standing example. Open-book examinations, in which candidates may bring whatever books they like to assist them, enjoy a vogue, but it is doubtful whether they give much assistance in a short examination; and they may give unfair advantage to those who can afford the best books of reference. There is growing use, particularly in higher education, of 'take-away' questions, in which students are given the question(s) and return the answer(s) at a specified date, one, two, or three weeks hence. During that time they can use whatever material they can find, but not usually the assistance of other people (a requirement which is almost impossible to control).

An avenue which is only just beginning to be explored is the use of electronic storage and retrieval systems. Electronic calculators have been in use for some time and on the whole they are welcomed by examiners and examined alike. A problem not yet resolved, however, is the more recent availability of hand-held devices which not only carry out simple arithmetical, algebraic and geometric functions, but can be programmed to provide data and to solve problems which normally the candidates would be expected to recall and solve without such assistance.

The advent of cheap but powerful electronic devices for storing, processing and retrieving information raises in an acute form a dilemma which has always faced examiners. On the one hand, they are encouraged to keep their examinations in touch with the realities of the classroom and the world at large. With this in mind they might be encouraged to allow all the aids which normally may be available for the abstraction of information and the solving of problems. These aids may range from the most powerful electronic devices to simple books of reference. On the other hand, to allow open use of these aids would contravene one of the traditional tenets of examinations which is to put individuals to the test alone and unaided.

It might appear self-evident that the alternatives do not present a true dilemma and that a compromise could be found. But in traditional examining such a compromise is not easily attained. If *some* aids are to be allowed but open access denied, the problem of ensuring that all candidates are equally advantaged almost defies solution at the present time. It was relatively easy in the past to ensure that everyone had the same mathematical tables, or dictionaries, or books of data. And even in practical examinations it was possible to prescribe minimum and maximum specifications of equipment and materials. But modern electronic devices look remarkably alike whether they be simple or the powerful programmable type. It is all very well for examiners to prescribe the minimum and maximum capacity of such instruments but, in practice, it is virtually impossible to police such a regulation. The hard-pressed invigilators have quite enough to contend with as it is and could not be expected either to have the knowledge or the time to examine all the electronic devices which candidates could well bring into the examination room. One solution might be to provide all candidates with the same device. But this is not nearly so satisfactory as it might sound. Apart from the expense, the device which might be appropriate for one subject is unlikely to be appropriate for all. And within a rapidly changing technology whatever device was provided would soon be obsolete anyway.

Faced with such problems, it is little surprising that examiners have tended to be unadventurous and have allowed either the absolute minimum of aids or more usually none at all.[2] In some respects the problem has been met by allowing at least a part of the assessment to take the form of coursework, that is, work done under the normal teacher/learning process.

The Media of Communication

The classification of types of question and answer which has just been attempted is intended to be sufficiently general to encompass all the familiar media of communication. Answers may be written or spoken or practical, but they can all be classified according to the degree to which the response is 'fixed' or 'free'. Nevertheless, the kind of communication which mediates between examiner and examined, in both directions, is important in its own right, independent of the types of question and answer which are being used: 'examinations should take as natural a form as possible; they should employ as nearly as possible the same *medium* as that in which the ... student will eventually make use of his attainment' (see Schools Council, 1964). This principle could be taken further to say that the examination medium should be the same as that used in the learning situation. In short, the medium of expression should make a contribution to the subsequent relevance of the examination and to its curriculum validity. Easily said, but difficult to accomplish.

A distinction could be made between the medium by which the question is conveyed, and that by which the answer is conveyed. For example, a written response can be made to an oral question – a technique still commonly used in the classroom but now rare, if not extinct, in examinations. The older ones among us, however, may remember the mental arithmetic and spelling-tests which we endured when sitting the scholarship examinations which could lead to a passage from the elementary to the grammar school. Regardless of the various permutations, it is instructive to consider a general classification of the media of communication which are available.

Inscriptive

I use this generic term to include all forms of writing, diagrams, graphs, calculations, indeed anything which is inscribed – usually on paper – even if it be simply a mark on an objective test answer sheet. It could be extended to electronic visual displays, although this particular form of communication is for the future rather than the present.[3] It is essentially abstract and symbolic, whether the symbols be words, numbers, mathematical, scientific, or figurative. It tends to be cognitive; and it is passive rather than active. Inscription is by far the most frequently used medium of communication for both questioning and answering, and this has been so ever since the advent of examining on a large scale in the middle of the nineteenth century. Indeed, mass examining would have been impossible without a change from the oral tradition.

Written questions, as they are colloquially called, allow a common paper to be set to a large number of candidates dispersed in different locations. They may be centrally devised by one or a small number of examiners and their application is relatively inexpensive and administratively convenient. They lend themselves to uniformity rather than to variety. As the choice between examination papers increases, and as the choice within them also increases, so do the costs and the administrative complexity. A small number of inscribed tests, with little or no choice within them, is the surest and cheapest way of ensuring a common curriculum and uniformity of standards of performance, assuming that both are thought to be desirable. Similarly, all the inscribed answers can be returned to a small number of examiners or even, in the case of responses to objective tests, to one machine. The answers readily can be stored, compared and consulted at standardizing meetings, marked in comparative leisure and subsequently used for research (Christie and Forrest, 1980, ch. 9). They are virtually imperishable. Even the questions can sometimes be classified and stored for re-use later, a practice which is common in the so-called item banks of objective test questions (Schools Council, 1976).

It is all very convenient, but all very remote. Not only remote in the sense that it tends to the abstract and academic rather than the concrete, but also in the sense that examiner and examined never meet. Once the questions have been written and dispatched, nothing can change them (unless some error is found). And once the candidates have put down their pens at the appointed time, second thoughts will avail nothing. No opportunity remains for further explanation or correction of error; they cannot change one jot or comma.

How unlike real life it is. Even classroom life allows more flexibility. And the inscriptive medium relies greatly on the mediating skills of reading, writing, drawing, and so on. If these are deficient, the *actual* knowledge of a candidate may remain largely hidden. This is particularly so if an examiner, consciously or unconsciously, ascribes an exaggerated value to the mediating skill: handwriting and spelling being perhaps the most common objects of excessive reward or penalty. If the main object of the examination is to test skill in use of the medium, that is another matter; but if it is not, candidates may be too readily advantaged or disadvantaged if that medium alone is used.

One could be forgiven for thinking that the inscriptive medium owes its near-total domination of all levels of examinations to technical and administrative convenience and to the traditions of the past 100 years or so. It would be wise, however, to consider the alternatives before allowing ourselves to be too carried away by deprecation of written examinations.

Keyboards and Electronics

Life after school can be full and prosperous without an individual ever inscribing much more than a signature and entries on a form. Writing and calculating, at any length, with pen on paper are activities confined to the very few. On the other hand, the need for 'keyboard competencies' is growing. Communication through keyboards and subsequently tapes, discs and visual displays is no longer a novelty, it is a feature of everyday life for a growing number of people; yet rarely is it a form used to communicate between examiner and examined in either direction.

There are, of course, examinations in which the use of a keyboard is an integral part. Typewriting is a case in point, so is the use of electronic calculating devices which are allowed to a limited extent in mathematics and related examinations. The present concern is not so much with them as with the possible use of combined keyboard and electronic devices as a normal form of communication in the examination of many other subjects.

Legibility of handwriting has always been a problem for examiners most of whom would acknowledge the strain which bad handwriting can put on eyes and patience. Some research has been undertaken in an attempt to estimate the effect of handwriting on the marks awarded (Briggs, 1980), but it is difficult to isolate this one factor from all the others. Whatever the problems which handwriting brings to the examiner, it is unlikely that there will be a change to typewriting in examinations. Expense and noise and great variations in speed would be sufficient to preclude it. There is, however, a growing use of typed submissions for coursework, particularly in higher education, and this could well become more widespread at school level by those who could afford to do so.

Despite the reservations about typing, the time is ripe for at least experimental use of electronic devices, linked to audio and visual displays as a means of communication between examiner and examined. The transport of tapes and discs is no more difficult than that of written papers and scripts; and display screens can provide a greater range of visual material, both static and mobile, for candidates to work on than can be achieved on paper. Moreover, the direct electronic recording of marks by the examiner could well supersede the present manual inscription of marks on a script, which has changed little since examinations began; it would also facilitate the subsequent abstraction and processing of scores for standardizing and awarding meetings.

There is another, less reputable, aspect to the introduction of electronic communication into examinations which should be mentioned. Miniature devices available now, and increasingly in the future, make it easier for candidates to gain access to unauthorized information in an examination room. Hitherto the use of books or notes has been relatively easy to detect. Very small transmitters and receivers and programmed data retrieval systems make the invigilation task much more difficult. Modern technology could well revolutionize examinations, but perhaps not always in ways which would be approved.

Oral

Apart from the examinations for the Chinese Civil Service, the tradition of examining by word of mouth is much older than written examinations. The ancient universities used it for centuries and vestiges of the tradition remain. (It is still strong in the Soviet Union and parts of Europe.) At school level it forms but a small part and that mainly in English and second languages.[4] Some experiments have been conducted in other subject areas (Schools Council, 1971b) and no doubt an element of assessment by word of mouth takes place in some internal examinations conducted by teachers.

The reasons for the apparent neglect of oral examinations are not difficult to find. Compared with written examinations, they are vastly more extravagant of human resources. Necessarily they involve a person-to-person communication. Recorded questions and recorded answers may appear to provide some advantage but they cannot be a substitute for real oral examining. Not only does recorded speech suffer from the inflexibility of written examinations, it precludes all the non-verbal communication which so greatly enriches normal conversation. It follows that the standardization of oral examinations is much more difficult unless reduced to a prescribed set of questions rather like an interview schedule. If that were to be the case, there is little advantage over the written examination.

At the higher levels of education, where the candidates are fewer, the problem of resources is less. Even here, university examiners would find first-degree examinations, if they were solely oral, more than a little daunting. For postgraduate work, where the numbers are still less, an element of oral examining is common; at doctoral level the viva voce is usually compulsory, although the written thesis must usually be the determining element in the assessment.

The question of the relative reliability of the oral and written media remains largely unresolved since the evidence on oral examining is scanty. It is widely assumed that oral examining is more subjective, and therefore less reliable, because it involves a direct assessment by one examiner who is present in person. But this remains to be proved. There seems no good reason why an oral examiner, confined by standard procedures and specific marking criteria, should be any more subjective than a single examiner reading an essay. There may be extraneous factors impinging on direct oral communication: appearance of the candidate, physical mannerisms, racial origin, accent, nervousness, speed, and so on, but why should these influence an examiner any more than, say, handwriting in an essay?

The problem may lie less with the subjectivity of oral assessment than with its validity. While the inclusion of an element of oral assessment may be thought to make a contribution to the overall validity of an examination simply because it widens its scope, the artificiality of the assessment remains. A one-to-one communication standardized on procedures, substance and scoring is not a bit like oral communication in social and working life. It may resemble a little more closely the communication in the classroom but that too can verge on unreality.

Of course, there are ways and means of reducing this unreality. The communication could be conducted within a group instead of by a dialogue; it could be open-ended with regard to content; and it could be judged by impression. But each one of these factors diminishes the standardization of the assessment and contributes to its unreliability. The relationship is close to that of structured written answers, coupled with a standardized mark scheme, compared with free-response answers marked by impression.

Perhaps another factor in the relegation of oral examining to so small a component in public examining is that it is thought to be relevant to only a small part of the curriculum, modern languages. The case for a substantial element of oral examining of second languages seems so self-evident that it barely needs to be pressed; it is strange that the case has been so strongly resisted in the use of a first language. Why should it be confined to second languages? In what walk in life and in what part of the school curriculum does not oral communication play at least as great a part as the written? But even if oral communication does dominate over the written, the telephone over the letter, the radio and television over newspapers and books, it does not necessarily follow that it must dominate our examinations. Considerations of convenience and cost and timing, and of pragmatism, may bear more heavily on mass examining than those of relevance.

Substantive
This is the most difficult medium to define. Other terms come to mind: 'direct observation', 'concrete', 'practical', 'assessment of product', none is quite inclusive enough. The implication of 'substantive' is that the assessment is to do with actual events or an actual product or performance in circumstances where competence can be directly observed and assessed and not inferred. It concerns *doing* rather than writing about or talking about. It may involve all three domains – cognitive, affective and motor – but it is more to do with *effectiveness* than with any one of them alone.

It may be that this medium of assessment is less applicable to those activities which in themselves are mainly to do with the use of the written or spoken word; for example, the learning of language, and the study of literature. In these it is the written and spoken products which are the only manifestation of the activity. The same could be said for 'pure' mathematics; the fact that the product is in mathematical symbols other than words does not really deflect from the point.

In other areas, however, the outcome is so obviously real rather than symbolic or abstract that simply writing about it or talking about it, or any other symbolic treatment, is not sufficient as a vehicle of communication between examiner and examined. The examinee has actually to do something or produce something manifestly nearer to material reality if the assessment is to have an acceptable validity. The practice of science and technology comes immediately to mind, so do medicine, agriculture and teaching (a case can be made for including the last three in technology).

Common sense points to an obvious conclusion that in these areas assessment is best done by observation of the candidates at work or of their final product, or preferably both. At once, however, there arises a conflict with those technical aspects of examining which has encouraged the application of a common test and common marking on a large scale: written papers and written answers are used, the papers are set and the answers marked centrally, while the candidates sit the examination at a distance. It is on this simple process that the whole of mass examining to a common standard depends, and it should be self-evident that it cannot sensibly be used when direct observation of process or product are required.

The inappropriateness of examining these attributes at a distance through written examinations has not been as readily accepted as one would have expected. Perhaps the best illustration is that of the traditional practical examination in science, which is still widely administered. The questions consist of centrally written instructions for the conduct of experiments at schools. The responses are also written in the form of observations and results and, possibly, comments and suggestions for experimental design. The school is responsible for providing material facilities, supervising the test and sometimes checking the results. But the communication between examiner and examined is *written*. It follows that what can be tested is limited to what can be used in a common test applied over the same short period of time and the results of which can be entirely reported in writing. This leaves out a good deal more of the real nature of scientific experiment than it includes. There are instances in which an artefact can be centrally assessed according to a prescribed specification: metalwork, woodwork and engineering workshop practice come to mind. In these cases a reliable assessment can be made by direct observation of the product by a panel of external examiners. But the limitations on the kind of artefacts, conforming to a common specification which can be required in these circumstances, and the organizational constraints of dispatch and storage, inevitably lead to a restriction on both range of work and number of candidates. This is not to deny the care with which these artefacts are assessed and the perceptive comments which are made by the examiners.

Try as we may, it is difficult to replicate real situations within the artificial conditions of examinations. The issue is specially acute in areas such as medicine. While every effort has to be made to bring medical education and assessment as close as possible to the real situations faced by qualified practitioners, the best which can be achieved must have some aspects of simulation and artificiality. The point is made with some force by Fleming (1976, p. 37): 'Surgical evaluation in the past has sometimes included the dissection of a cadaver but even this does not give very satisfactory evidence of what a man can do with a living body.' It may be that examinations, and formal education itself, are so far removed from real life as to be moribund if not actually dead. The 'deschoolers' would certainly have us think so: 'The pupil is thereby "schooled" to confuse teaching with learning, grade advancement with education, a diploma with competence, and fluency with the ability to say something new' (Illich, 1971, p. 9).

The vicarious nature of school and examinations is difficult to deny; but that in itself does not make a case for abolition. There *are* ways of widening the concept of examining and of bringing it closer to real life (see Chapters 11 and 12). There are, however, two strongly opposed sets of forces, which by pulling equally in opposite directions tend to inhibit radical change in examining. On the one hand, there is the demand for common standards on a national scale, leading to crude categorization of large groups of candidates. On the other, there is the demand for evidence of individual effectiveness when one young person seeks to find one niche in life. It would be unduly optimistic to look to a revolutionary new technique of examining to resolve this dilemma. The techniques of mass examining, which have been the main burden of this chapter, have almost reached their limit, certainly in written and oral examining. There is at least novelty still to be found in electronic and keyboard techniques; but whether their use would amount to a revolutionary breakthrough in examining remains to be proved.

Notes: Chapter 7

1   Structured questions are long, complex and consume much space. It is not possible, therefore, to give a representative sample in this book. There are many examples available in books of published papers and a fuller discussion of them in Mathews, 1974.
2   Examination boards are responding to changing circumstances albeit slowly. The Joint Matriculation Board (1985) have made a significant step in acknowledging that in some subjects the lack of an electronic device could place candidates at a disadvantage in an examination. The Board now assumes that all candidates will have a device, with a specified minimum capacity, at their disposal.
3   It is of interest to note that at the time of writing the Youth Training Scheme, designed to bridge school and the world of work, has made keyboard skills an essential element.
4   The GCE and CSE Boards' Joint Council for 16+ national criteria found that in English (January 1983) much of their discussion and disagreement centred on the assessment of oral ability. In the end it was decided that 'Opportunities must be provided for pupils to

develop the skills of oral communication in situations where individuals are both listeners and speakers': GCE and CSE Boards' Joint Council for 16+, 1983a, p. 2. The technical and organizational problems were recognized: 'The assessment of oral communication in English will be shown separately on the certificate, using a grade scale still to be determined': loc. cit.

8

Are They Fair?
I   Social Bias

The concept of fairness in examinations is one which, though often used colloquially, is rarely to be found in the academic literature.[1] To the public at large, however, the concept has a commonsense meaning which may be paramount. It implies equity and justice and consistency. It implies also that examinations should not be susceptible to abuse by particular individuals or groups; and that if they are to be instruments of social mobility, they should be applied with an acceptable degree of uniformity and in accordance with acceptable purposes of education.

It is proper, then, that fairness should occupy a commanding position in any general work on examinations. But the concept is not simple; many factors impinge upon it. These may be considered as two kinds. There are those *social* factors of class, school organization, sex and race which are the subject of this chapter. Then there are the factors more directly associated with examination systems themselves: agencies, techniques, reporting, stability over time and equity between subjects; these will be grouped under the general head of *comparability* and will be the subject of Chapter 9.

The reader should not expect a definitive answer to the question: 'are they fair?', certainly not in the form of yes or no. The most that can be done is to identify those aspects which may be associated with the question of fairness, to report on some relevant research and at least to illuminate the often heated and prejudiced discussions which they engender. Whether that will be sufficient to give reassurance to those who have anxieties on the matter is something which only individual readers can decide.

Have They a Class Bias?

It might be thought that if examinations favour a particular class of society, or conversely if they place another class at a disadvantage, they are to be regarded as unfair. Before developing this issue, the point should be made that some degree of social bias is inevitable. There are some groups within society, distinguished by wealth, class, creed, or culture, which must gain or be denied advantage by some aspects of any process of assessment and selection. If our society were culturally homogeneous, then perhaps bias could be avoided. But it is not, and not likely to be. Even if it were, our inherent differences are sufficient for some to take advantage of any assessment and selection system which leads to the more desirable careers, while others cannot.

That examinations have been instrumental in upward social mobility there can be no doubt.[2] Slowly in the nineteenth century, and in increasing numbers in the twentieth, children of the poorer classes gained access to secondary and higher education, and then to the professions, by competing in examinations, which otherwise would have been denied them. It was not just a matter of obtaining academic qualifications. The scholarship and free-place system provided the necessary financial assistance to maintain the pupils and students throughout the long period of competition. Generations of teachers, civil servants, doctors, lawyers, scientists and technologists owe their professional status to their skill in climbing the examination ladder; and there are many distinguished individuals to make the point.

Despite this, the degree of upward mobility in the education system does not reflect the relative numbers in the social classes. Little and Westergaard (1964) in their analysis of three national surveys of the educational careers of children born in the late 1930s showed the great disparity in proportions of each social class who gained access to grammar school education; a disparity which increased still more in access to higher education. So much so that the chances of an unskilled manual worker's child of that generation attaining a university education was thirty times less than that of a child of a non-manual worker. (The percentage of girls of unskilled manual workers entering university was so small that it was not recorded.)

There appears still to be a high level of social inequality in access to educational opportunity. Since that opportunity is largely controlled by performance in examinations, the question asked at the head of this section is pertinent. It does appear that the children of some working-class parents either cannot or do not take as much advantage of the competitive examination system as do those of the other classes. It does not necessarily follow, however, that examinations are *deliberately* biased to maintain this state of affairs.

Hargreaves (1982) rightly points out that examinations deal almost exclusively with 'cognitive–intellectual' skills to the almost total exclusion of other kinds of skill: 'artistic–aesthetic, affective–emotional, physical–manual and personal–social' (ibid., p. 51). He also maintains that the children of the middle classes can take advantage of this bias, drawing on the cultural capital of their parents:

> middle class parents are highly skilled in the cognitive–intellectual mode, partly because they are themselves products of such an

educational system. It is transmitted before the child ever reaches school and continues to be transmitted throughout the child's educational career. (ibid., p. 72)

This may well be so, but it does not follow that a change of emphasis in the school curriculum, and the assessment system related to it, will put the matter to rights; although it may shift the bias. It is true that the present curriculum and examinations are biased to the cognitive–intellectual mode. If the other four modes were accorded an equal place, a happier balance *may* be achieved. To assume, however, that such a change would necessarily dispel the present social inequalities could be misguided; indeed, it could aggravate them. Would not the children of the middle classes continue to draw on their cultural capital and possibly strengthen their advantage by achieving disproportionately better in all the other four modes?

The development work which is presently taking place in alternative or complementary forms of assessment such as profile reports and graded tests has been seized hopefully by some as a way to offset the social bias of examinations. Blackstone and Mortimore take a similar line to Hargreaves:

The examination system is also expensive to operate and, in terms of consumer benefit, must be considered a resource that is disproportionately used by the middle classes and which benefits the disadvantaged hardly at all. (Blackstone and Mortimore, 1982, p. 76)

Referring to the development of profile reporting, and graded and criterion-referenced tests, they suggest that these initiatives 'may prevent the institutionalisation of that disadvantage by the structure of the examination system' (ibid., p. 77). The pros and cons of these new initiatives will be taken up at greater length in Chapters 11 and 12. But the point must be made now that any claim that alternative systems of reporting student attributes will rectify social injustice to any great degree is nothing more than speculation at present.

In any event, the social divisiveness of our educational system is largely effected before the age when most of our children sit their first public examinations. The 11+ examination undoubtedly did so and continues to do so in those places where it still operates. But even in comprehensive schools, and even where mixed ability teaching is practised, the fact remains that children of the lower classes perform proportionately less well than those of the middle classes in the curriculum between the ages of 11 and 14. And at that time, when critical decisions are made about curricular options, there is evidence that a greater proportion of middle-class children take those subjects which have public examination status, while a greater proportion of working-class children and other disadvantaged groups take the non-examined options. The possible causal factors: home background, lack of motivation, lack of facilities, teacher prejudice, and so on, have been widely researched and documented and cannot concern us here; the fact remains that by the time the first public examination arrives a disproportionate number of children from the lower social classes are either no longer part of the population of examination candidates or are entered for lower-level examinations.

The influence of social class on performance declines in later years (at age 18 and thereafter), although it is reiterated that those working-class children who remain in the education system at that stage have been highly selected by passing through increasingly narrow examination hoops (Halsey *et al.*, 1980; Brimer *et al.*, 1978). If public examinations at 16 plus were to be abolished, examinations in later years would almost cease to be a divisive social influence. This is not to say that differential access of the various classes in society to higher education and high-status careers would not still take place; it almost certainly would, but public examinations could no longer be held to blame and social engineers would have to seek a different scapegoat.

Have They a School Bias?

The relative examination performance of students from different types of educational institution has become an emotive political issue in recent years. In particular, attempts have been made to compare the performance of candidates from comprehensive schools with those from selective schools. The findings have been confused by the difficulty of controlling all the variables inherent in the research, allowing full rein to the prejudgements which most commentators bring to their evaluation of the research findings and other statistics. Despite all the dangers which attend the use of examination results in making judgements about individual schools and comparisons between types of schools, the practice persists. It is possible to use examination results to maintain a precommitment to almost any partisan educational or political standpoint.

One of the more balanced commentaries on the relationship between type of school and examination performance is that of Auriol Stevens, who recognizes that

> The exams debate itself resembles most closely in its abstruseness those medieval theological arguments about the number of angels which can be accommodated on a pin's head – except that it matters more. Such evidence as there is is patchy and contentious. Nothing is certain. (Stevens, 1980, p. 76)

She goes on to say somewhat guardedly,

> Given all of these complications, pronouncements about standards are

extremely unsafe. However, from these figures and from tramping the schools, I have the impression that the rise of certificated achievement for the middle ability children does owe something to comprehensive schools rather than only to the invention of new certificates and the lengthening of school life. But I have the impression, too, that this gain has to some extent been achieved at the expense of the brightest students. (ibid., p. 89)

More recently the requirement that the examination results of individual schools must be made public has added fuel to the debate.[3] It is understandable at present that parents will seek to place their children into those schools which appear to give the best chance of examination success. It is also natural that the decision will be based on totals of examination successes rather than on a finer analysis of the complex statistics of the grades of various groups of children in various subjects and in various kinds of learning situations.

Such an analysis was attempted by Rutter *et al.* (1979), who studied in depth the attainment of children in different schools. This study confined the number of schools and its geographic area to twelve from Inner London. While this limits the degree to which the findings can be generalized, the researchers did control the many variables as far as possible and the results do throw light on the issue. Even so, Rutter himself points to the need for further work before direct causal relationships can be established between the attainment of children and the many influences which impinge upon them.[4]

Rutter was not concerned with examination results alone; he measured other outcomes: attendance, behaviour in school and delinquency. One of the main contributions of the research was to relate attainment to detailed characteristics of the schools rather than simply to the type of school implied by its name. In other words, he went beyond what the school was called to such things as the characteristics of the individual pupils, the social processes and organization within the schools, and the social environment in which each school was set.

Perhaps the most interesting findings and discussion in Rutter's work concerned the effect of what he called the 'processes' of the school on the outcomes of education. The kinds of processes he considered are too numerous to be listed here but they included such things as relationships between teachers and pupils and the policy of the schools towards homework in general: 'those features of the social organisation of school life which create the context for teaching and learning' (ibid., p. 106). He found that

There was a very strong and highly consistent correlation (0·92) between overall school processes and pupil behaviour. The correlation with academic attainment (0·76) was also very substantial indeed. (ibid., p. 134)

I have quoted at some length from Rutter's work because, despite its limitations, it does get to the heart of the matter and beyond the crude slanging-match between the advocates of selective and non-selective education. Some schools do get better examination results – and further attainment – than others and this success has been shown to be related to particular features of their internal organization, management and social interactions. Of course, the prerequisites for examination success do not lie entirely with the school processes. There are other factors which lie beyond the control of the school, for example:

> Examination success tended to be better in schools with a substantial nucleus of children of at least average intellectual ability and delinquency rates were higher in those with a heavy preponderance of the least able. (ibid., p. 178)

In passing, however, it is interesting to note that Rutter did not find any relationship between the various educational outcomes and the physical resources of the schools or – rather unexpectedly – with continuity of teaching staff (see DES, 1983c).

Of course, all this begs the question of whether examination success, and the other attainments which Rutter measured, are desirable and that they are suitable criteria for making judgements about schools (Plewis *et al.*, 1981). This, however, is a fairly safe assumption at the present time and parents who value examination success must accept that the kind of school which their children attend *will* have an effect on their examination results. If examination results are high among their educational goals, choice of school will be important. But that choice will require a deeper and more subtle evaluation of the school than the blanket evaluations which have tended to be attached nationally to independent, grammar, secondary modern and comprehensive secondary schools, particularly those based solely on grand totals or percentages of examination passes.

A more informed evaluation is possible at local level, although the necessary information is not always readily available. It would include information about the admissions to the school, the degree of importance attached to academic work and examination subjects within the general curriculum, and the school's policy on the choice of options within the curriculum. Added to this is the policy on entering candidates for the examinations. Does the school, for example, enter everyone even if they have little chance of success or does it enter only those likely to succeed. The two policies can give rise to a very different appearance in the published statistics of results. Then there are all the less tangible factors which contribute to the attainment of the school: the social relations between staff and pupils and between pupils and pupils, and even within the staff, the complex processes which contribute to the ethos of the school.

Even though these issues are the central ones in the minds of parents, I have wandered from the point a little. If society chooses to judge schools by examination performance, so be it; there is not much that can be done about that except by fundamentally altering the function of examinations in education and in selection processes. That is a more general political issue than the immediate one of whether examinations are equitable across various kinds of schools.

It is easy enough to find a statistic which appears to show that our examination system favours one kind of school rather than another. Selective secondary schools, whether they be independent or former direct grant or maintained, can claim a degree of examination success in proportion to their numbers greater than non-selective schools. That fact may or may not point to class divisions and social inequality in our education system. It does not demonstrate, however, that in themselves examinations are unfair. They are divisive in the sense that they distinguish one candidate from another, that is one of their functions; but to lay all the real or imagined ills of education and social inequality on the examination system is in itself unfair. If a comprehensive school, given a balanced intake, chooses to put examination success at the head of its aims, it can so organize its curriculum and select its staff as to compete effectively with any other type of school of similar intake of pupils (Boyson, 1969). If, on the other hand, it chooses to give prominence to wider educational and social goals, and to apply greater resources to the less able in the community, it may have to accept lower examination performance. Given finite resources, there is a price to be paid for either alternative.

There is another point to be made on the relationship between schools and examinations. Examinations are not only competitions between candidates; they involve competition between schools and even competition between teachers within a school. In one sense it could be thought that all three competitions are to the good. If extended to all pupils, to all schools and all teachers, a rise could be expected in the overall quality and quantity of examination performance – *but it would not necessarily enhance the prospects of any individual candidate.* The competition for limited education and employment opportunities would remain; the increased number of certificates awarded would simply add to 'certificate inflation', increasing the price of access (see Chapter 2).

Nor would greater emphasis on examination success in all schools necessarily further the cause of educational equality. Indeed, an overall rise in performance may *increase* the difference in attainment between students: 'We found the variations in attainment between pupils to be least (i.e. the greatest reduction in inequality) in the schools with the poorest level of attainment' (Rutter *et al.*, 1979, p. 170). In other words, it seems to be easier to make everyone equally bad than to make everyone equally good.

The overall totals of examination grades might rise and the differences between schools even out, but the other factors in examination success remain and the dominant ones attach to the individuals themselves: inherited characteristics, early childhood education, social and family background, and so on. So although schools could become more alike in examination performance, it does not follow that individuals would do likewise:

> The differences in attainment between children within any one school are much greater than any differences in average attainment between schools. Raising the quality of education does not have the effect of making everyone alike. This is because children vary (as a result of both genetic endowment and home experiences) in their ability to profit from educational opportunities. Improving schools will not necessarily make any difference to individual variations. But it may have a decisive impact in raising overall standards of attainment. (ibid., p. 7)

The same kinds of people, then, would continue to win the prizes. The examination system has long outlived its early image as the one great vehicle for greater social mobility and educational equality; and for several decades it has been made a scapegoat for a creaking educational system. In many ways examinations have provided the only generally applicable measure of success to all kinds of school. The fact that the measure is limited in its function and that it is given influence beyond its narrow confines, and used to make judgements beyond its capacity, has to be recognized. But this does not justify making it a repository for all our past and present errors and dispatching it to the wilderness. Auriol Stevens (1980, p. 54) points to the ambivalent attitude to the problem among many educationists, not least in the Inspectorate: 'There are no signs yet of any national willingness to argue out the relative values of breadth and academic specialisation in terms removed from active political battles about standards.'

If those who have control in these matters wish to see secondary schools put more effort into public examinations, no doubt that could be arranged. Of course, there would be a price to pay in a decline in other areas of the curriculum which are not appropriate to this sort of competition. The emphasis on one or the other has political as well as educational overtones. Meanwhile the examination system endures the blame until society makes up its mind on what kinds of school it wants and what qualities it wants its young people to develop.

Are They Sexually Biased?

Access to the new public examinations in the mid-nineteenth century was at first only for men and boys. The reasons for this lie deep in the social structure of the period and were yet another manifestation of strongly differentiated roles conventionally attached to men and women (Burstyn, 1980). While men could seek upward social mobility through academic and commercial competition, women were largely confined to whatever competition the marriage market allowed. Formal education – at what would now be called the secondary education level – was not entirely denied to girls, but the curriculum was not designed to provide for subsequent careers in industry, commerce, politics, the civil service, or the church, all of which at that time were the provinces of men.[5] This being so, access of girls to examinations would serve no function. So at first they were excluded; there seemed no point in allowing girls to enter a race for which there would be no prize.

For a while examinations remained yet another instance of sexual apartheid. But later in the century when the seeds of feminism began to germinate, and the women's teaching profession grew, the exclusion of girls from public academic examinations began to be questioned. The first steps to gain access to Local Examinations were taken by Emily Davies, who in 1863 succeeded in persuading Cambridge University, but not Oxford, to allow girls' schools to have copies of the examination papers, so that they could use them in private (Fletcher, 1980). Later that formidable pair, Miss Buss and Miss Beale, entered the debate, but with different points of view.

One of the early points of division was whether girls should enter for the existing examination to compete on the same ground in an examination designed by men for men, or whether a special examination should be devised to suit the needs of women in particular. Roach (1971) gives a more detailed account of the discussion at the time than is possible here. The essence of it was whether girls should enter for the Locals and be judged by the same standards as boys, hence providing the impetus for a curriculum common to boys' and girls' schools, or whether boys and girls were sufficiently different to warrant a different curriculum and examinations specially designed for them. For a while both approaches coexisted, the parallel development being reflected at Cambridge in the foundation of Girton College where Miss Davies insisted on competition on equal terms with men, and Newnham College where Miss Clough supported the Women's Examination.

Although the two schools of thought were in opposition on whether there should be separate or single development of examinations and curricula for the two sexes, they were united in working for access of women to higher education through competitive examinations of some sort; they both sought the academic advancement of women. Others, more committed to maintaining the separate roles of men and women, raised objections to women's access to examinations on social, psychological and even physiological grounds. The objectors had to be convinced that the female candidates 'would suffer no harmful effects from the excitement of the examination' (ibid., p. 111). And Roach reports an examiner at the London centre after the 1865 examination, who wrote with apparent surprise:

> I was struck by the easy way in which they bore the stress of the examination. I could not detect any flagging interest in it, or any sign of weariness, or any ill effect upon them whatever. (ibid., p. 112)

Such statements may sound bizarre to modern ears; but the idea that the frailty of women was an obstacle to examination competition persisted long afterwards. Sutherland (1981, p. 26) recalls the Report of the Consultative Committee of the Board of Education in 1923 which recommended that 'care should be taken not to overstrain girls: girls should, as a rule, be encouraged to take the First School Examination about a year later than boys'.

The statistics of GCE O-level entry still show a slightly higher average age for girls; traditionally also girls have offered fewer subjects than boys. The long-standing assumption that girls are more prone to examination stress may be associated with menstruation; but little research has been done to provide evidence to justify it. Even if it were so, it is difficult to see how examiners could make allowance for that event any more than they can for hay fever.

Although it was many more years before women could gain that ultimate prize of examination success, admission to the degree courses of Oxford and Cambridge, they were at least accepted as competitors in the examinations. The effect was twofold: women slowly gained access to careers previously limited to men, and the secondary school curriculum for boys and girls became more uniform. The uniformity of curricula, however, is still not complete even in these days of comprehensive, mixed-sex schools. A glance at the statistics reveals that entry to many examination subjects is sexually biased, showing that the curriculum option system still allows a distinction between male subjects and female subjects. In 1951, for example, 18,820 boys entered for O-level physics compared with 2,730 girls. Whereas in biology 22,080 girls entered compared with 6,940 boys. Murphy has shown that the bias is declining in

Table 8.1

	Boys	Girls
Physics	114,270	31,540
Biology	84,600	136,590

Source: Murphy, 1980.

most of the major subjects; the 1977 figures were as shown in Table 8.1. (In passing, the massive increase in entries to both subjects is worthy of note.) Nevertheless, over 100 years after girls obtained access to public examinations there are still examination subjects which show an unequal distribution of male and female candidates.

This unequal and changing distribution of *entry* makes the comparison of *performance* of males and females rather difficult at the national level. This was recognized by Murphy, who suggested that a more restricted inquiry with one examining board might be fruitful. Forrest had already demonstrated that in some subjects there were differences in mixed schools between the examination performance of males and females, and in the general ability of the male and female populations (as measured by a reference test) which entered for them:

> It may be seen that girls achieve better mean grades than the boys in all subjects except Mathematics and the Sciences. On the other hand, the boys scored more highly in the reference test in every subject sample. (Forrest, 1971, p. 25)

He attributes this apparent discrepancy to 'factors of motivation and industry'. There is also evidence that the form of examination can favour either males or females (Wood, 1978).

Differences between the performance of males and females in some cognitive skills has been established for some time, although the reasons are more elusive than the facts. Some research indicates that boys perform better in mathematical and spatial abilities, while girls show higher verbal ability.[6] Given the variation in the education of boys and girls, the different choices which they make and the variation within the examination system itself, it is difficult to establish that differences in examination performance can be definitely associated with sex difference rather than acquired characteristics.

In a study of JMB examination results (1963–80) in the twelve subjects attracting the greatest number of candidates, Price (1981) was able to show some patterns of performance which subsequent research on a larger scale might prove to be general. He confirmed, in accordance with previous findings, that in general boys did better in mathematics and related subjects while girls did better in subjects which required mainly verbal ability. But rather more important, he was able to show that some subjects gave anomalous results and the differences in performance showed various trends over the years, particularly when related to changing patterns of examination entries. For example, between 1963 and 1980 the number of boys entering for JMB O-level physics increased by about 27 per cent (after reaching the peak of a 35 per cent increase in 1972). Over the same period the entry of girls for the same examination increased by 236 per cent. The *actual* number of girls taking physics in

1980 was still less than one-half that of boys (11,465 : 28,426). For every year except 1963, the average performance of the girls was better than that of the boys.

Over the same period Price showed that the entry of girls to both JMB O-level mathematics and English language increased by over 20 per cent, while the entry of boys decreased in both by about 10 per cent. In mathematics the average performance of boys was always greater and in English language it was always less than that of girls. These differences fluctuated greatly from year to year, however, and Price's discussion emphasizes the complexity of any argument which seeks to attach *reasons* to the variation in performance. These arguments must involve such factors as changes in entry policy (including entry to CSE), the availability of teachers and the quality of teaching, changes in career prospects and motivation, and changes in examination content and format, among many others. However, some trends are clear. Girls are increasingly entering for what were traditionally male subjects: mathematics, physics and chemistry, while the entry of boys to these subjects has tended to level off. On the other hand, there has been a substantial increase of boys entering for biology, religious studies and music, traditionally the province of females.

Whether these patterns of entry arise from intrinsic differences in the sexes is doubtful, to say the least. Ironically there is evidence (HMI, 1975) that the blurring of the distinction between 'male' and 'female' subjects is greatest in single-sex schools. In these schools it appears that boys and girls are less inhibited in choosing subjects which traditionally have been the province of the opposite sex, while in coeducational schools the sex-typing of subjects persists to such a degree that Sutherland (1981, p. 30) remarks: 'In fact, co-education does not give equal opportunity or identical education.'

Price (1981) studied average pass rates of males and females in twelve A-level subjects over eighteen years. Of the 216 examinations, there was a significant difference in the pass rates of males and females in 112 of them. Some examples may be of interest, but it must be emphasized that conclusions are dangerous unless they are linked to other factors such as different entry policies. Boys did consistently better than girls in general studies, biology and economics, while girls did better than boys in English literature, statistics and mathematics. It does not follow that girls are *in general* better at, for example, mathematics and statistics examinations: it simply means that those girls who *entered* for them did better, and it should be noted that the entry of girls was much more selective than the entry of boys. The overall picture of A level revealed in Price's work is that, in the 112 examinations in twelve main subjects where there was a significant difference, 'the majority of the differences favour the girls in the ratio of 2:1' (ibid., p. 62). Even this may reflect not a general difference in the inherent ability of boys and girls to pass examinations, but a difference in numbers of candidates. In any event the pattern of differences is not stable. Price points to 'the overall decline in the performance of girls relative to boys since 1969' (ibid., p. 63) and reflects on the complex array of factors which might have brought it about. One of these factors is that since about that time there has been an increase in the use of objective tests in examinations and a decrease in the use of essays. And further to confuse the issue all researchers have assumed that to pass in any subject is equally difficult. This is by no means so, as will be explored in Chapter 9. If it could be shown that either males or females tend as a group to enter for the 'hard' or 'easy' subjects, attempts to investigate sexual bias in examinations would be made even more difficult.

The research work reviewed in this section raises far more questions than it answers. Rather like the work on the performance of different social groups, the different examination performance of males and females can be used selectively to substantiate many prejudgements about the sexes. That differences do exist is undeniable, but to use the global figures to substantiate hypotheses about the roles of the sexes and the biases of their education is likely to be misleading. Furthermore, it is not reasonable to expect examination authorities to deliberately change their examinations in order to decrease these differences. The control which examiners can exert on all the various factors which operate on the examination performance of the sexes is slight indeed. Any attempt to iron out differences is likely to produce unforeseen and perhaps even less acceptable side-effects. In such circumstances it is small wonder that the examination boards base their syllabus and examination design on other premises and let the sexes take care of themselves.

Are They Racially Biased?

Research on the relative educational achievement of ethnic groups in Britain has been reviewed by Tomlinson (1981, 1983). It should be treated with caution. Some of the earlier research was on a small scale, localized and sometimes unwarranted generalizations on causes of underachievement have been made from it.

The first statistics on a more substantial level, involving examination performance, were those of the Department of Education and Science in its school-leaving survey of 1978–9. The statistics provided information on the examination performance of children in six large education authorities and they were used subsequently by the Committee of Inquiry into the Education of Children from Ethnic Minority Groups, the Rampton Report (1981).

The information used by the committee of inquiry did not cover the whole country and was not completely generalizable. The six authorities, however, did contain a large number of children from ethnic minorities.

The performance of all the children was a little lower than the national average; nevertheless, the relative average performance between ethnic groups was established and the figures confirmed that there was cause for concern, for example: 'In English 9% of West Indians scored higher grades compared with 21% of Asians (for many of whom English may have been a second language) and 29% of other leavers' (ibid., tables A and B). ('Higher grades' means GCE O-level grades A, B and C, and CSE grade 1.) In mathematics the figures were 5 per cent West Indians, 20 per cent Asians and 19 per cent all other leavers. And over all subjects, '3% of West Indians obtained 5 or more higher grades compared with 18% of Asians and 16% of other leavers' (ibid., table C). The Report continues with statistics which show a similar pattern at A level and in entry to degree courses.

Despite the scale of the research on which such findings are based, there is still need for caution in their interpretation, particularly in deducing causes. For example, the general categories 'West Indian', 'Asian' and 'other leavers' conceal the performance of subgroups within them. There are, for example, differences in performance between males and females, between the various social classes, and between the cultural and geographic origins within the main ethnic groups (Tomlinson, 1983). Furthermore, the information was mainly based on city schools in which the 'white population' may not be typical of that in the country as a whole. Nor is sufficient known about the different choice of the ethnic minorities among the various examination subjects. Nevertheless, sufficient has been done to establish the fact that 'West Indian pupils are under-achieving in relation to their peers, not least in obtaining the examination qualification needed to give them equality of opportunity in the employment market' (Rampton Report, 1981, p. 10). But it is a big step from statements like this to the identification of causes and attaching blame, and a still bigger step to the prescription of remedies. Tomlinson, (1983 p. 136) suggests the need for research to place less emphasis on underachievement and to 'concentrate on providing a more effective education for all pupils in multi-ethnic schools'.)

The Rampton Report lists and discusses several factors which could contribute to underachievement: parental influence, language problems (particularly with Creole) and bias in textbooks, the curriculum and in examinations: 'we have found evidence of an exclusively euro-centric bias in some examination papers' (Rampton Report, 1981, ch. 2).[7] As the Report acknowledges, however, the committee of inquiry was not able to investigate this last charge to any extent. It would be extraordinary if some examination syllabuses, given their origins, did not show a bias towards the culture and antecedents of the majority of the population. Even if such a bias could be thought to place ethnic minorities at a disadvantage in such subjects as English literature, history, geography and the arts, it would be difficult to use it to substantiate differences in performance in such subjects as mathematics and the sciences which are less rooted in an indigenous culture.[8] In any event the near-equality of performance of students of Asian origin with that of English students would be difficult to explain if cultural bias were the main determining factor. Vellins (1982, p. 212) suggests: 'hard work and high aspirations can lead to considerable success in passing public examinations, despite the presence of many obstacles.'

But given that there is a problem in the relative performance of ethnic minorities in public examinations, what should be the reaction of examination boards? The Schools Council (1982, p. 10) thought that a reappraisal of syllabuses and examinations should be undertaken 'to ensure that they reflect and meet the needs of our multicultural society' and suggests twelve questions which those responsible for examinations should attend to. Four of these[9] are directed 'towards culturally fairer examinations':

(1)   Is there within the examinations a variety of forms of assessment (projects, coursework, and so on) to enable teachers to encourage pupils to use skills or follow up interests which arise from particular cultural backgrounds?

(2)   Does the language, particularly the idiomatic, used for examination questions, minimize difficulties of comprehension?

(3)   Are examiners sensitive to the difficulties candidates can have in demonstrating abilities if their first language is not English?

(4)   Is marking empathetic to candidates, rewarding attainment demonstrated through various cultural forms and responsive to the full range of acceptable language?

The first two questions are general and should inform the design and construction of all examinations whether or not there is to be special consideration of the strengths and weaknesses of ethnic groups. The last two, however, are different. Once examiners go beyond the evidence and attempt an exercise in empathy by projecting themselves into the mind and culture of individual candidates, they stand at risk of being accused of applying different standards to match preconceived estimates of a candidate's linguistic and cultural background; the preconceptions being based perhaps on little more than the name at the head of the script.

An extrapolation of the suggestions in the last two questions is that examinations for ethnic minorities should be set and marked separately. The population of candidates would at least be more clearly identified. This might be logical but, if generally applied, would be divisive and likely to hinder the cause of ethnic minorities rather than enhance it, just as it did that of women in the nineteenth century. This is not to say that some examinations or options within them should not, in their content and objectives, allow the expression of minority interests, including those of ethnic minorities. But that is already the case. The Mode III systems within the CSE allow this opportunity and there are a number of instances quoted in the Rampton Report (1981) and in the School Council Report (1981). And it should not be forgotten that similar schemes exist within the GCE boards; the JMB O-level English language alternative D is an obvious vehicle by which work with minority cultures can be undertaken without loss of status in the award itself.

If one looks at the statistics of entries to separate examinations and options, there is to be seen a fairly clear division between large-scale and small-scale entries. In some the number of candidates is very small indeed.[10] If the cost of examining per candidate were to be calculated, it would not be surprising to find that an examining board ran most of its examinations at a loss, supporting that loss by a smaller number of large-entry staple commodities. It is a little hard, then, to accuse examination boards of bias against minorities in general. There does seem to be a growing awareness of the need for sensitivity, however. The Working Party on National Criteria for English at 16+ is convinced that

> subject examinations in English will only do justice to the needs of a multi-cultural society in so far as Examining Groups ensure that questions and materials used in assessments are carefully chosen and sensitive to the differing cultural backgrounds of the candidates. (GCE and CSE Boards' Joint Council for 16+, 1983a, p. 4)

It may be that they could respond more actively to suggestions for syllabuses and examinations from the ethnic minorities. There are examples of this already in existence and these could be increased. But examination boards do respond to approaches made by various bodies, particularly groups of teachers, which make out a case for syllabuses designed for special minorities; and they do instigate their own developments in minority areas if they perceive a need. The needs have to be established before examination boards can assign substantial resources to the development and to some extent this leaves the onus on the minority groups themselves.

Are They Socially Biased?

The whole problem of discrimination against or in favour of various groups in society is emotive and politically loaded. Intervention in the substance and form of examinations could exacerbate the situation and produce unexpected side-effects, even when done with the best of intentions. The dangers of separate provision for various kinds of candidates are as great as that of a single set of common examinations. Furthermore, the problem in examinations is but a reflection of the problem in the curriculum itself. This may be stated quite simply: how may a balance be achieved between on the one hand studies which are based on a culture and a structure of knowledge common to all, and on the other hand studies based on particular interests and cultures. To what extent do we aim for commonality and cohesion in society and to what extent do we aim for cultural pluralism and diversity?

So to return to the point with which this chapter began: examinations can never be fair in the sense that every individual or group of individuals has an equal chance to do well. Even supposing that everyone comes to the examination endowed with the same inherited ability, the factors associated with examination performance are so numerous that the best possible inherited ability can be submerged. There is now a great deal of evidence that performance also depends on the effects of early childhood, parental attitude, gender, social class, ethnic origins, schools' aims and ethos, quality of teaching and more besides. Furthermore, these various factors are so linked together that their interaction would make deliberate allowance for any one of them a hazardous, unpredictable intervention.[11] A candidate of West Indian origin who lives in the inner city, and who is poor and attends a school in which the proportion of able children is low, starts with a disadvantage which there is little a public examination system alone can do to alleviate.

Examinations are no more or less fair than schools are fair, or society is fair. If unfairness there be, it lies in fixing the blame for the inequities of society on the educational system in general, and the examination system in particular. For many years now both have served as whipping boys, conveniently institutionalized, serving to deflect blame from where it properly lies: with the actions and attitudes of us all.

Notes: Chapter 8

1   It is pleasing to find the term in Bardell *et al.*, 1978. This admirably precise booklet summarizes the methods and results of the studies undertaken to monitor the equivalence of standards between the boards.

2   Hargreaves, 1982, makes the point that the mobility was mainly one way. The increasing number of middle-class jobs provided opportunities for the working classes to attain the more desirable professions without causing a reverse downward flow. Hargreaves also points out that in more recent years occupational structure is stabilizing and with it the opportunity for upward social mobility through academic competition will decline.

3   A recent study has made use of the published GCE and CSE results. It has been criticized on methodological grounds, and the authors acknowledge some limitations of the data analysis: see Marks *et al.*, 1983, pp. 123–9. However, the work was based on a very large population and some of the findings deserve serious attention. For example: 'the data support the common-sense view that it is the quality of the teaching which is probably much more important than the size of class' (p. 15); and 'The results of these calculations show consistently and robustly, that substantially higher O-level, CSE and A-level examination results are to be expected for pupils in a fully selective system than in a fully comprehensive system' (p. 18).

4   For criticism of the methodological and other alleged weaknesses of the research,

together with Rutter's response, see Acton and Rutter, 1980; Bennett and Rutter, 1980.

5   The curriculum of Cowan Bridge School, which the Brontë sisters attended, was probably typical, 'The system of education comprehends history, geography, the use of globes, writing and arithmetic, all kinds of needlework, and the nicer kinds of household work': Gaskell, 1975, p. 97.

6   There is an extensive literature; as good a starting-point as any is: Maccoby and Jacklin, 1974.

7   See also Verma and Bagley, 1982; in particular, the contribution of S. Tomlinson, 'A case of non-achievement: West Indians and ESN-M schooling'.

8   Mathematics and the sciences are not entirely 'culture-free', particularly when in teaching concepts are developed from concrete examples; see Schools Council, 1981, p. 10.

9   A fuller report is to be found in Schools Council, 1981, a report of the conference held at the Schools Council, September 1981. A thorough study of the implications for examinations for social sciences in a multicultural society is found in Mukhopadhyay, 1984.

10   The Joint Matriculation Board offers at O level: Manx, Modern Hebrew, Punjabi, Polish and Ukranian for which the numbers of candidates in 1983 were respectively 8, 37, 212, 111 and 22.

11   Christie and Forrest, 1981, p. 29, refer to the so-called Bayesian theory applied to the German *Abitur*; for the calculation of a candidate's final examination score, 'factors concerning the student's social background and method of preparing for the Abitur may be fed into the computer along with his grades on periodic and terminal examinations in a group of subjects'. They go on to say that there is little possibility that a similar allowance for non-academic factors would be made in the single-subject system of the GCE and CSE.

9

Are They Fair?
II Comparability

In Chapter 8 the concept of fairness in examinations was discussed in relation to the possibility of bias for or against various groups of candidates. Chapter 9 considers some features of examinations themselves which can act against equity, consistency and uniformity, and hence detract from their fairness.

One possible source of inconsistency lies in the marking. The point has already been made in earlier chapters that this can never be totally reliable. Reliability, in a limited sense of consistency of marking, has dominated the work of examiners and examination boards for schools and it has now reached a level at which further refinements could only be achieved by extravagant use of resources. This chapter will be concerned with reliability in the wider sense of equivalence, or comparability as it is sometimes called, between other aspects of public examinations. These have been identified as:

(1)   between examining boards in the same subject and year;
(2)   between years in the same subject within an examination board;
(3)   between modes of examining in the same subject and year within an examination board;
(4)   between alternative syllabuses in the same subject and year;
(5)   between subjects in the same year within an examining board (see Nuttall *et al.*, 1974, p. 11).

If it can be shown that standards vary between boards, between subjects or modes, or over time, then it could be said that there is some degree of unfairness within the system itself. At the same time, it should not be forgotten that research into equivalence between these variables depends ultimately on the accuracy of the original marking.

The Boards

Is There a Best Buy?
There exists among the consumers of examinations a certain amount of

gossip about the 'standards' of the various school examining boards in England and Wales, particularly the GCE boards (Stevens, 1980, p. 88). This usually amounts to no more than a feeling that some boards are more generous or more severe than others either in general or in particular subjects. As with most gossip, these impressions usually start with a small element of fact and spread with much embellishment.

Hearsay of this kind is to be expected in a free and competitive market, which is the case in GCE examinations.[1] It is less so in single systems, in which candidates are restricted to one board which operates in their region, as for CSE examinations. It operates too in higher education, in the comparison of degrees from different universities and other degree-awarding bodies. The gossip has, perhaps, a firmer foundation in higher education, where the numbers of students are much smaller in each subject and where the staff and work of each institution may be known by reputation. Even so, the labelling of applicants according to the institution from which they graduated is familiar enough to those who have experienced selection from both sides of the process and it is not always conducive to fairness.

At school level the effects of labelling particular examining agencies in this way, whether it is justified or not, can lead to discrimination for or against candidates on a much larger scale. It is not surprising, therefore, that individual schools, parents and students should seek to take advantage of the open market. But where does advantage lie? Should one go for the board which is supposed to be lenient in the hope of obtaining a higher grade than would have been possible elsewhere? Or should one go for the board which is supposed to be severe in the hope of gaining an award which will carry more weight with the selectors?

Even if there were no speculation of this kind, the problem of equivalence between the various agencies would still remain and the examining boards are well aware of it. The National Foundation of Educational Research and the Schools Council have conducted investigations into the comparability of standards between the CSE boards; and the GCE boards acting jointly have conducted similar investigations.[2] Bardell *et al.* (1978) have discussed the relative merits of three methods by which the equivalence of standards between examining boards may be investigated, as outlined below.

The Analysis of Examination Results Alone

It might appear that the proportion of candidates passing a particular subject should be the same in all examining boards; but this is not necessarily so. If the sample of candidates and schools had the same characteristics in all boards, and if all the subjects were identical and taught in an identical way, then the results should be exactly the same. But none of these factors is necessarily the same in all boards. There may be regional differences, and differences in type of school, in the cultural background of the candidates and of their sex, together with differences in subject-matter and objectives, despite a subject's common title.

It is not surprising, therefore, that the proportion of candidates passing a particular subject in any one year varies from board to board and that this variation is reasonably stable from year to year. This might reflect differences in standard, but it is more likely that it reflects differences between the types of candidate and types of subject.[3] Bardell *et al.* report:

> There is, for example, a common pattern which shows that candidates from independent schools tend to achieve higher grades than those from maintained schools. It is therefore to be expected that a board such as O & C, which draws most of its candidates from the independent sector, will award a greater percentage of high grades than a board which draws its candidates principally from maintained schools. (ibid., p. 15)

If this is so, a direct comparison of pass rates between the various boards is unlikely to be helpful in the attempt to equate standards.

Some of the public prejudgement of the relative standards of examining boards sprang from apparently anomalous results arising from small groups of candidates who sat for the same subject with two different examining boards in the same year. In the public mind each candidate should have got the same grade with both boards. But that assumes that the syllabuses were identical; that the required skills were equally weighted; that candidates were equally prepared for both; that the types of question were the same; and that the performance of each candidate did not vary from one occasion to the next. None of these conditions could be assured. In any event, the candidates who submit dual entry are likely to be those whose attainment is doubted and hence not typical of the whole population.

The Use of Monitor Tests

One technique for comparing standards between two boards is to compare the performance of the two groups of candidates (or a representative sample of them) in the two different examinations with their performance in a third test or examination which they all sit. The common test is known as a 'monitor' or 'reference' test. It is usually one of two kinds: a test in the subject under investigation or a general test of aptitude which is not based on a particular body of knowledge.

The validity of this technique rests on two main assumptions. The first is that it does not favour one group of candidates more than the other; that is, it should not be *biased*. For example, if the monitor were an aptitude test on which boys tended to score better than girls, it would favour any board whose candidates contained a high proportion of boys.[4] Similarly, if the monitor were a test of subject-matter, it would disadvantage a board whose syllabus did not cover all aspects of that subject-matter or did not give it emphasis.

The second assumption is that the monitor is equally *relevant* to both of the examinations which are being compared. In other words, the kinds of abilities which the candidates are expected to demonstrate in their examination should closely resemble those which are required in the monitor. A test of mathematical aptitude would not be thought relevant, for example, if it were used to compare the standards of two examining boards in French. If, on the other hand, the monitor took the form of a general test in linguistic skills, its relevance is likely to be higher, although still not perfect.

A simple expedient might appear to be to require examining boards to include an element common to them all in each of their examinations. This common element could then be used as a monitor to compare the standards of the boards in the examinations as a whole. Newbould and Massey (1979) point out that logically a common element may be no more relevant to the two non-common parts than a separate test might be. Furthermore, if the two examinations allocated different weights to the common element, its use would not be free from bias. So with different amounts of overlap and different weighting, a common element could prove to be a misleading indicator of comparability, despite its apparently high face validity. The use of a common element, however, does have advantage; it would be easier and cheaper to administer and it could provide a national benchmark for comparing the standards of the examination boards, at least in the more popular subjects. Even so, the results would need to be interpreted with caution and used along with other evidence rather than rigidly used in a statistical way.

Marks on monitor or reference tests of whatever type are related to the examination marks in a particular subject by the statistical process of regression analysis. This is done by plotting all the candidates' marks on a graph, one set on each axis (see Figure 9.1). In practice the plotted marks would not all lie on a straight line; a line of best fit would have to be drawn through them; and the lines representing the marks of the candidates of each board are unlikely to be exactly parallel.[5] Nevertheless, the simple relationship shown in the figure will serve to demonstrate the principle.

If we consider those candidates who obtained the same mark x on the monitor test, the graphs show that they would have got a higher mark or grade z in the subject examination of board A than the candidates in board B, who would have got a mark or grade y. It would seem, on the face of it, that the standards of the two boards in that subject are 'out of line'; if the two lines had coincided, then they would have been 'in line'.

In the very simplicity of such an analysis there lies the danger of unjustified inferences. It seems obvious that the further apart are the regression lines of the two boards, the greater is the difference between their standards in that subject. But this assumes that the monitor is equally

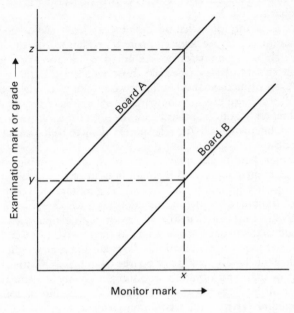

Figure 9.1

relevant to both examinations, that it does not favour one board's candidates to the disadvantage of the other and that all the tests – both examinations and the monitor – are totally reliable, that is, consistent and free from error of measurement. None of these conditions can be exactly met and, rightly, Newbould and Massey advocate caution: 'whilst it [the common element] is a ready vehicle for emphasising common ground, and hence implying a similarity of examinations, it may tempt people into adopting over-simplistic views of the nature and meaning of the concept of comparability' (ibid., p. 51).

Cross-Moderation

The examining boards themselves appear to view purely statistical techniques of comparability with some doubt (Bardell *et al.*, 1978, p. 27), and in view of the limitations mentioned above this is not surprising. It is natural, therefore, that the boards have come to rely more heavily on the process which all of them use in their final award of grades meetings: the judgement of their chief examiners. It is on this judgement that the cross-moderation investigations depend:

Cross-moderation studies are founded on the assumption that subject experts (in practice usually board examiners), on the basis of their professional judgements and despite the numerous differences between examinations, can decide from a scrutiny of scripts whether comparable grades are being awarded by the boards to candidates of comparable levels of attainment. (ibid., p. 27)

Between 1964 and 1978 the GCE examining boards conducted sixteen investigations using cross-moderation, covering most of the subjects which attract large numbers of candidates. During the period they have changed and improved this research technique considerably but many of the problems associated with it remain. If the examiners of board A re-mark the scripts of board B, using the mark scheme of board B, they are simply checking the accuracy of marking. On the other hand, if the board A examiners apply the mark scheme *they* would have used, they might well arrive at different marks. Neither of these methods takes note of the process by which each board converts marks into grades; and in the final event it is the grades, not the marks, which matter. So more recent investigations have concentrated on the award of grades rather than marks.

Bardell *et al.* point to two kinds of investigation into the equivalence of grades: 'examiners ... can be asked either to identify borderlines or to ratify them' (ibid., p. 28). In the first, identification of 'borderlines', the examiners of one board are provided with a range of scripts covering the grades on which decisions have to be made. They then have to decide where to draw each grade boundary; in effect, they are exercising the same function as they would do at an award meeting. In the second kind the examiners are given a sample of scripts on or about each 'borderline' and asked to judge whether the original decision was lenient or severe, or correct.

A problem which besets all such moderation exercises is how to define the criteria by which the grade boundaries are to be judged. Is each moderator to use his own criteria or those of the board whose scripts he is scrutinizing or special criteria for the exercise itself? Indeed, is it possible to formulate criteria in such a way as to allow the application of an agreed standard? The experience gained from several of the GCE studies indicates that the formulation of such criteria is difficult and their application even more so.

Another difficulty in cross-moderation is that it is time-consuming and expensive since the moderators have to be paid and scrutiny script by script cannot be hurried. It follows that the sample of scripts in any one exercise has to be small, whereas in the statistical methods much larger samples – sometimes the whole population – can be used. What is more, the exercise is confined to scripts of the traditional kind; other evidence, particularly that from objective tests and internal assessment, is not suitable for the same kind of treatment. With the introduction of new examining techniques and the consequent decline in the weight attached to traditional scripts, the cross-moderation technique has an inescapable limitation. An added problem is that the scrutineers are usually both practising examiners and teachers with little time to spare for further calls on their time.

While acknowledging various problems associated with cross-moderation exercises, the GCE boards point to an incidental advantage. The actual process of discussing one another's examination techniques, marking and awarding procedures, and the criteria for grading leads to fruitful debate and feedback to their own boards. The examining boards' preference for the cross-moderation comparability is understandable because it replicates their traditional, subjective awarding procedures in which the judgement of experienced examiners can override statistical evidence. Whether cross-moderation provides sufficiently hard evidence on which to base changes in awarding procedures and standards is, to say the least, uncertain. The boards point to some such changes (ibid., p. 36); but having in mind the many published studies the number of published changes is small. There must be some doubt about the effectiveness of controlling national standards with much precision by this method alone. If the aim is to produce national subject criteria and standards of performance, the statistical use of a common element in all the main subjects for the purpose of comparability is a temptation which is going to be difficult to resist.

At the time of writing, the issue of national standards and comparability between the many school examining agencies in England and Wales has impinged more strongly on the public mind. There is a cautious hint in government reaction to the Tenth Report of the Expenditure Committee of the House of Commons (1977) that closer comparability could be achieved at the expense of diversification of boards and syllabuses. A move in this direction is unlikely to endear itself to the various boards which over the years have engendered an ethos and understandably are anxious to preserve their autonomy.

Can Different Be the Same?
There can be no doubt that the examining boards themselves are concerned to establish parity of standards. They also want to establish sufficiently different syllabuses and examinations to give a real choice to their clients and to justify their own existence as separate bodies. The degree of comparability between these two aims is limited. The greater the similarity in content and techniques, the easier it is to establish comparability between examinations. The more syllabuses, the more examinations, and the more agencies there are, the greater the difficulty in equating one with another. If there were only one national examination in each subject, the question of equivalence would not arise. If it is true that there are substantial differences between the offerings of the examining boards, even if they use the same titles, then in comparability exercises like

is not being compared with like: 'although a pass in one board may be different from a pass in another, to claim that one is better is a value judgement like the preference of one picture over another' (Bardell *et al.*, 1978, p. 35).

To sum up: the examining boards are trying to make the best they can of two opposing requirements. One is to provide alternative examinations which are substantially different from each other, thus offering a real choice to their clients. The other is to ensure that the performance in each, as represented by a particular grade, is the same. In effect they are trying to make good the claim that although board A's English language, for example, is different from board B's English language, a grade C from board A is the same as a grade C from board B. This is like claiming that a kilo of cheese is the same as a kilo of butter because they cost the same and are both made from milk. The two grade Cs may have the same *value*, but they cannot denote attainment of the same *skills* if the two examinations are different in substance.

Clearly the two positions cannot be totally reconciled. The many and various comparability exercises which the examining boards and others have conducted indicate that they are concerned to reconcile them as far as possible and to reassure the public that although what they offer is different it has, as far as they are able to judge, the same value. They elevate the freedom to choose above the need to establish an absolute parity in grades. They are saying that there is no 'best buy' as far as the value of the grades is concerned; it is the substance of the goods themselves, that is, the syllabus, on which customers should base their choice as to which best suits their needs:

> There are several ways of dealing with the situation, from, at one extreme, the introduction of a single national syllabus and examination in each subject, to the full exploitation of the variety which exists today, at the other. The former is not likely to receive much support from teachers used to the flexibility of British education, particularly those who believe in teacher responsibility for syllabus content; the latter demands more forthright acceptance both by boards and by users of the approximate nature of examination results in general. (ibid., p. 37)

The last phrase is significant, and it is noteworthy that the 'approximate nature' of examination grades is recognized by the examination profession if not always by their clients.

The Subjects

Are Some Subjects 'Harder' than Others?

A case can be made that this question has no meaning; that subjects are sufficiently different to invalidate any attempt to equate the standard of one with the standard of another. To put it another way, 'hardness' is a particular not a universal concept. If it is accepted that performance in each subject should be judged by criteria peculiar to each, then comparability between awards made in more than one subject is logically not possible. If, on the other hand, it is assumed that there are general criteria which can be applied to the standards in all subjects, then comparability between them should be possible. In practice it is the latter assumption which is usually made, and this section seeks to examine some methods by which it may be investigated.

In order to make a meaningful comparison between subjects it is necessary to assume that performance in them all depends primarily on one characteristic of the candidates which may be called 'general ability'. Other terms are used almost synonymously, 'calibre' is one often to be heard at meetings of examiners. What general ability actually is is an interesting point for psychometricians and others to consider but it need not concern us at length here; it may be no more than a general ability to pass examinations. The point has already been made that some users of examinations, especially those who are not concerned with specific subjects, seem quite happy to take an array of marks or grades or even the sum of the marks as an indication of a general ability to do almost anything.[6]

It does not follow from this that an individual will do equally well in all subjects since performance will also depend on specific abilities in each. But if a sufficiently large number of candidates is considered it could be assumed that *on average* they should do equally well in all subjects if an equivalent performance is demanded by each one. Thus if a large group of candidates takes both subject *x* and subject *y*, it should, if standards in *x* and *y* are equivalent, attain the same average grade in both. The distribution of grades should also be the same; that is, the proportion of candidates awarded each grade should be the same in both *x* and *y*.

Of the methods used in comparability between boards, that of cross-moderation cannot usually be applied to the comparison of subjects unless these are closely related. This is because it would be unreasonable to expect a group of examiners to exercise judgement in subjects in which they have little or no experience. Nuttall *et al.* (1974) describe five methods, two of which involve the use of a reference test as the basis for comparison, the test being entirely external to the examination system. The other three use internal evidence as the basis for comparison, that is, the scores of the candidates in other subjects in the examination.

Reference Tests

The use of reference tests was found to be the least satisfactory by Nuttall *et al.* (1974). It is based on the assumption that performance on a test of general scholastic aptitude can be used to predict the grades attained in examinations in various subjects.[7] In other words, those who perform equally well on the aptitude test should get, on average, the same grades in the various examinations. The research demonstrated that this was not so; candidates in some subjects, for example, physics and chemistry, attained high average aptitude test scores and low average examination grades, whereas for candidates in English the position was reversed: 'There can be no doubt that some sort of difference between subjects exists' (ibid., p. 20).

Two methods have been used to estimate the size of the differences between subjects as revealed by aptitude tests: the regression method, and the structural regression method (also called the guideline method).[8] Although the two methods differ in their quantitative findings, the general pattern is the same. Both reveal that given the assumptions involved in the use of reference tests, some subjects such as French, physics and chemistry are severely graded, while others such as art and English language are leniently graded. In some instances the difference amounted to a whole O-level grade. It must be said, however, that the researchers do not advocate the use of these findings to apply statistical adjustments to awards in order to bring subjects into line. Among the many reasons for this is the likelihood of bias in the tests which were used, particularly a bias which favours some kinds of subject over others and boys or girls.

Subject Pairs
This technique is one of three which makes use of the internal evidence of examination grades rather than an external test as a basis for comparison. It is given prominence here because it has been extensively developed and used over many years at the operational level by the Joint Matriculation Board.

The percentage of passes in each subject or the percentage attaining each grade is of no value in itself for comparing standards between subjects because it does not take note of the differing levels of general ability between the groups of candidates which take each subject. If all candidates took all subjects, then a percentage of passes could be used; but that is not the case. However, in most of the subjects which attract a large entry there is considerable overlap in the candidates who take any *pair* of subjects. This being so, for candidates who all take a pair of subjects A and B, one can legitimately compare their average grade in A with their average grade in B. An illustration may help to explain the principle (Forrest and Vickerman, 1982, p. 10).

To take two examples, Table 9.1 shows that all those candidates who took both biology and English language alternative A achieved an average grade of 3·7 in biology and an average grade of 4·3 in English language (A).[9] Likewise all the candidates who took both biology and physics achieved an average grade of 4·2 in both biology and physics. The composition of the two groups is unlikely to be identical, but there will be some membership common to both. For each pair of subjects, biology always being one of the pair, the mean grade in each subject is then plotted on a graph on which one axis shows the mean grades in biology for each pair, and the other the mean grade in each of the other subjects offered with biology (ibid., p. 11). If there was an exact correspondence between the biology grades in the other subjects, the points on the graph would all lie on the line AB in Figure 9.2.

Table 9.1 *JMB: Biology (Ordinary), 1978*

Other subject	Mean grade in biology	Mean grade in other subject	Correlation coefficient
English language (A)	3·7	4·3	0·379
English language (B)	3·5	3·9	0·386
English literature (A)	3·7	4·0	0·411
Geography (A)	3·7	3·9	0·579
French (A)	4·1	3·8	0·449
Mathematics (B)	3·9	3·9	0·602
Physics	4·2	4·2	0·709
Chemistry	4·3	3·9	0·664

Note: Biology candidates in fact took, as a group, more than sixty other subjects. The examples given are limited to those pairs of subjects which attracted more than 10,000 candidates. (A and B refer to alternative syllabuses.)
Source: See Forrest and Vickerman, 1982, p. 10.

As might be expected, such exact correspondence was not achieved in practice. In fact most of the points in this case lay in the area within the circle above and to the left of the line AB. This occurred for fifty-one out of the seventy-four subjects paired with biology. This means that the average grade achieved by the biology candidates in these fifty-one other subjects which they took was *higher* than they achieved in biology itself. It is significant that these fifty-one were non-science subjects. (See Figure 9.2.) A small number of points lie below and to the right of the line AB. In these subjects the average grades achieved by the biology candidates were lower than they achieved in biology itself. These subjects were in science or mathematics.

Both Table 9.1 and Figure 9.2 show the differences between the mean grades in biology and the mean grades in the other subjects which a large number of candidates took in addition to biology. These differences were not only positive and negative, they differed in amount; some were close to the line AB, others further away. The amount of difference, however, may arise partly from the error of measurement in the examinations as well as differences in standards. To meet this point two more lines are drawn: CD and EF parallel to BA, and two-thirds of a grade above and below it. Two-thirds of a grade is arbitrarily chosen and maybe used as a

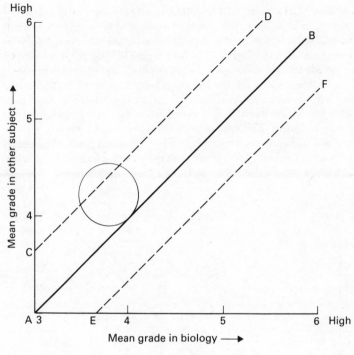

Figure 9.2

notional limit of tolerance. Any subject points lying outside these limits could receive special consideration.[10]

The differences in the grades awarded between one subject and all the others can be further summarized. For example, suppose the average grade awarded in subject x is 3·8 and the average grade obtained in all the other subjects taken by the group of candidates who took x was 3·9. One conclusion could be that candidates in subject x performed slightly better (by 0·1 of a grade) in their other subjects. This difference could be regarded as negligible. Suppose, however, that candidates in subject y obtained on average a grade of 4·5 in y but only an average grade of 3·5 in all the other subjects which they took. There is now a difference of one whole grade between the average performances. And since the grade in y itself is the one which is considerably higher, it could be concluded that y is an easy subject or that it is leniently graded compared with the other subjects with which it is taken. In these circumstances it might be thought that some action should be taken to bring the examination in subject y into line, that is, make it 'harder'.

The Joint Matriculation Board, as a matter of course, calculate the mean grade obtained in each subject and the mean grade obtained in all other subjects which that group of candidates took. The results of these calculations can be shown in the form of a graph, in which the mean grade in the named subject is plotted against the mean grade in the other subjects taken with that subject (ibid., p. 16) (see Figure 9.3). A subject in which the mean grade was the same as the mean grade in all subjects taken with it would lie on the central diagonal line; and subjects which lie above that line show a lower mean grade in the subjects taken with it. The amount of this difference is the vertical difference from the plotted point to the central diagonal line. The two broken lines are placed two-thirds of a grade above and below the central line. Thus the mean grade obtained by candidates taking subject ÿ was more than two-thirds of a grade more than the mean grade which they obtained in all their other subjects.

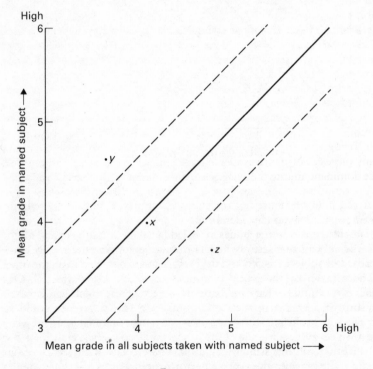

Figure 9.3

Subjects x and z, lying below the central diagonal line, show a higher mean grade in the subjects taken with them. Thus the candidates taking subject z obtained a mean grade in z *less* (by more than two-thirds of a grade) than the mean grade they achieved in all the other subjects which they took. Candidates taking x also got a lower mean grade in that subject, but in this case the difference between it and the mean grade in their other subjects was less than two-thirds of a grade. The Joint Matriculation Board uses the two broken lines in Figure 9.3 'to give some indication of the significance of deviations from the central line' (ibid., pp. 46–7). This is an 'arbitrary choice', and it is not strictly applied as a tolerance limit because divergence from the central line can arise for reasons unconnected with the concept of difficulty: for example, the different distribution of marks in the various examinations, their different reliabilities and the different correlations of performance one with another. Examinations which consistently lie outside the $\pm\frac{2}{3}$ grade lines, however, are likely to be at least subject to discussion within the Examination Council and Subject Committee, and possibly to action intended to bring them more into line.

It might seem at first sight that the kind of analysis which has been outlined provides an exact means of comparing standards between subjects and regulating those standards statistically. In practice it is used much more cautiously. It is given as a matter of routine, together with other statistical information about the examination as a whole and about its parts, to each Subject Committee. In turn the Subject Committee can, if it wishes, pass to the examiners 'views or advice', but 'The Subject Committee's observations are never a precise instruction, such as, for instance that the standard of award must be raised or lowered by a given number of marks or a given proportion of a grade' (ibid., p. 21). Forrest and Vickerman emphasize that the subject pair analysis is only one among many pieces of evidence available to examiners at the award meeting and that dominant among the evidence is the examiners' firsthand knowledge of the questions, of the answers and of the candidates themselves.

A more vigorous use of subject pairs analysis would require certain assumptions to be made, as follows.

(1)   That the distribution of grades is the same for each subject. In other words, that the award of grades is norm-referenced to a predetermined proportion of candidates in each grade. In the GCE and CSE examinations this is not exactly so. It is true that in many of the large-entry subjects there is a similarity in the proportions; but a glance at the statistics of awards in any one subject reveals differences from subject to subject, board to board and year to year.

(2)   It follows from assumption 1 that subject pairs analysis could not be used if the awarding system were strictly criterion-referenced (see Chapter 10). That is, if the award of each grade were made on the basis of attainment of a predetermined performance. Although there is a degree to which this operates in most public examinations, it is far from being exact. Nevertheless, there is a sense in which the award of grades must be based on criteria of performance, however vague and unquantified they may be. It follows that an examiner in, say, English could defend his award of grades in terms of *performance in English*, and possibly in defiance of the

evidence of how the same candidates performed in, say, mathematics.

(3) The third assumption is that on average the candidates in all the subjects are equally motivated; that they have received teaching which has been equivalent in quality and quantity if not in kind; and that they have had access to equivalent resources in each subject. This is plainly not so. It is common knowledge, for example, that students involved in one of the big national curriculum projects will have the additional incentive to work which comes from identification with a pioneering project at least in its early years. This is even more discernible in their teachers who have a strong commitment to the project and a vested interest in its success. Furthermore, it has been a feature of many such projects that they have attracted additional equipment and other resources. Given these factors, it could be assumed (although difficult to prove) that this group of students would perform at a higher level in that examination than in all the others for which they had entered. This being so, a subject pairs analysis might well reveal an *apparent* leniency in the examination of the curriculum project.

(4) Subject pairs analysis is essentially a special case of the use of a reference test. It involves the use of average performance in one other examination subject, or the average performance in all other subjects, as the basis for comparison rather than a specially designed external test. And just as the use of an external reference test is only valid if there is a strong relation between performance in it and performance in the particular subject under investigation, there should be a strong relation between the subject and whatever subject or group of subjects is being used as the reference. If a strong relation does not exist, then the use of subject pairs analysis must be suspect.[11]

Forrest and Vickerman make reference to 'great stability in correlation coefficients between subjects from year to year'. They identify three levels of correlation:

(1) the highest correlation coefficients occur among the languages (classical and modern) and also between the science and mathematical subjects ($+0 \cdot 6$ to $+0 \cdot 8$);
(2) in general, low correlations ($+0 \cdot 2$ and $+0 \cdot 4$) occur between the technical and domestic subjects on the one hand, and those subjects which may loosely be described as 'academic' on the other;
(3) the lowest correlations ($+0 \cdot 1$ to $+0 \cdot 3$) involve art (see ibid., p. 22).

Art and some of the technical and domestic subjects epitomize one of the problems associated with single-subject examinations such as the GCE and CSE. Notionally the standards in all subjects are deemed to be equivalent – a grade C in art is equivalent to a grade C in, for example, physics – and in this sense they should be subject to the same criteria. But it is evident that art is not physics, and a strong case can be made for accepting that most of those students who opt to take art have different characteristics from those taking physics and may have particularly strong motivation for the subject itself. In these circumstances it is not surprising that the correlation between performance in art and other subjects is low and that candidates will do better, in general, in art than they do in their other subjects.

The problem becomes more complex when subjects such as mathematics, the sciences and modern languages are considered. There is no reason to suppose that motivation may be equally high in all of them. Yet correlation of performance with other subjects remains high and subject pairs analysis reveals that, on average, their candidates actually achieve higher grades in other subjects. The reason must lie in the essentially intellectual or cognitive nature of these subjects and most other examined subjects. The apparently anomalous relationship of art and technical and domestic subjects lies not so much in their difficulty or easiness, but in the different skills which they demand. Christie and Forrest (1981) make the point that the particularly anomalous subjects in this respect, art, domestic science, and geometrical and engineering drawing, all have a large 'performance component'. It is clear that the attempt to encompass such widely different human activities as equivalent subjects within the same examination grading system may be stretching the system beyond its limits of coherence.

It seems, then, that performance in each subject, although related to some general ability, is not solely dependent on it, but on other factors specific to that subject. It follows that the process of grading – while it may take note of such evidence of general ability as reference tests or subject pairs analysis provide on its standards – is ultimately dependent on criteria inherent in the subject and on those who teach and examine it. In effect, the grading process as we know it in school examinations works on a compromise between evidence of specific performance and evidence of general performance of which subject pairs analysis is one; and the weight placed on general performance is related to the nature of the subject.

In subjects which are widely different in kind, for example, art, mathematics and English, a case can be made for grading entirely on the internal criteria of the subject without reference to external criteria such as evidence of general ability. If, however, subjects are closely related, most of the objections to the use of reference tests and subject pairs carry less weight. For example, when several options for English language or mathematics are offered, it becomes more acceptable to use subject pairs analysis to judge the relative standards of awards across the options *within* each subject.

In England and Wales comparisons of standards between subjects, whether by reference tests or internal standardization such as subject pairs analysis, serve as one of many pieces of information on the basis of which subject committees and examiners may adjust their standards in future examinations. They do not serve as moderating instruments for the statistical scaling of marks *during* the awarding process. There are, however, examination systems which do apply statistical procedures of this kind at the time of awarding in an attempt to attain equivalence between subjects. One such is the Matriculation Examination of South Australia which introduced a scaling procedure in 1978:

> to achieve comparability of marks between subjects by an internally consistent system which ensures as far as possible that the choice of subject does not of itself (that is independently of the candidate's abilities) significantly affect the final score. (Education Department of South Australia, 1981, p. 6)

The 'final score' is the aggregate score of performance in five matriculation subjects. If these five scores were the raw scores for each examination, the lenient or easy subjects would contribute more marks than the severe or hard subjects. This would give an advantage to candidates who opted to take the lenient subjects since entry to university depends on a candidate's position in the list of the five aggregated scores.

The South Australian system for achieving comparability of standards between subjects resembles the subject pairs analysis outlined above. The standard used for comparison lies in performance in the various examinations within the examination system itself, not on an external reference test. It differs from the JMB subject pairs analysis, in that it uses scaled marks rather than grades and that it makes comparisons within and between groups of subjects classified according to the degree of correlation of performance in the subjects. It openly acknowledges that some subjects attract candidates of higher general ability than others; something which is often said in the English system but not always acted upon. The statistical adjustments in the South Australian scheme are thought to be necessary to ensure that candidates qualifying for higher education are not only competent in particular subjects, but are in general the most able.[12] It is one of the few schemes which acts upon the evidence that some subjects are easier or harder than others.

To return to the general issue: any demand for more stringent equivalence between subjects and between options within subjects can be met, but at a price. That price is more conformity and uniformity in examinations and hence in the curriculum. Certainty of equivalence is in inverse proportion to diversity of curriculum. The Schools Council (1979, p. 15) has put the matter plainly: 'A reduction and rationalisation of the present diversity of syllabuses and examinations would help to make a more precise comparability possible.'

Over the Years

The problem of comparing examination standards over a period of years is one of the most intractable of all the studies of comparability. Given one subject in one board, with no changes in syllabus or in general calibre of candidates, or in examiners, it is just possible that some well-planned re-marking and re-grading could produce reliable comparison of standards over a period of years. Changes in standards from one year to the next may be so slight as to be imperceptible. Over a longer period, provided that the trend was in the same direction throughout, the change might be more apparent. But the longer the period, the more difficult it will be to hold constant the variables listed above.

The methodological problems are daunting. Yet the demand for comparability over time remains. It is perhaps the one form of comparability which gives rise to the most opinions on the least evidence. Examinations are not alone in this. In any field of human endeavour the desire to compare the performance of this generation with that of a former generation seems to be irrepressible. 'Things aren't what they used to be' is easily said but less easily proved. It *is* said, however, and when it comes so frequently from those who use examinations to select for employment and further education, it behoves those in the examination system to try to answer it.

The difficulties of such an investigation have not encouraged researchers to rush to make the attempt. Christie and Forrest (1980, p. xi) comment: 'Lack of work is due not so much to lack of interest as to the obvious difficulty in producing reliable answers when neither the examinations, nor the candidates, nor the conditions are held constant.' Not only is it difficult to hold the various conditions constant, or to allow for their change, there is the purely practical problem of retaining the evidence. It was only the foresight of the Joint Matriculation Board in retaining a sample of scripts for ten years which allowed Christie and Forrest's research to take place. (Normally examination boards are only too anxious to dispose of the great bulk of scripts once the possibility of individual appeals has gone – usually after one year.) In the event it was possible to investigate standards in three subjects, English literature, mathematics and chemistry, at GCE A level over the 1963 to 1973 examinations.

The work of Christie and Forrest was essentially a pilot study of the methodological problems. Although some findings of interest did arise within the specific subjects, it was the *method* of research rather than its particular findings which provided the focus and which made the main contribution. In essence the method involved panels of senior 1973 examiners re-marking 1963 scripts and subjecting the marks to the same procedures as if they were awarding 1973 grades. Allowance was made, where possible, for changes in syllabuses, objectives and examination format. The research was further complicated by using groups of examiners from other boards as well as JMB examiners, thus introducing inter-board comparability as an additional dimension.

This is not the place to record all the details of the Christie–Forrest research; its strong and weak points were precisely analysed by the authors. They set out with admirable clarity the conditions necessary for any future comparability exercises of this kind. It is likely that if considerable resources were to be allocated to such an exercise, and if the necessary procedural conditions were foreseen and met, a more refined research could be implemented. The point at issue, however, is not whether the instrument of comparability could be refined, but whether anything of significance would arise even if it were. In short, is it worth while expending large resources, and possibly distorting the examination process in the attempt, in order to investigate whether an indefinable standard is going up or down with time?

It might *appear* to be desirable to maintain constant standards over time, so that, for example, a grade C in A-level mathematics would indicate the same performance in 1984 as it did in 1974. On the contrary, it can be argued that standards *should* change over time. Mathematics has changed and the teaching of mathematics has changed, so mathematical performance should change even if all the other factors remain constant. In any event a grade C in, say, mathematics could be obtained (since it is probably equivalent to no more than 50 per cent of the marks) by any one of a large number of combinations of specific mathematical skills. Thus any attempt under the present system to hold the 'standard' constant would be a nonsense.

But even if grade C could be held constant in terms of definite performances, there would be little point if those who use examination results for purposes of selection are not primarily concerned with *actual* performance standards. They may simply use the examinations as a competition, taking that proportion of candidates they happen to need from as high in the order of merit as they can get them. Such a procedure has little to do with real, operational standards of performance. If the number of candidates for the examination goes up or if the number of candidates to be selected goes down, selectors may simply raise the grades required for selection.

This is not to say that those who use examination results have no regard for the actual knowledge and skills of their applicants. Obviously there will be a requirement for a basic attainment sufficient for further study or employment in addition to evidence of general ability; this is the principle on which candidates are admitted to most faculties in universities and colleges. One can see that it is important that the level of essential knowledge and skills is not eroded over the years. However, the need to maintain a specific basic performance is not met by attempts to determine whether the general standard represented by, say, an overall grade C has changed. It can only be done by, first of all, more closely defining the essential skills and knowledge in a concrete rather than conceptual form, and then so designing the examination that they can be assessed without too much interference from other aspects of the examination. Until this is done efforts to check the change over time are bound to founder because what is being sought has been inadequately described. This point is taken further in Chapter 10.

Between the Modes

The term 'mode' was launched into the examination system at the time of the introduction of the Certificate of Secondary Education. The practice of distinguishing between internal and external assessment agencies was not new; it has a long history, although rather more so in colleges and universities than in schools. It has crystallized more recently into three modes:

Mode I   Syllabus and examination produced by an agency external to the educational institution.

Mode II   Syllabus produced within the institution, examination produced by an external agency.

Mode III   Syllabus and examination produced within the educational institution.

The real situation is not as neat as this. In practice teachers have a say in what goes into Mode I and examining boards retain a moderating function in Mode III. And increasingly a school-based element is creeping into many so-called Mode I examinations in various proportions, the external element usually dominating.

The purpose of this section is not to debate the relative merits of the modes, but to comment on the problems of comparability in their standards. To simplify the issues this will be undertaken in two parts: the first deals with the relation between notionally pure Mode I and Mode III forms, the second with the problems which arise when an element of internal assessment is used in a predominantly Mode I examination.

Mode I and Mode III
While it has been customary to allow institutions of higher education, and to a lesser extent further education, a strong measure of internal autonomy in producing and assessing their own examinations, society has been reluctant to place similar trust in its schools. The vestiges of internal assessment in schools in the nineteenth century were soon eroded and remained so until the bold attempt to re-establish it for the middle ranges of ability in secondary schools in the 1960s.

The success of the move has been at best patchy. The suspicion remained,[13] and possibly grew, that if teachers were given the responsibility for deciding what to teach and devise questions on the basis of what had been taught, and then to mark the answers of their own pupils, the pupils would gain an unfair advantage. In the sense that such a system could more exactly match the curriculum with the examination that might be so. But it is unreasonable to disparage Mode III examinations on the grounds that they have high curriculum validity; unless, of course, the unfairness has amounted to malpractice. The more serious charge is that in Mode III 'standards are lower', and there can be little doubt that in the public mind this is held to be the case.

Such an attitude has been especially galling to those concerned with the Certificate of Secondary Education, particularly in those regions which have given Mode III the highest priority. It has to be recognized, however, that there are some grounds for concern. Mode III was heralded as a breakthrough in curriculum development, a liberating system allowing teachers to develop curricula appropriate to the needs of their pupils. But if this is so, it is strange that the developments have been applied almost entirely to those of lower ability. Mode III would generate less suspicion if it were seen to be applied to all levels of ability. The need to inject some objective evidence into a subjective and emotive argument is apparent. It was to this end that the West Yorkshire and Lindsey Regional Examining Board commissioned research in this area (Nuttall, 1973).

The fact that research on comparability was commissioned does not imply that the boards do nothing themselves to ensure that standards are maintained. Research into comparability produces findings which are necessarily after the event. Research findings may influence examinations in the future – although instances of their direct influence are not easy to find; meanwhile examination boards are required to ensure at the time of examination that there is a reasonable equivalence between the various modes.

The objectives, syllabuses and form of assessment of Mode III examinations are normally scrutinized by the board's Examinations Committee, or a subcommittee of it. This is essentially a validating process and suffers from the limitations of all such exercises, in that it is restricted to a consideration of intentions and design. Anyone who has participated in validation of course design at any level of education knows very well that a submission of design can hide more than it reveals: an impressive façade may obscure a flimsy structure; conversely, a less pretentious submission may fail to reveal some imaginative curriculum development and teaching and rigorous assessment at the operational level.

Despite the shortcomings of the process, validation requires an external body to make the judgement that a submission for a Mode III examination is educationally desirable and feasible. More than that, it usually has to decide whether the submission is sufficiently different from an existing

Mode I examination to allow the provision of a special examination for one institution. Herein lies a dilemma and a possible source of conflict. On the one hand the validating body has to ensure that the submission is sufficiently similar to other Mode III and Mode I examinations in the same area to allow comparability, and on the other that it is sufficiently different to justify separate provision. The dilemma has become even more acute in recent years with the growth of the demand for a common element within those subjects which command a large entry from schools (DES, 1982). The more immediate problem is: once validation has been agreed, how can sufficient equivalence be demonstrated between the modes at the operational level rather than the research level to give confidence in the standards across the modes. Practice varies in detail but has some principal features in common.[14] Just as the chief examiner is the main repository of the standard *within* an external examination, so the chief moderator has the responsibility for equivalence of standards between Mode I and Mode III, and between various Mode III examinations in different educational institutions.

While moderators and chief moderators almost invariably are practising teachers, they could be considered to have some of the functions of inspectors. In practice, this aspect is not emphasized; exchange of ideas, consultation and advice predominate. Nevertheless, in the final outcome moderation would be little more than a public relations exercise if it did not carry some powers to change examination design and grade boundaries:

> Moderators should recognize that, in the last resort, a school is likely to be free to proceed with its own scheme. It is no part of the moderator's duty to suggest to a school what it should teach or how it should teach it. However, should the shortcomings of the scheme be such as to be likely to affect the standard of attainment, these should be made clear to the school.
>
> Normally the moderator will not alter the school's order of merit but may suggest the moving up or down of grade boundaries. (Associated Lancashire School Examining Board, 1979, pp. 4, 9)

It is ironic that those called moderators for the school examinations would be called external examiners in higher education (Williams, 1979). In fact their functions are very similar. In essence both involve members of the same profession visiting each other's institution to ensure as best they can that what is being done and the awards which are offered have an acceptable equivalence with what is being done and awarded elsewhere. The procedures they adopt have a degree of formality and the limits of their actions are defined partly by regulation but mainly by custom. The moderator normally receives a cordial welcome; outright conflict is rare, offence not given or taken, and such changes as are made by the visitor are usually modest.

The status of visiting moderators be it at CSE or PhD level is but temporary. On another occasion they may well receive a return visit with the roles reversed. At its best moderation is a model of how a profession should maintain its standards by an internal system of self-accountability. At its worst it is an introverted, cosy and expensive[15] way of hiding the real standards from the real world.

Yet what alternative can objective, empirical research offer? During the period of an examination nothing. The constraint of time alone would not allow the application of the reference test or the rigorously controlled cross-moderation exercises which have been outlined above; and subject pairs analysis is unlikely to have validity because of the small number of candidates taking any one Mode III scheme. Researchers – given time – could probably drive a coach and horses through the sampling and standardizing methods used by moderators at any level of education. No matter. Given the need for some form of internal assessment, one must accept that moderation is the practice of what is possible rather than an exact science. Maybe the strength of such a system lies not so much in the maintenance of exact and constant standards, but in the discussions between colleagues at regional meetings, or with moderators during their visits, on what constitutes good professional practice and goals. An optimistic view is that such a system, while going some way to preserving acceptable standards of candidates' grades, goes much further in advancing good teaching. It is in the latter, then, that its main justification may lie, and in any judgement of it the defects and influence on teaching of an entirely external, alternative system of examining should not be overlooked.

The foregoing paragraph could be dismissed as merely pious; certainly it does not absolve internal systems of examining from scrutiny by more objective measures of comparability, at least after the event when time allows a more leisurely investigation. These investigations can be of two kinds. The first looks into the actual procedures of moderation and group standardization, and the second applies some form of external standardizing instrument to the candidates themselves or their work.

The research of Nuttall (1973) rejected the use of a crude comparison between the mean grades awarded in Modes I and III. The use of a subject-specific test was also rejected.[16] A scholastic aptitude test was used,[17] assuming that performance in different subjects should be equally and closely related to the concept of general ability. A subsequent investigation used subject-specific reference tests as well as the same test of general scholastic ability to compare mode standards within two examining boards in biology and geography. In one board the grading of biology was found to be severe in Mode I and lenient in Mode III but there were no significant differences in the other comparisons. But another interesting finding arose incidentally: that the average awards 'hid considerable differences between schools'. This is somewhat disconcerting for selectors because it means that even if it could be established that, on average, one mode was more severe or lenient than another, they could not rely on this when considering individual candidates from individual schools (Smith, 1976).

The findings cannot in themselves be used to form a precise judgement about the relative standards of Modes I and III. On the assumption that the average performance of a large number of candidates in the test of scholastic aptitude is an acceptable indication of the average grade they should be given in a subject examination it was found that

> there is a trend towards leniency in every subject except English. This trend is sufficiently marked to be worthy of note even though only two of the leniency estimates fall outside the tolerance limits. (Nuttall, 1973, p. 17)

The most telling part of the report, however, lies not so much in the finding, but in the explanation offered:

> [the] tendency towards leniency in standards in Mode 3 ... is very probably but not necessarily wholly explainable in terms of differences in the average level of motivation and other attributes undetectable by the scholastic aptitude test between candidates in different modes. (ibid., pp. 17–18)

Linked to motivation of the candidates, of course, could be the enthusiasm of the teacher who designed the course. If such an explanation is accepted, and there is no evidence that it is not true, it effectively undermines most comparability research except cross-moderation (to which a different set of objections have been raised). In effect it claims that performance in each subject should be judged largely by criteria intrinsic to each subject; and that general ability, whether it be shown in a reference test or performance in other examinations, should be a secondary basis for judgement. This further undermines any confidence which selectors may still have in the equivalence within an array of grades in a variety of modes and subjects.

In the special case of comparability between Modes I and III other explanations of differences in the award of grades could be put forward. It could be argued that apparently high performance in Mode III is only to be expected when a teacher decides not only what to teach, but what to assess and how and when it should be assessed. The evidence on this is no firmer than that on motivation. Nevertheless, it would be surprising if a Mode III assessment was based in part on something which had not been taught, an occurrence not unknown when the examination is entirely external. An even more contentious explanation is referred to, but not necessarily supported, in Schools Council Examinations Bulletin No. 36:

> For instance, it could be argued that, since Mode III allows teachers a larger degree of control over the precise methods of assessment used to examine their pupils, teachers will use Mode III particularly for those pupils who do not respond well to traditional techniques of examining. (Bloomfield *et al.*, 1976, p. 16)

In other words, Mode III may be used to give advantage to pupils who are not good at conventional external examinations.

There is not much profit in speculation on this or any other explanation of an apparent lack of equivalence of standards. For any one finding many justifications can be put forward. As a result, one could be forgiven for some scepticism on the value of comparability exercises in general.[18] In some fields of study – for example, economics and chemistry – the concept of equal value has had some meaning and a definable standard. Not so in the currency of educational performance. There is no 'gold standard' or '1 g of hydrogen' to serve even as an arbitrary standard of equivalence.[19] But in the technology of education a criterion of equivalence has never existed either in terms of general ability or in specific ability, or in attainment. The situation is nicely epitomized in the form of an unanswerable question posed by the Schools Council (1980): 'A candidate has received a grade C at O level in both mathematics and art. Can she be expected to multiply as well as she can paint?'

It could be supposed, if criteria for actual performance could be devised and applied either generally or specifically, that we could be taken a step nearer to genuine comparability in its various forms. The search for a more absolute standard, however, takes us from present to future practice and another chapter. Meanwhile it is not unfair to say that despite considerable effort and expenditure all comparability studies conducted so far are to some degree methodologically inadequate. Whatever findings they produce can be offset by selecting from an array of explanations most of which remain unproven but have sufficient force to prevent the research being used to adjust standards. It is small wonder that research on comparability is running out of steam. But in the long run perhaps that is not a bad thing. Perhaps the time has come to call a halt to the crunching of the numbers which come out of the assessment machine and to turn more to the quality of what goes into it (Christie and Forrest, 1981, p. 80)?

Notes: Chapter 9

1   For a discussion of the issue of centralized or diversified examinations see the Schools Council Focus on Examinations series of pamphlets. The sixth pamphlet states: 'It is clear that the local character of education in this country, together with the existence of several examining boards, makes it difficult to establish national grade standards.'

2 The main references are Nuttall, 1971; Skurnik and Connaughton, 1970; Willmott, 1977; Bardell *et al.*, 1978.

3 Bardell *et al.*, 1978, p. 14, give a summary of the different types of centres which use the various examining boards. For example, in the 1977 O-level examinations the percentage of entries from direct grant and independent schools for the Joint Matriculation Board and the Oxford and Cambridge Board was 10·2 and 89·6 per cent respectively. Similarly, the percentage of entries from further education for the Associated Board was 36·6 per cent compared with 1·3 per cent for the Cambridge Board. In the same publication differences in the percentage of candidates achieving grade C or better in some of the main subjects (O level, 1977) is given. In English language, for example, this percentage ranged from 45·9 per cent (AEB) to 67·8 per cent (Northern Ireland); while in Latin in ranged from 46·8 per cent (AEB) to 83·7 per cent (Oxford and Cambridge).

4 This seems to have occurred in the NFER comparability studies of CSE and GCE: see Willmott, 1977.

5 For an intricate but clear exposition of the significance of 'parallelism' and other statistical matters see Newbould and Massey, 1979. They also set out the arguments for and against the use of monitor tests in comparability studies.

6 A recent example is provided by the University Grants Committee which used as one criterion of the standing of university subject departments the numerical sum of the A-level grades of students entering each department regardless of the nature of the subjects in which they were attained.

7 See Nuttall *et al.*, 1974, and Forrest, 1971, in both of which the NFER Aptitude Test 100 was used. This test contains eighty items equally weighted to test verbal and quantitative ability. The correlations between test performance and performance in eleven O-level examinations are given by Forrest (p. 33) and Nuttall (p. 99); they show a positive but modest relationship, fairly uniform for many major subjects but especially low in some, for example, art.

8 For details see Nuttall *et al.*, 1974, pp. 20–4, and Forrest, 1971, pp. 24–7.

9 The average O-level grades are obtained by equating the literal grades A, B, C, D and E (unclassified) with the numerical scores 6, 5, 4, 3, 2 and 1. This quantitative relationship is difficult to justify but is frequently used in this type of research: see Forrest and Vickerman, 1982, p. 9. It assumes, for example, that the difference in performance from each grade to the next is quantitatively the same.

10 Forrest and Vickerman, 1982, p. 14, list the subjects which deviate from biology. The extremes were:

	No. of candidates	mean grade in biology	mean grade in subject listed	difference
Pure mathematics with mechanics AO	527	4·9	3·4	+1·5
Commerce 16+	248	2·9	4·2	−1·3

It would be inadvisable, however, to arrive at any immediate judgement from these figures. It would not be legitimate to conclude that on average pure mathematics with mechanics AO is 1·5 grade more severe than biology, and that biology is 1·3 grade more severe than commerce 16+, therefore pure mathematics with mechanics AO is 2·8 grade more severe than commerce 16+. The candidates are few in number and, in view of the subjects concerned, are not likely to be representative of all candidates.

11 The converse, that if there is a strong relation a reference test is necessarily valid, does not apply. There may well be a strong correlation between the ability to play cricket and the ability to play soccer but this does not make it legitimate to judge a performance in one by watching the other.

12   The South Australian system is quite open about its procedures. It even published the median-scaled scores which indicate the relative contribution each subject makes to the aggregated score which is used for matriculation purposes. For example, in the 1980 Matriculation Examination some median-scaled scores were: art 60·7, biology 60·1, chemistry 70·9, French 70·8, geography 59·5, mathematics I 73·1 and physics 70·2.

13   This suspicion is not confined to employers. A survey conducted by the Schools Council found that 'There is also suspicion within the teaching profession in that some staff who are committed to the Mode I philosophy have doubts about the motives of their colleagues who use Mode III procedures': Smith, 1976, p. 31.

14   A concise account and balanced comment on the use of moderators in two CSE boards is given in Schools Council Examinations Bulletin No. 36: see Bloomfield *et al.*, 1976. In addition, most individual examination boards publish regulations and guidelines for the practice of moderation.

15   Smith, 1976, writes: 'Mode III is an expensive method of examining both in money terms and in the boards' staff in preparing and operating Mode III schemes. It is estimated that, whereas in 1974, Mode III accounted for about 17% of the total entry, about 70% of office time and resources is devoted to it' (p. 54).

16   Nuttall, 1973, p. 4, gives an example that in the 1972 TWYLREB French the mean grade in Mode III was one-third of a grade better than in Mode I, but points out that the statement has no meaning unless it can be related to the nature of the two populations of candidates. Nuttall points to the difficulty of finding an external test in, say, French which would be equally fair to all candidates.

17   The NFER Aptitude Test 100 comprises eighty multiple-choice items which in itself casts doubts on its suitability for comparing standards of attainment in areas in which the kinds of work are so manifestly different from multiple choice.

18   Bloomfield *et al.*, 1976, write: 'Factors of this kind may be regarded as illustrations of a common methodological problem in social science research, that is, control of the data is lost when subjects are not randomly assigned to treatments' (p. 16).

19   It must be acknowledged that the fixed standards of equivalence in both economics and chemistry have suffered a decline in recent years; not altogether without loss to chemistry since it allowed the calculation of equivalence even between opposites such as acids and bases.

10
Standards

Standard of Aptitude or Standard of Attainment?

Chapter 9 ended on a note of scepticism on the methods used for comparing examination standards. Christie and Forrest (1981) make the point that the problems arise, at least in part, from the failure to decide which of two functions of the examination system should predominate: the *prognostic* function in which the results are used as measures of general *aptitude*, and the *descriptive* function in which the results are based on actual *achievement*[1] in whatever specified area is being taught and tested. If the latter function predominates, then the use of reference tests of general ability becomes invalid; furthermore, attempts to equate subjects become fruitless since the level of attainment represented by a single grade will be specific to each subject. It is an unfortunate characteristic of most examination systems to pretend that one system can perform both the prognostic and descriptive functions equally well.

The conceptual and psychometric problems involved in trying to distinguish between aptitude and attainment are daunting and, at present, far from resolution. Aptitude presumably means some inherent quality which enables a person to do something. But is it a single generalized quality? If so, to what activities is it generalizable and to what degree? Or is it a set of specific aptitudes each related to a particular activity? Does a measure of it indicate how much aptitude someone has or is it relative, simply indicating that one person has more or less of it than another?

A definition and measurement of educational attainment is no easier. If it means the knowledge and skills which have been acquired, the difficulties which attend their specification referred to in Chapter 4 remain. Even if they could be defined, the question of *when* they were acquired and for what *period* of time they are retained is still not answered. Then there is the question of whether attainment, like aptitude, is divisible or indivisible. In the days of group certificates, like the School Certificate, the concept of attainment had a degree of wholeness in that it was only recognized by a certificate for a total, balanced performance. The advent of single-subject examinations appears to assume that attainment is infinitely divisible; in that case are all the bits of attainment equal and can they be added together? Is there any way in which an *amount* of attainment can be conceived? The terms 'level' and 'depth' are often synonymously used to try to attach a quantity to attainment. Occasionally they can be given a quantitative meaning such as 'x has a vocabulary of 1,000 words'. But that is rare and suspect in its accuracy. Usually levels, even in such closely prescribed performances as graded tests in music, mean no more than one quality of performance has to be attained before going on to the next.

Finally, is there a relation between aptitude and attainment or are they distinct? It would seem self-evident that there is a relation. A personal, inherent aptitude cannot be solely something with which one is born; it must be a function of inherited attributes and of learning. In other words, aptitude is enhanced by attainment and stunted by lack of attainment. Did someone have the same aptitude for French after one week of attainment as he did after ten years of attainment? The answer is unlikely to be yes.

The Dual Function of Examinations

Christie and Forrest (1981, p. 46) while still maintaining that the issue of standards and the various forms of comparability will not be resolved until the dual function of examinations is resolved come to the commonsense conclusion that 'Public examination grades as currently conceived reflect both aptitude and attainment: they represent both, the cause and effect of educational achievement'. This takes us back to the historic dual purpose for the institution of public examinations in schools: to exercise a *competitive* function for the purpose of selection for employment or further education, and a *formative* function to exercise some control on the curriculum of schools and hence on the actual attainment of those who attended them. Provided that selectors did no more than base their selection on the position of a candidate on a scale of grades, without much regard for performance (that is, what the candidates could actually do), then a competitive examination system which reflected the relative general aptitude of its candidates would serve well enough. If, on the other hand, the selectors or society at large were more concerned with actual performance, with the doing of certain things (preferably over a long period of time and not just at the moment of an examination), then a form of reporting which simply reflects a candidate's position in an order of merit of all candidates would not suffice. The examination results would have to be reported in such a way as to describe what candidates could actually *do* in order to qualify[2] to go on to do something else.

In the past most examination systems have contrived to fudge this issue. Content to exercise sufficient influence on the curriculum through the published syllabuses, they have then functioned very largely as a service for selectors by producing orders of merit. They have assumed the need for equivalence between subjects and, therefore, tacitly accepted that what is being tested is predominantly general ability. When the nature of actual performances required to achieve certain grades has been questioned, they have resorted to general, non-operational statements of grade criteria (see Chapter 6). In other words, they rely on the skill of experienced examiners to make consistent judgements of the quality of work at the borderlines between grades – without, however, those examiners being able or required to specify the nature and level of these qualities in operational terms.

Over the past few years one senses a growing uneasiness with this state of affairs.[3] While it appears that the examination system determines what is *taught*, it cannot explicitly give an account of what has been *learned* even at the time of the examination, let alone over a longer period. It is this uneasiness which has found expression in movements towards the so-called 'criterion referencing' of grades.

This tension between the two functions of examinations has developed into a debate to which the terms 'norm reference' and 'criterion reference' have come to be applied. These terms have proved to be of little more worth than those of aptitude and attainment. But they do serve to make a distinction between two purposes of examinations, so a little space needs to be devoted to them. It is rather more important at present to discuss this issue than to repeat the rather academic studies of validity and reliability. For one thing, there is a substantial literature on the latter two[4] and, in any event, both reliability and validity are subordinate to purpose in the sense that reliability is a part of validity and a valid test is one which fulfils its purpose. So until purpose has been adequately defined there is not much point in debating the other two. Thyne (1974, p. 4)[5] writes: 'no matter how well the examination fulfils its actual purpose it cannot be good if the purpose is bad.'

Norm-Referenced

This may be approached by asking how may the value of a mark or score be described? Suppose two groups of candidates each take the same test in which the maximum score is 10 (see Table 10.1). And suppose the question is asked; what is the *value* of the score of 5? Assuming for the moment that the value of a score is determined by its standing in relation to the other scores, then candidate F in group I has a *low* score of 5 on the first test. On the other hand, candidate P in group II has a *high* score of 5 on the same test. If the two groups are combined, candidates F and P can be said to have the *median* score of 5 because they are midway in the order of merit, five candidates above them and five below them.

So what *is* the value of score 5? The answer is that if the basis of value is its position in an order of merit, then it has not got an absolute value. It can be high or low, or in between, depending on the scores of the other candidates of the group in which it rests.

Table 10.1

Group I candidates	Mark in test I	Group II candidates	Mark in test I
A	10	P	5
B	9	Q	4
C	8	R	3
D	7	S	2
E	6	T	1
F	5	U	0

This is the essence of norm-referenced assessment. The value of a mark depends on its standing among the other marks in a *specified group of candidates.*

It follows that if the main purpose of a test or examination is to produce an order of merit to be used for the selection of candidates who came highest, it is the position of a candidate's mark in relation to all the other marks which is decisive. A system of norm referencing is then appropriate.

The mark awarded, although it is used to determine the position of a candidate in an order of performance, is of no use in itself for reporting the position unless all the other marks are given. The reporting has to be done in other ways. If Table 10.1 represents the results of a class test, P could go home and say 'I came top'; F, if he was honest, might say 'I came bottom', but might opt for the more prudent 'I got 5 out of 10'.

These, of course, are oversimplified examples; but in large-scale examining the same principles operate. Meaningful reporting in the form of a grade is possible only if the recipients know, at least approximately, what proportion of candidates were assigned to each grade; if this is not known, then a grade has no more meaning than a mark has. Since in public examinations in schools in England and Wales there is a considerable degree of conformity in the proportion of candidates assigned to grades from one year to another, the system of reporting by grades is essentially norm-based. Of course, there are other, more explicit ways of doing it. The actual position in the order of merit could be reported: 2,121st out of 50,000, for example (although of little practical use on this scale). Candidates could be assigned to, say, the top quartile, denoting that they are among the top quarter of candidates in the order of merit; or it could be said that they are in the twentieth percentile, that is, among the top 20 per cent of candidates in order of merit.

At a cruder level a candidate could be said to be in the top half in order of merit. This candidate could be said to be above average; but the term is meaningless unless the population of candidates against whom he has competed is specified. (It certainly does not mean that an above-average candidate necessarily has above-average marks, as a glance at the marks of the group II candidates in the first test will demonstrate.)

To emphasize the point and to bring out others suppose that the same two groups of candidates took another test (see Table 10.2), the maximum score again being 10. What, then, is the value of a mark of 5? Assuming that the purpose of the test is again solely to produce an order of merit and that norm referencing is applied, candidate F in group I now has a *high* mark of 5 on test 2, while P has a *low* mark of 5 on the same test. They have scored 5 on all occasions but on test 2 the value of their mark of 5 has been inverted simply because the marks scored by their fellow candidates have changed. If the two groups are considered as a whole, 5 becomes the *median* mark because there are five candidates with a mark above it and five candidates with a mark below it. So once again a mark may be high, low, or intermediate provided that *the frame of reference for its value is the performance of the other candidates in the group.*

Table 10.2

Group I candidates	Mark in test 2	Group II candidates	Mark in test 2
A	0	P	5
B	1	Q	6
C	2	R	7
D	3	S	8
E	4	T	9
F	5	U	10

One further aspect should be apparent. If a mark is to have any norm-referenced value, it is essential that at least some of the candidates should get different marks. This is illustrated in Table 10.3 (maximum mark 10). In group I all candidates have the same mark on test 3, so none is higher or lower than another. The test cannot now serve a selective function because it has not discriminated between the candidates. The same point applies to group II candidates who on this test all scored zero marks. Tests which do this have no function in terms of solely norm-referenced assessment. This is not to say that they have no function at all. If test 3 were a valid test of the ability to land an aircraft, and the candidates were pilots in training, the test would have a very important function in *qualification* procedures.

If the two groups are put together, a norm-referenced standard can again apply. Since 10 is higher than 0, all group I candidates have performed better than group II candidates. More can be read into the marks: it could be said that group I candidates could do perfectly whatever it was that test 3 required, whereas group II candidates failed totally to do so. It is now possible to use test 3 with a norm frame of reference for both groups together on an all-or-nothing basis. (All the foregoing assumes, of course, that the tests are marked with total reliability; the standing of any score whether it be norm-referenced or criterion-referenced acquires some degree of uncertainty if complete accuracy and consistency of marking is not attainable – and it never is!)

Table 10.3

Group I candidates	Mark in test 3	Group II candidates	Mark in test 3
A	10	P	0
B	10	Q	0
C	10	R	0
D	10	S	0
E	10	T	0
F	10	U	0

Table 10.3 in a crude way brings out a dominant principle in most public examinations, that is, the need to get a wide distribution of marks. This is a revealing principle because, together with the grading system, it amounts to an admission that the emphasis in public examinations is on obtaining norm-referenced results; that is, an admission that the dominant function is competitive.

Distribution and Discrimination

Whether by chance or design, marks in an examination do not take the all-or-nothing form illustrated in Table 10.3; they are distributed over a range of scores. The distribution can take many different forms three of which are illustrated in Table 10.4, showing the marks obtained by eleven candidates in three tests. In all three sets of marks the average (mean) mark is nearly the same (about 5). In test 4 the maximum possible range of marks is used (0–10) and no candidate has the same score, whereas in test 5 the marks range from only 4 to 6 and several candidates have the same score, all bunched near the average of 5. It follows that the scores in test 4 are more widely distributed than those in test 5 and the performance of each candidate can be distinguished from all the others in test 4 but not in test 5. (Again it is assumed that the scores are a sufficiently accurate measure of performance. If they are not, the discrimination may be apparent but not real.)

Test 6 represents a rather odd case. The full range of marks is used in the sense that the two extremes 0 and 10 are recorded; and the marks are widely distributed in the sense that 0 and 10 are as far as possible from the mean mark (50 ÷ 11 = 4·5). It differs from test 4, however, in that it discriminates between two *groups* of candidates, A to E and F to K.

These, of course, are oversimplified illustrations of distribution and discrimination. In large-scale examinations published tables showing the marks of each candidate would simply confuse. The distribution of the marks is better shown in the form of tables or diagrams in which candidates are grouped according to subdivisions of the range of marks.

Table 10.4

Candidates	Mark in test 4	Mark in test 5	Mark in test 6
A	10	6	10
B	9	6	10
C	8	6	10
D	7	5	10
E	6	5	10
F	5	5	0
G	4	5	0
H	3	5	0
I	2	4	0
J	1	4	0
K	0	4	0

This is illustrated in Table 10.5 and Figure 10.1. Table 10.5 shows the distribution in groups of 5 or 10 marks. Thus 2·5 per cent of all the candidates got a mark between 0 and 5 out of 100, 5 per cent of all candidates got a mark between 6 and 15 (inclusive) and 10 per cent got between 16 and 25 marks, and so on. The curve in Figure 10.1 represents what may be called the general *shape* of the distribution. It is symmetrical either side of the mean mark of 50. The full range of marks is used, in that some candidates got between 0 and 5 and some between 95 and 100.

Figure 10.2 represents the distribution of the marks given in Table 10.6. The curve again shows the general shape representing the way in which the marks are distributed among the candidates. In this example it is again symmetrical either side of a mean mark of 50, but in this case the full range of marks is not used and the marks are bunched closely around the mean mark.

The two figures are rather neater and more symmetrical than those representing the distribution of marks in an actual examination but correspond reasonably closely to the two extreme distributions which actually arise. Figure 10.1 resembles the distribution usually obtained in mathematics and related subjects; Figure 10.2 resembles that obtained in history, English literature and related subjects.

The shape of the distribution reflects an examination's effectiveness in

Table 10.5

Percentage of candidates	Marks attained out of 100
2·5	0–5
5	6–15
10	16–25
10	26–35
15	36–45
15	46–55
15	56–65
10	66–75
10	76–85
5	86–95
2·5	96–100

discriminationg between candidates. The more widely the marks are distributed, the easier it is to discriminate – in other words, the more effective will be the ranking function of the examination. On the assumption that the main purpose is competitive an examination which distributes the marks in similar fashion to that in Figure 10.1 is more efficient than one similar to Figure 10.2.

Table 10.6

Percentage of candidates	Marks attained out of 100
5	16–25
10	26–35
20	36–45
30	46–55
20	56–65
10	66–75
5	76–85

If this is so, the question arises what causes the different distributions? The Joint Matriculation Board (1983a) and others have demonstrated from the data from many years of examinations that the kind of distribution appears to be related to the nature of the subject, the shape of the distribution being fairly constant from year to year. The JMB uses its A-level mathematics syllabus A and English literature as examples of wide and narrow distributions.

It may be premature, however, to conclude that it is an entirely intrinsic

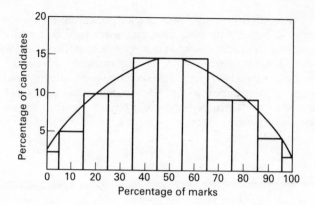

Figure 10.1

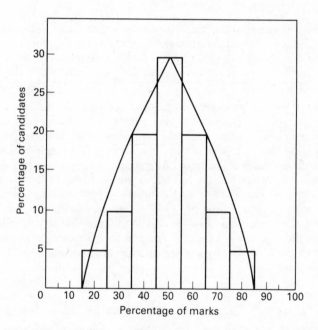

Figure 10.2

attribute of the subjects themselves which brings about this state of affairs. It may also be a function of the way in which they are examined, particularly the kinds of questions which are set and the way in which the answers are marked. Traditionally subjects like English literature and history are examined through open-ended questions and a wide choice of syllabus, answered by essay and marked subjectively. In these circumstances it is not surprising that examiners tend to bunch their marks near to the middle and not to use the two extremes of the possible range; an essay is never worth 0 or 100. It is not inconceivable that a fixed-response test, closely tied to a very limited compulsory syllabus, could be devised to give a distribution to a history examination much more like that traditional to mathematics. Similarly if physics were to be examined solely by essays on a wide range of topics, distribution like that of English literature could be achieved.

Table 10.7

Candidates	Marks on part 1 (5)	Marks on part 2 (5)	Total marks (10)
A	5	0	5
B	4	1	5
C	3	2	5
D	2	3	5
E	1	4	5
F	0	5	5

A feature of examining in recent years has been the increasing use of several parts to a single examination, each part testing different skills and knowledge and the final score being the sum of the scores in each part. It can be expected that individual candidates perform differently on each part the result of which is illustrated by a simple, extreme case in Table 10.7. In each part separately the candidates are distributed widely; each part discriminates well. But the performances in part 1 are completely reversed in part 2 (a correlation of -1). The result on addition is that all candidates get the same total mark with no distribution and no possibility of discrimination (a severe case of regression to the mean!). If there is complete correlation between parts, the problem does not arise (see Table 10.8).

Table 10.8

Candidates	Marks on part 1 (5)	Marks on part 2 (5)	Total marks (10)
A	5	5	10
B	4	4	8
C	3	3	6
D	2	2	4
E	1	1	2
F	0	0	0

A closer look at Table 10.8 reveals that although the total marks have gone up (except for the unfortunate candidate F), the total scores give no better discrimination than either parts 1 or 2 separately. It could be said that one or other of the two parts is redundant. This is so *provided that the assessment is completely normative and that the sole purpose of the examination is to discriminate.* It may not be so if the examination has other purposes, but more of that later. The point being made here is that if the correlation between the parts of an examination is anything less than perfect (and this is usually so), the total score will show a bunching round the mean mark, a decrease in the distribution of marks around the mean and, consequently, less effective discrimination between the candidates.

Table 10.9

Candidates	Marks on part 1 (5)	Marks on part 2 (5)	Marks on part 3 (10)	Total marks (20)
A	5	0	5	10
B	4	1	5	10
C	3	2	5	10
D	2	3	5	10
E	1	4	5	10
F	0	5	5	10

One peripheral point needs to be made in connection with the effect on distribution of the various parts of an examination. Suppose a third part, marked out of 10, is added to Tables 10.7 and 10.8 in which all the candidates do equally well, scoring 5 out of 10. In terms of ranking the candidates the addition of part 3 has no effect in either case. In Tables 10.7 and 10.9, although their total marks have gone up, all candidates still achieve the same marks and there is still no discrimination between them. In Tables 10.8 and 10.10 the discrimination remains the same; the only effect of adding part 3 is to raise each candidate's total score, and incidentally giving candidate F some reward even if he still remains at the bottom. Not that candidate F will ever be aware of this; if the assessment is norm-referenced he will be told only that he is bottom, or has the bottom grade, and what he *actually* did will remain hidden.

This state of affairs is now common if not in quite such an extreme form as these simple illustrations. It is generally found that if a part of an examination is internally assessed practical work, the marks awarded tend to be bunched round the mean mark for that part. (They also tend to have a higher mean than the externally assessed parts, but that is not relevant to the present discussion.) It follows that the internally assessed part has less effect on the distribution of the total scores than might appear from the proportion of the total allocated to it. Table 10.10, for example, shows

Table 10.10

Candidates	Marks on part 1 (5)	Marks on part 2 (5)	Marks on part 3 (10)	Total marks (20)
A	5	5	5	15
B	4	4	5	13
C	3	3	5	11
D	2	2	5	9
E	1	1	5	7
F	0	0	5	5

that part 3 although allocated an apparent weight of one-half the total marks (10 out of 20) has no effect on distribution; the distribution and discrimination of the examination as a whole is effectively determined by either parts 1 or 2 each of which was allocated only one-quarter of the total marks, 5 out of 20. In the ranking sense part 3 was a waste of effort. In short, the *published* weightings of each part of an examination design as shown in a specification may bear little relation to their *effective* weighting.

The kind of anomalies which can arise if assessment is considered to be purely norm-referenced have been illustrated almost to the point of absurdity by some admittedly simplified and extreme sets of marks. In real examinations the data are not simple, nor are the effects so extreme. Nevertheless, the general points remain and are well known. The anomalies of norm referencing have led to the search for an alternative basis for determining standards. From the depths of psychometrics the term 'criterion referencing' (or better, 'criteria referencing') was discovered, dusted down and, by some, hailed as a new approach to examining. The time has come to subject it to the same scrutiny to which norm referencing has been exposed.

Criterion-Referenced

It is easier to say what the definition of standard by criterion referencing is *not* than what it *is*. One of the more readable reviews of criterion-referenced assessment is that of Brown; for those who like brief definitions to focus the mind, hers is better than most:

> Assessment that provides information about specific knowledge and abilities of pupils through their performance on various kinds of tasks that are interpretable in terms of what the pupils know or can do, without reference to the performance of others. (Brown, 1981, p. vii)

The status of a criterion-referenced mark of a candidate is not determined by the marks of any of the other candidates. It follows that it is not dependent on its position in an array of scores. It does not depend on its position relative to the mean score or median score or percentiles or quartiles or any other way of indicating a position in an order of merit. A score could be at the top of a list and still not meet a criterion-referenced standard; it might be at the bottom and still meet such a standard.

It might also be helpful at this stage to balance the argument by pointing to some shortcomings of a norm-referenced standard. The principal defect is that although it indicates the standing of a score in relation to those of the other candidates, it says nothing about the *actual* performance which it represents. Refer back to Table 10.1 for a moment which illustrated that the score of 5, if viewed normatively, could be relatively good, bad, or intermediate depending on the group of candidates in which it finds itself. Of the skills it represents, and whether those skills are up to 'standard' or not, it says nothing. The most that could be said from the arrays of scores in Table 10.1 is that group I performed better than group II. It is tempting, then, to say that candidate F is the worst of a good lot and candidate P is the best of a bad lot. But then when one turns again to Table 10.2, the positions are reversed. So the statement about the performance of the two groups has to be modified: group I is better than group II in whatever it is that test 1 tests, but in test 2 it is worse.

Bringing the argument to real examinations, the bald statement that a candidate obtained a grade A in mathematics means no more than that that candidate was placed within a top group of candidates. It says nothing about what the candidate can actually do in mathematics. It also says very little about his relative performance, unless the whole population of mathematics candidates is defined together with the proportion of them to which grade A was awarded.

The solution to the difficulties which arise in applying purely norm-referenced standards looks at first glance deceptively inviting. Why not specify what performance each mark represents, or if that is not possible, specify what performance a range of marks represents? Thus the range of marks comprising grade A could represent the attainment of a particular performance or set of performances, similarly with grade B, and so on:

> Criteria-referenced grading is intended to describe a system under which grades are defined and awarded in terms of predetermined standards of performance specific to the subject concerned. Candidates are required to demonstrate predetermined levels of competence in specified aspects of the subject in order to be awarded a particular grade. (GCE and CSE Boards' Joint Council for 16+, 1981, p. 7)

But therein lies the rub: how can actual performances be attached to a particular mark or range of marks? If that could be done, then criterion referencing becomes feasible: the description of an individual's performance in relation to a defined *standard of performance*; indeed, it might be better if it were called 'performance referencing'.

The traditional examiner's response might well be that that is exactly what happens. That the 'borderlines' between the various grades are determined by an evaluation of the actual performances as manifested in the scripts or projects or practical work or whatever form the final outcome of an examination takes. Up to a point that may be so. Certainly a good deal of time is spent in looking at actual performances, particularly near the borderlines between grades, during the assessment procedure. It is not the only factor, however, and it is not difficult to list the various aspects of public examining which combine to deflate extravagant claims that the standards of awards are based on prescribed criteria formulated in terms of actual performances, as given below.

(1) In Chapter 6 the various other factors which impinge on the decision to fix grade borders were described. These are mostly normative: a knowledge of what candidates are likely to be awarded in other subjects, in other boards and in previous and subsequent years. All these are norm-based standards and it is idle to pretend that they do not influence the award of grades.

(2) Then there is an element of hindsight in the present system even when actual performances are being discussed by the awarding group. One of the requirements of criterion-referenced standards is that the standards be *predetermined*, not massaged into shape afterwards. True, mark schemes are predetermined, but they simply allocate scores to expected answers; even they are modified after some of the scripts have been seen and in no case do they predetermine what marks are required to attain each grade.

(3) Even when examiners are pressed to describe performance standards, they have to fall back on generalities which are difficult to perceive as actual performances.[6] An example has been given already in Chapter 6; to press the point home another will not come amiss:

> Grade 6
> The candidate can be expected to have demonstrated competence in:
> (i) understanding and conveying information at a straightforward level;
> (ii) understanding basic facts, ideas and opinions, and presenting them with a degree of coherence ...;
> (vii) writing in simple sentences – weaknesses in punctuation, spelling and the construction of complex sentences will be apparent, but will not seriously impair communication.

> Grade 3
> The candidate can be expected to have demonstrated competence in:

(i) understanding and conveying information both at a straightforward and at a more complex level;

(ii) understanding facts, ideas and opinions, and ordering and presenting them with a degree of clarity and accuracy ...;

(vii) writing in paragraphs using sentences of various kinds and exercising care over punctuation and spelling. (GCE and CSE Boards' Joint Council for 16+, 1983b, pp. 5–6)

There is an appearance in such statements of performance-based standards: words like 'competence' are used and each of these statements relates to a recognizable language skill. But it is only skin deep. What is meant by 'more complex', for example, and how does it differ from 'a straightforward level'? (All language, even a grunt, has some complexity and what is complex for a grade 3 16-year-old pupil may be straightforward for a 3rd class honours graduate.) What the authors are really saying is that they know from their experience what a grade 3 candidate can be expected to produce, and can recognize it when they see it. Their judgement is based on performance relative to that of many other candidates past and present; in other words, it is essentially normative. The argument is becoming circular: the performance of a grade 3 candidate is what grade 3 candidates can do.

(4) But let us suppose that the examination outcomes can be prescribed with exactness and detail in a specification which sets the skills and the content and the nominated weighting of them all in advance of the examination. Surely, then, the standard of each grade can be described in performance terms. Not so, except for those who get nearly full marks or nearly zero marks. To use Table 10.1 yet again it might be thought that candidates F and P, both having 5 marks on the same test, had given the same performance (even though one was top and the other bottom of their respective groups). This is not justified unless all the questions test the same thing, that is, the test is homogeneous. It is possible – although certainly not easy – to devise reasonably homogeneous tests; but it is obvious that examinations are far from homogeneous. Different parts, and different questions within parts, test different things – as they are intended to do. So if candidate F answered correctly the five questions which candidate P answered incorrectly, their performances may be far from equal; and so the equal mark deceives. Since grading decisions are at present usually made on the aggregated marks of all the different parts and different questions, it is obvious that very little can be said with certainty about what candidates in each grade can or cannot do.

Hobson's Choice?

It could be thought that what has been written so far in this chapter is somewhat nihilistic. The exposure of the defects of both approaches has been not so much to criticize examinations as we know them as to call attention to the fallacy of thinking that norm-referenced and criterion-referenced assessment are alternative kinds of test. They are not. It is possible to perceive and indeed design for a bias to one or the other, but not to have either in a pure form. The real point of importance is that a trend towards one or other is essentially a trend towards one or other of the two main *purposes* of examinations, the competitive and descriptive.

It is not possible to devise a norm-referenced test which does not provide some information about what a candidate can do, even though it may be difficult to say what it is. Nor is it possible to devise a criterion-referenced test without giving rise to an order of merit and hence some discrimination between the candidates. Simply by looking at the test itself reveals nothing about whether it is norm-referenced or criterion-referenced, or what its bias to one or the other is. Most tests could fit either description – although not both equally well. The examination in itself is neutral in this matter, it is not until its main purpose is revealed that it may be nominated as being predominantly one or the other. And that purpose must be deduced from the *use* to which the marks or grades are put, not what the examining boards *say* about their purposes in the course of public relations.

Par for the Course

Other kinds of test may help to emphasize the point: golf, for example. Par for the course could be said to be a criterion, a standard of performance of, say, 72 strokes; a high standard in the sense that few golfers can attain it, but a standard none the less. It also serves as a fixed performance to which other performances can be related. So the standard of performance of someone who on average requires 10 over par to complete a course could be said to have a performance of 82. So several dependent criteria of performance can be established, hence a handicap system in which those with the same handicap can be said to play at the same standard of performance. There are, of course, all the many factors which bring about variation in performance from day to day even among those with the same handicap, and thus some unreliability in the measurement; these apply equally well to examinations, but do not concern us here.

Is, then, golf norm-referenced or criterion-referenced? The answer is that you cannot tell merely by reading the rules (the examination regulations) or talking with the committee (the examining board) or walking the course (the examination syllabus) or even watching a game (the examination itself). The answer rests in the reasons for playing. An open championship is predominantly norm-referenced. A score is judged not in relation to par (although that is a convenient, but not necessary, way of stating the scores), but in relation to the scores of the other competitors, that is, the distribution of scores. It may be a matter of passing interest to know what someone's *actual* performance is in terms of number of strokes. But at the end of the day it is the order of merit only that matters; from that the consequences, that is, the prizes, are determined. It matters not whether the winner was 10 over or 10 under par.

If, on the other hand, the purpose of the game is to complete a card to establish a handicap (a performance standard), the game could be said to be criterion-referenced. In the course of the game one player is likely to do better than the others; but that would not be significant if he failed to reach the performance to which he aspired and which would have been necessary to establish him as a player who could play at a designated standard.

It is tempting to push our golf analogy still further. Is par on one course the same as par on another (are the standards across the examining boards the same)? Was the standard of entry in the United States Open as good as that in the British Open (what are the characteristics of different examination populations)? Did the redesign of the course make it more difficult (is Nuffield biology more difficult than JMB biology)? If he is good at golf, will he be good at snooker (is a grade A in chemistry a good indicator that she will be a good doctor)? The most intriguing analogy is with the handicapping system, so arranged that players of different abilities (for various reasons including different education and social background) are scored differently in order to bring them, on average, to the same score at the end of the examination. (The relation to positive discrimination is close.) But perhaps to continue would be to trivialize an important matter.[7] Anyway there is one significant difference: the outcome of a game of golf is precisely determined, the number of shots required to put a small ball into eighteen small holes. For no examination is the outcome so simple (I write here of *outcome* not *process*, the latter seems infinitely more complex in golf). Nor would any system of positive discrimination be so easy to agree and apply.

It is relevant to note, however, that there appears to be a deep-seated public demand for a *winner* in all manner of competitions, indicating a strong bias to norm referencing. It is so in all sport (there is, for example, no television coverage for a group of golfers trying to establish a particular performance to get a handicap). Even in the arts, particularly music,[8] there is great public interest in competitions designed to produce an order of merit and a winner. Agricultural and horticultural shows, beauty contests, athletics competitions, political elections, even angling, all show a strong public preference for competitive norm-referenced assessment. It is not too fanciful to suggest that this preference is reflected in the academic competition of public examinations. The reasons must lie deep in our cultural history. The attitude will not be easily reversed.

Defining a Standard of Performance

The nearest we have got so far in defining a standard of performance is in Chapter 4, in which examination specifications were discussed; and in Chapter 6, where it was established that the interpretation of that specification and its application as a set of standards (grades) rests in the minds of chief examiners, who while capable of applying the standards with reasonable consistency, have difficulty in saying what they are.

When one analyses the substance and the kinds of task and activity which comprise a curriculum, they are remarkably complex in nature and varied in their manifestations. If it were not so, it would have been impossible to produce different questions year after year even in comparatively elementary school examinations. There are a very large number of variations in tests of so simple a task as that of multiplication. It is small wonder, then, that examiners have found it impossible to specify with any exactness the performances which are required to attain a particular grade.

This is not to say that description of the performances is impossible. It has already been established in Chapter 4 that the various parts of an examination and the questions within each part can be classified in terms of their subject-matter and the kinds of activity that are demanded. The point has also been made that in recent years there has been considerable progress towards establishing a consensus among teachers and examiners on what that subject-matter and those activities should be and so enhancing the curriculum validity of examinations. In this sense, then, the performances required in an examination *are* specified in advance. Various authors have applied the term 'domain' of behaviours to such a specification, hence *domain-referenced* assessment.[9]

Agreement on what constitutes the domain is only the first step. What matters in the long run to someone who wishes to make use of the reported outcomes is what an individual candidate has done or can do (not always the same thing) out of the whole domain of possible things that may be achieved. This is a good deal more difficult, and it is made even more so by some of the practices of public examining, as outlined below.

(1)   Although the specification of the domain of performances may be acceptable, many examinations are so constructed that they allow candidates to ignore large parts of it. This comes about through the provision of choice of question or even choice of parts within the examination; indeed, candidates may have to confine themselves to questions unrepresentative of the domain as a whole.

(2) Even if candidates are compelled to answer questions from each of the main elements of the domain specification, they may be able to neglect part of it and still achieve a respectable grade. This arises from the practice of adding all the marks in the various questions and parts and using the total score to provide an order of merit and subsequently to decide on the boundary scores between grades. It follows that candidates who achieve the same total score and grade have probably done so through different kinds of performance in different parts of the paper.

(3) Finally, there is the difficulty of determining what the marks actually mean in terms of *levels* of performance. Two candidates may answer identical questions in an examination and so have attempted to show the same *kind* of performance. If one candidate gets 40 marks and another 80, what do those marks actually tell us? No one knows. It does not necessarily mean that the first performs half as well as the second.

In the present state of the game all the examiners can do is to specify the domain of performances which they test, describe in general terms the level of performances associated with each grade and then say that, in their judgement, those levels of performance have been attained by the candidates allocated to each grade. In effect examiners are doing little more than describing what they examine and then reporting that they have awarded, for instance, the top 10 per cent of candidates a grade A. In short, the pressures of norm referencing and the need for comparability have been too strong to resist.

There is no doubt that public examinations could be so designed as to allow more definite statements of candidates' performance to be made, and we now have the political intention to do so (Joseph, 1984a). But it will not be easy; it will require radical development work and changes to both the design and operation of examinations. I fear that the developments towards the General Certificate of Secondary Education (GCSE, a single system to replace GCE and CSE) have not sufficiently anticipated these radical changes (with the exception of modern languages). This point will be taken up again in Chapters 12 and 13. Meanwhile in answer to the question 'what is the standard?' we should be honest and admit that it is not known and that, in both concept and practice, the term has little meaning.

It is all very difficult. And it is not very reassuring for one who has engaged professionally in the examination system for half a lifetime to read:

> Judge not, that ye be not judged.
> For with what judgement ye judge, ye shall be judged.

Notes: Chapter 10

1   I am aware that distinctions can be made between achievement and attainment. In much of the literature, however, the two terms seem to be used as if synonymous. The same applies to the terms 'ability' and 'aptitude'. I will do likewise, using the first two terms to denote that which has been actually accomplished and the second two to denote a capacity for accomplishing something.

2   The word 'qualify' is used in its literal sense as a statement of competence, implying a standard of qualities necessary as a statement of fitness to do something or proceed to do something.

3   The Secretary of State for Education – Joseph, 1984b – voiced this unease in his address to the North of England Education Conference, and in *The Times*, 9 January 1984: 'It should be possible to devise examination syllabuses and assessments which give a reasonable assurance that a pupil awarded a particular grade knows, understands, and can do certain things.' On another point he goes on to write: 'The examination system is designed to deny success to many.'

4   For a good exposition of these concepts and also criteria and norm referencing see Satterley, 1981.

5   An excellent, logical analysis of the essential purposes of examinations and the nature of norm and criterion referencing to which I am indebted.

6   In fairness it has to be pointed out that the authors now call such statements 'grade descriptions', not 'grade criteria', but this is little more than a semantic device.

7   I leave readers to decide which of the two is the important matter.

8   Those who have a preference for a criterion-referenced bias will be encouraged by Yehudi Menuhin's support. In his Paris competition he awards an equal prize to all who reach his criteria for excellence: European String Teachers' Association, 1984.

9   Christie and Forrest, 1981, pp. 27–9; see also Popham, 1978, p. 93, who writes 'A criterion-referenced test is used to ascertain an individual's status with respect to a well defined behavioural domain'.

11

New Ventures: I Recording Personal Achievement

Public examinations for schools are now over 100 years old and one must acknowledge some hardening of the arteries despite periodic efforts to rejuvenate them. The introduction of the single-subject certificate to replace the grouped certificate in the 1950s was one of the more fundamental changes. There was the introduction of internal assessment as an optional alternative in the 1960s, together with a widening and refinement of examination techniques. There was the move to widen the social base of the examination population in the 1960s. Now in the 1980s there is the introduction of a comprehensive, single system of examinations at the statutory school-leaving age, to match the comprehensive organization of secondary education, coupled with the move towards criterion-referenced grades. All such ventures have been welcomed by those professionally involved in the system; there has been little opposition to new ideas. Some of us were thought to have extravagant designs in the early, heady days of innovatory curriculum projects. In the event, compromise and assimilation were achieved without revolution.

It would be harsh to dismiss the changes of recent years as cosmetic, hiding the inevitable ageing process which afflicts any public institution. Yet there remains the uneasy feeling that this product of nineteenth-century enterprise, which did more than anything else to give the mass of young people access to a wider education and the opportunity to climb the social ladder, is being maintained partly by its own momentum and partly by society's inability to find viable alternatives. It resembles in many respects some of the industries which were our staple in the nineteenth century and now find it difficult to come to terms with the late twentieth. One thing is certain; the innovations of the past three decades, useful and progressive though they are, have not had the radical effects which might have been anticipated. Those, like Mode III examinations, which may with justification claim to be radical, have had only partial success; they have solved some old problems at the expense of spawning new ones.

Public examinations over recent years 'have been refined rather than reformed' (Goacher, 1983a, p. 7). Many of the incipient shortcomings, evident from the earliest years, are still there:

(1)   Their substance is predominantly intellectual, based on a classification of knowledge which though long standing in academic circles is not a comprehensive sample of human experience.

(2)   Formal education, being strongly supported by examinations, reflects the same limited view of human experience.

(3)   Achievement in examinations is expressed in competitive terms, dependent on the relative achievement of others at the *end* of the educational process rather than in terms of actual long-term competences.

(4)   Society has used examinations competitively as a primary instrument for selection for high-status education and employment, regardless of the lack of correspondence between the skills required to do well in examinations and those required subsequently.

(5)   There remains the need to strengthen other means by which a fuller curriculum can be maintained, teachers and students motivated, and young people guided into occupations appropriate to both personal and societal needs.

The more general issues of the future of examination systems, and their relation to education and society, will be discussed in the concluding chapter. Meanwhile, in chapters 11 and 12, it is necessary to set in perspective some of the more recent proposals for making good the limitations listed above.

The Growth of Individualism

Over the past thirty years or so there has been a trend for both curriculum and examinations to become more fragmented and individualized. The move from pass or fail in a single certificate, in a nationally prescribed group of subjects, to grades of achievement in a wide range of single subjects started and typified this trend. The Mode III system of courses and examinations, designed to meet the needs of children and teachers within individual schools, was another instance. At a higher level modular degree systems, as in the Open University, reported achievement in different parts of the curriculum and at different levels as well as within a single class of degree. There has been a continuing division of the subjects of the curriculum, and of the examinations and the groups of students who participate in them. With this differentiating trend has gone an inevitable increase in complexity and a decrease in commonality which has made equivalence difficult to maintain between the various fragments.

Most of the new ventures at the time of writing have sought to continue this trend of individualization and differentiation. They make even more personal and detailed the reports on what young people have achieved during and at the end of their formal education. The feature that they all have in common is that they are more specific, more personalized and more fragmented, hence the term 'personal profile' which is sometimes applied to the kind of report to which they give rise. 'Profiling' can be used in a more exact sense, so 'record of personal achievement' has been adopted in this chapter since it is more inclusive.

Comprehensive records of personal achievement may cover all aspects of formal education: a portfolio ranging from performance in public examinations through various kinds of graded or modular tests used during the teaching process to the more personal and social attributes of the individual. This chapter will deal with some of the general issues which arise from records of personal achievement with special reference to the personal and social attributes which may be included in them. Chapter 12 will be concerned with other aspects which could also form part of a record: profiled examination results, graded tests and credit accumulation.

Personal and Social Attributes

Various titles have been given to this rather ill-defined area: 'work-related characteristics', 'life and social skills', 'personal characteristics', 'attitudes and relations' and 'affective qualities' to name only the better known. Within them are to be found many diverse 'behaviours': confidence, reliability, co-operation, enterprise ... the list is endless. It is perhaps more meaningful to think of them as those attributes of students, which while properly the concern of formal education are not directly assessed by subject-based examinations or tests.

There is nothing new, of course, in reporting these personal attributes. School reports (Goacher and Reid, 1983) have a long history and have always made statements, usually in well-worn clichés about 'effort' and 'conduct' and 'extracurricular activities'. Writing a multitude of reports continues to be a hurried end-of-term chore for jaded teachers. (Do headteachers still sign them all and maybe add a phrase of exhortation to that of a particular worthy or unworthy individual?) And no doubt parents still ponder on the subtle differences between 'B for effort' and 'C for achievement', and read far more into the clichés than the harassed teachers ever intended.

More seriously, there are the *confidential* reports and references. These may range from the semi-formal reports on the personal attributes of applicants for university places to the written reference, or even telephone call, from teacher to employer or tutor about an individual student. These hidden value judgements by individuals about individuals to individuals is the ultimate in subjective and specific reporting of achievement and characteristics of students (and later in life of employees). It is the subsoil of assessment lying hidden beneath the topsoil of the examination results. It has a powerful, and often decisive, function in the allocation of people to their future education and work. It is informal and non-standardized, and by its very nature impervious to research. Its existence is a tacit recognition of the limitations of public examinations. It has its own fineness of grading and subtlety of language (did anyone ever accept, or even interview, a candidate whose bland reference ended with 'X is worth an interview'?).

It is tempting to dwell on the ancient secret garden of the confidential reference. It has been the cause of advancement of many a worthy student whose only published achievement was a '3rd'; and no doubt it has prevented the unsuitable employment of others with a brilliant '1st'. But my immediate purpose is to describe and discuss more formal and overt attempts to make good the deficiencies of traditional examinations by means of records of personal and social attributes, particularly at the time of the statutory age of leaving school.

The need for a record of educational achievement wider than examination results, more open than the confidential reference, and more standardized and carefully prepared than the school report has long been recognized.[1] There has been plenty of talk; the Royal Society, no less, has recently weighed in:

> There is also a widespread feeling that undue emphasis on such paper qualifications tends to obscure the value of truthful recording of other valuable qualities such as honesty, perseverance and common sense. (One employer produced quite persuasive arguments for regarding personal cleanliness as the most useful single criterion for certain jobs.) (Royal Society, 1982, p. 43)

Action, however, has been slow to follow and even now in Britain has not got beyond experimental projects and reviews of present practice. Yet the need seems so obvious. Though an increasing proportion of school-leavers take public examinations, there are many who do not and more who have little or no success to demonstrate when they do. Even those who do well in examinations must be aware that their certificates are inadequate statements of what kind of people they are and of what they are capable in different circumstances.

One of the first positive moves came from Scotland (Scottish Council for Research in Education, 1977) with a trendsetting project in a small number of schools in 1974. Since then there have been reports of individual initiatives (Burgess and Adams, 1980) and Balogh (1982) reviewed the experience of those schools in England which had attempted some form of record of personal achievement. Goacher (1983a) reports a rather hurried project for school-leavers mounted by the Schools Council. In further education there is considerable interest in records of personal achievements for students who have studied for one year after the statutory end of compulsory schooling; this has been reviewed in 1982 by the Further Education Curriculum Review and Development

Unit (1982). There are also initiatives overseas, for example, by the Education Department of South Australia (1981).

Perhaps most significantly, the public examination boards are beginning to show an interest in radical alternatives to traditional examinations. The Oxford Delegacy[2] has made one of the first moves towards establishing such an alternative on a large scale. Much of the other work which has been done has been fragmentary and on a small scale. There is, however, sufficient evidence to allow a disinterested commentary on some of the fundamental issues. Indeed, it would be as well if these issues were discussed and resolved nationally before hasty judgements are made and the issues lost in details of organization and administration. The elements of the discussion should be the same as those which have formed the basis of the commentary on traditional examinations in this book: why? – what? – who? – how?, and to what effect?

Why?

The negative reasons for introducing a record of personal achievement have been the subject of the early part of this chapter: the inadequacies of the present examination system on three main counts: the limited range of achievements reported; the limiting effect on the curriculum; and the limited group of young people who actually derive benefit from them. The view is now widely held, rightly or wrongly, that examinations can go no further in their original functions of widening the curriculum and widening life opportunities for young people; and that they now constrain rather than liberate.

But the shortcomings of the present system are insufficient justification for the introduction of a new one. Nor are mere enthusiasm for something new or political prejudgement proper substitutes for reasoned evaluation. But it would be unwise to dismiss records of achievement simply because they are new, or rather because they are purveyed in a new form. So what positive benefits may be expected to give sufficient purpose to the new venture?

The first is as old as examinations themselves: to give advantage to those who at present are disadvantaged; and to allow those who cannot advance through traditional examinations the opportunity to display their merit through other qualities, by different criteria of assessment and by a different kind of report. The realization of such a purpose depends on two things. First, the willingness of those who are in a position to select young people, and to give effect to their advancement, to accept the new reports and act upon them. Secondly, it rests on the ability of those who get low grades in examinations to get high grades in other attributes. The likelihood of these two conditions being met will be discussed later.

The second main purpose is also held in common with traditional examinations: to use the record of achievement as a formative influence on the curriculum. This was certainly successful in the case of examinations; too successful, indeed improper, in many people's view. But perhaps those who seek radical curriculum reform through the growth of personal and social education might be prepared to swallow the dictum that the curriculum should come first if it could be demonstrated that the new forms of assessment brought about the changes which they seek.

The third reason is that records of personal achievement could be used to motivate students. In this, examinations have been a powerful agent and teachers' reluctance to abandon this carrot-cum-stick has already been noted. Would a record of attributes of personal and social behaviour be equally effective? At first sight it is tempting to think so. If young people know that their punctuality, attitude to discipline, perseverance, and so on, are to be recorded and publicly reported, would they not more readily become punctual, disciplined, persevering, and so on? There is little evidence one way or the other; but if it worked with academic examinations, would it not work with more personal reports? The answer is by no means certain.

There is a fourth purpose which is not held in common with the public examinations: records of personal achievement could be used to guide students towards the best courses of action throughout their time in schools and colleges? This points to an uncertainty at present apparent among those who are developing these new systems of assessment: whether the records are to serve as certificates for use at the *end* of a period of education or to serve as diagnostic tools for guidance *during* a period of education.[3] This, however, is related to two other questions: who should assemble the record, and who should use it?

Who?

Although it may seem obvious that teachers should do the assessing, recording and reporting, in practice it is not so simple. The source of the information on the record can range from the students alone, through joint teacher – student consultation to a record compiled solely by teachers.

It has been noted earlier that control of traditional examinations may range from control by individual teachers or schools to a single external system; and that in Britain a compromise between the two is now common practice. In all the research and development on examinations in the past two decades, however, the direct involvement of students in their own assessment has been negligible. Yet there is nothing to justify the assumption that those who are taught are any less honest and reliable in their own assessment than are those who teach them. Admittedly self-perception by the young may be distorted – usually in underestimating rather than overestimating their own ability – but this is often the result of insensitive, misinformed attitudes of parents and teachers. One does not have to work for very long with young people without coming to realize that often they are a good deal more honest about themselves than are many of their elders; self-deception is an adult trait: 'People see in their own record a statement of their own identity and they do not want this to be untrue' (Burgess and Adams, 1980, p. 44). The 'people' here are schoolchildren in a project on personally compiled records reported by Stansbury.

It may be that for reporting intellectual performance externally devised tests are the most appropriate. But for attributes of personality and attitudes to people, work and social institutions, and the whole range of characteristics which go to making a whole person, teachers – still less public examination boards – may be less reliable assessors of a student's worth than the students themselves. After all, we usually accept the curriculum vitae of adults without question and the self-evaluation of young and old during interview, why not a record of personal experience written by the young?

The evidence reported so far does not show total confidence in teachers' ability to assess activities and attributes of a more personal nature. In any event, those attributes are being manifested in the somewhat artificial social atmosphere of a school. Goacher (1983a, p. 35) reports a telling remark of a pupil on reading his record of achievement: 'This is not really a view of us as human beings but as school children.' What the young people do in school may be the lesser part of their lives.

Perhaps the most sensible way forward would be a compromise in which the report would be a matter for negotiation between teacher and student. This would help at least to prevent gross omission or inaccuracy. Given the present workload in schools, however, the prospect of such negotiations with a large number of assertive teenagers is a daunting prospect for teachers; it could become a battle of wills for changes in both directions.

The question of *who should be assessed* seems to have been resolved already. Although in the early years of development these records of achievement were seen as relevant only to those who had not got significant examination results to show, it now seems generally agreed that if applied to one student they should be applied to all:

> a document issued to a limited target group assists in the perpetuation of labelling of the less able. It may well limit pupil chances rather than enhance them. (Goacher, 1983a, p. 50)

So much for who should write the reports; the issue of who should receive and use them is no less fraught with problems. There are several groups of recipients ranging on a scale of openness of access from the individual students alone to the world at large. Which is the most appropriate depends on the prime purpose of the record. If the sole purpose is to motivate and guide students, then no one else need see it; although if the student has written it himself, little point would be served. More realistically it could be open to students, parents and anyone on the staff with a legitimate interest in it. More contentiously it could be denied to students and parents and restricted to staff. An extension of the secret report would be to allow access to employers and further educators; this is similar to the present situation in university applications.[4] Or it could be open to all, with the possible variation of the students being allowed the right to withhold it if they wished.

Where on this scale of openness access to a record of achievement should lie depends ultimately on its purpose. If it is primarily to diagnose and guide students to the most appropriate activities within the school, then there is no reason why anyone outside the school, other than parents, should have it. If, on the other hand, it is primarily a terminal report designed to improve the information available to prospective educators or employers, then access could either be totally open or available only to those who will use it to select or reject (which excludes the student). The parallel with the conflicting purposes of traditional examinations is close: either to improve the educational process or to improve the selection process. One anticipates that the issue will be blurred as it is in the present examination system. Instead of deciding which purpose should dominate, the best of both worlds will be attempted. The debate on records of achievement within the world of education is only just beginning, but uncertainty on this crucial issue is already apparent. Until it is resolved little useful progress will be made because on the definition of purpose hangs not only the question of *who* should have and use records of personal achievement, but *what* should go into them.

What?

Inevitably the development work on records of achievement has concentrated on those attributes which are not directly assessed in traditional examinations. Whether or not examination results, as now reported, are included in the records is not important; the attainment or lack of examination success will be evident anyway. This does not preclude the reporting of achievement in traditional examinations in a different and more informative manner; that possibility is discussed in Chapter 12.

The 'profile' published by the Scottish Council for Research in Education (1977) after several changes during the trials, has three main sections: 'Basic skills', 'Performance' and 'Work related characteristics'. Each is further divided: basic skills are specified as oral, written, graphic, aesthetic (one wonders what constitutes aesthetic skill), numerical, physical co-ordination and dexterity. Performance is concerned with the more traditional subject learning, but recorded in terms of general skills:

knowledge, reasoning and creativity, together with a composite grade embracing all three. Work-related characteristics comprised perseverance, enterprise, carefulness, interest, reliability, confidence, social competence and leadership. The Scottish profile is mentioned simply because it was one of the first to be published, and although others are different in detail, it is typical of what is being attempted. Some common characteristics are evident among them all.

The first is the *personal* nature of many of the attributes which are assessed and reported. The Inner London Education Authority (1982) has suggested eight elements for personal assessment: confidence, initiative, reliability, co-operation with staff, sociability with peers, punctuality, attendance and health. It is quite likely that some of these have a bearing on examination performance; anyone who lacks confidence, does not co-operate with staff, plays truant, or has bad health is not likely to do well in traditional examinations. Society has come to accept the publication of individuals' academic success or failure; the more personal attributes exemplified above could be thought to be a more private matter.

A second characteristic is the *fineness of division* of what is assessed, both at the specification and reporting stages. Some of the specifications and reports of records of achievements make the most complex examination specifications look simple. Unlike examinations, these divisions are carried to the reporting stage. It follows that those who may use the records are confronted not with one grade, but with many – hence the term 'profile'.[5] It has been said with some justification that the single-grade method of reporting examination results hides the finer elements of performance. Records of achievement, on the face of it, may provide much more detail at the price of much more confusion.

The last point raises another: how real are the more personal categories which the records of achievement claim to report? There has been much criticism of examination specifications (see Chapter 4) on the grounds of the artificiality of both of their dimensions: the classification of subjects, and the generalized abilities. Little has been heard yet of the same kind of criticism levelled at the nature of the personal characteristics which make up part of records of achievement. When the early waves of enthusiasm are spent, no doubt these categories will be subject to the same kind of critical analysis. Meanwhile it is assumed that such things as perseverance, initiative and creativity are real, separable and assessable entities. Some clearly defy definition: 'How honest is "honest"? Hands in a fiver, pockets 50p?' (Balogh, 1982, p. 26).

The third aspect of much of the subject-matter of records is its dependence on its *context*. Someone who is unco-operative with staff in school will not necessarily be unco-operative in business. That kind of extrapolation would be every bit as dangerous as that which assumes that those with the best A levels will make the best doctors.

The complexity and lack of definition of some of the things assessed and reported in records of achievement, and their dependence on behaviours manifested in the somewhat unreal environment of educational institutions, must cast doubt on their effectiveness as terminal records. Those produced so far are unlikely to commend themselves to people who have been used to making their first selections on the basis of a set of single examination grades. That in itself is not a reason for abandoning the initiatives, but it should not be overlooked that reports of achievement which do not communicate conveniently and meaningfully will remain still-born.

The problems of complexity, lack of definition and context dependence do not weigh so heavily if the purpose of the record is solely for guidance within the school or college. The house style and implicit meanings would become familiar, forming a useful internal language; its idiosyncrasies would then matter less. A common specification of content and a common terminology, allowing national communication, would be more difficult (see DES, 1983b, p. 45).

How?

For such matters as basic skills and ability in traditional academic subjects, the usual array of techniques applicable to conventional examinations is available to teachers (see Chapter 7). While there may be room for improvement in the use of conventional tests by teachers, there is not much new which can be said about the techniques themselves. The problems associated with records of achievement lie more in the methods of assessment of personal qualities and with the system whereby all the information is recorded, processed and reported.

By what technique(s) does a teacher assess such qualities as sociability with peers or understanding society? No one knows. It is simply assumed that teachers, by observing their students, can become competent to detect and describe or grade that kind of quality. No doubt some standardized, inscriptive tests are available to measure these things, particularly in selection for commercial and industrial posts. But it has not been seriously suggested that teachers should use them, even if suitable tests were available for schools.

So we return to the question, what goes through a teacher's mind when he records an assessment of a personal attribute of a student? Not everyone will hold so sceptical a view as one teacher: 'I think the assessment of things like initiative, potential and level of basic skills are in most cases inaccurate and in some cases sheer fabrication' (Balogh, 1982, p. 26). Nevertheless, it is to be hoped that some day, if formal records of achievement are established, the validity of the techniques will be subjected to as rigorous research as those which have been applied to the traditional examination techniques. The problem of validity (which includes reliability) will not go away even if the present developments in records of achievement come to nothing; we are still left with the uncertain techniques within the confidential reference and the interview which will gain importance if traditional examinations decline.

In the development trials of records of achievement, investigations into techniques have concentrated on the recording and processing aspects rather than on the techniques of the actual assessment itself. All the recent projects report at some length on such matters as how often and in what form the assessments are made and recorded. Readers are referred to the individual projects for the details; I am concerned here with the general issues which arise in all of them.

Foremost is the demand on teachers' time. All teachers at some time have experienced systems of recording marks in tests and producing termly, monthly, or even weekly reports on the students on the basis of our 'markbooks'. This was tedious and time-consuming enough, but it was a routine part of classroom teaching and as nothing compared with some of the more ambitious records of achievement. This is not in itself a reason for abandoning records of achievement. On the contrary, it could be said that teachers' time might be better occupied in giving more attention to these attributes of their students rather than to some of the activities in which at present they engage. But that assumes a substantial shift in the emphasis in the curriculum; a point which will arise later.

The sheer volume of clerical work in maintaining records of achievement must be discouraging (this is still a problem encountered in many of the internally assessed elements of the present examination system). Predictably proponents look to computers for some alleviation of this load. No doubt this would be possible at the price of generating further suspicions about records of achievement. To record an assessment of personal attributes on paper is sufficient in itself to raise opposition; to commit it to tape and electronic processes of storage and retrieval would be to invite still greater, if less rational, resistance.

On this matter there is a significant point, made almost as an aside, in the report on the Scottish 'Pupils in profile' project which included one independent boarding school among the trial schools because of its experience in the field:

> Unlike teachers in many day-schools, these teachers saw their concerns as extending far beyond cognitive development alone and were thus accustomed to writing comprehensive reports on pupils' progress. (Scottish Council for Research in Education, 1977, p. 64)

The point is that if such personal attainments are explicitly or implicitly acknowledged to be part of the work of all members of the institution, then the recording and reporting of them are not likely to be regarded as an unacceptable burden. To make the point even clearer: it is insufficient to have such attainments as part of a school's 'aims and objectives'; unless

they are acted upon and become a reality, records of personal
achievement are not going to be worth much more than the paper (or
tape) on which they are written (or recorded).

Grading. There is one equally significant phrase to be added to the
quotation given in the previous section: 'some feared the dehumanising
effect of numbers.' This brings us to the *form* in which the assessment is
made and the now familiar question: is the bias to be *norm*-referenced or
criterion-referenced? In other words, is the standard to be described in
terms of position in relation to other people or is it to be described in
terms of actual performance? The Scottish project favoured a norm-based
grading system: four grades are awarded in the performance section with
25 per cent of pupils being allocated to each grade. Others have a stronger
bias towards criterion referencing; the City and Guilds of London
Institute designed a profile report for the Youth Opportunities
Programme in which each attribute and level of attainment was described
on the report itself. For example, one trainee's ability to cope with
problems in a work context was described in the following terms:
'Arranged meeting point for a new job and coped with phoning round
when things went wrong' (Further Education Curriculum Review and
Development Unit, 1982, p. 21).

Although the context is different, the problems associated with either
norm referencing or criterion referencing in records of achievement are
essentially the same as in traditional examinations (see Chapter 10). If the
bias is towards norm referencing, the standing of a grade is dependent on
the group of people who are being assessed by the same process. With so
personal an assessment as a record of achievement which may be made on
a single student by a very few teachers in a single institution, the group
which constitutes the standard is not only small, but may bear no
relationship to those in other institutions, still less to any general, national
norms. What, then, is a user of the record to make of statements such as
'student A is in the top 25 per cent of students in language skills'?

The problems associated with criterion-referenced records of achievement in this context are different but no less severe. If the assessor seeks to
describe in qualitative terms what a student has done, there is the
immediate problem of the *amount* of material – not only the amount
recorded, but the amount not recorded. It matters not whether the
assessments are made by teachers of the students themselves or whether
they be biography or autobiography, they will present a formidable
amount of material to the reader. In the event, it is to be feared that the
record will go unread or, at best, undigested.

Then there is the problem of establishing agreed *meanings*. Goacher
(1983a, appendix B) quotes criterion-referenced assessments such as 'has
legible handwriting', 'can write simple sentence', 'can read and understand
a popular newspaper' and 'can use simple punctuation correctly'. All such

statements assume commonly accepted meanings, which is far from being so. How legible is 'legible', how simple is 'simple'? Such criteria are no better or worse than those attached to examination grades, but they do differ in one important respect. Whereas the criteria applied by chief examiners to a traditional examination are applied on a large scale with reasonable uniformity, the criteria on a record of achievement are applied by an individual and will be interpreted by an individual; the scope for subjective divergence of meaning is great.

Sins of omission.   There are those selectors who read curricula vitae not so much to seek what is there, but what is not there. What is left out of a record of achievement may be thought to be more significant than what is put in. This has concerned developers of records of achievement since their inception. The general feeling is that records should contain only 'positive' statements, not 'negative' ones. Disregarding the misuse of the terms (to say that someone is dishonest is a very positive statement), such a policy could well undermine records of achievement. Suppose, for example, that a record makes no statement about the ability to 'read a popular newspaper'. Does this mean that the student never reads newspapers or only reads unpopular newspapers or that such a statement has been deliberately left out as a matter of policy? If there is no statement about a student's enterprise, is the reader to assume that he is unenterprising?

To What Effect?

It is too early to judge the effectiveness of records of achievement; those in use are wide in scope but small in scale. It would be prudent, however, to anticipate some of their strengths and weaknesses.[6] Effectiveness must be judged against purpose. Three purposes have been discerned: guidance and motivation for students and their teachers through their progress within an educational institution; information for those who will select students for future activities; and a formative influence on the curriculum.

The first of these lies outside the scope of this book since it does not fall directly within the scope of public examinations as we know them at present. In passing, however, one can see many advantages in a comprehensive record of progress, particularly if it were to involve discussion between staff and students; both could come to know each other better and more constructively. This is a matter for individual institutions and it is encouraging to see so many projects in this field. But a record for public use is another matter; that has to be judged by its usefulness and acceptability by society at large.

Seen as instruments to ameliorate disadvantage, I fear that they may prove to be neither effective nor equitable. They could, of course, record the disadvantage itself and leave it to the users to exercise positive discrimination and compensate for lower performance. Against this must be set the reluctance some may have to the publication on a formal document the fact that the disadvantaged are in a particular ethnic group, come from a broken home, or are working class. Similarly, those who are advantaged may not wish to have the fact recorded lest they are subject to negative discrimination from selectors who seek to help the disadvantaged. The complexity of the social and ethical and even the legal aspects is self-evident.

It has been argued that the disadvantaged could still gain from a record of achievement since they could demonstrate attributes which lie outside the scope of public examinations. The point has already been made that this assumes that non-examined attributes are in inverse relation to examined attributes. If this is *not* so, if records of achievement simply allow successful examinees to demonstrate that they are good at a whole range of other things, then records of achievement may simply accelerate the polarization of society into the successful and the unsuccessful.

So the deliberate use of records of achievement to achieve the sort of social mobility which follows from traditional examinations may prove to be less effective than their champions anticipate and, moreover, give rise to some unexpected and unwanted side-effects. That apart, there may be still good reason for publishing comprehensive records of achievement. The limitations of the attributes which are assessed and reported by examinations have been reiterated throughout this book; examinations report only a fragment of worthwhile human activity. Consequently, if the need for a more comprehensive report is self-evident, is this not a case for records of achievement on a national scale?

That question gives rise to two more: is the record to be open or confidential, and is the record to be nationally standardized? To the first there can surely be only one answer: in a free society it must be open; we have sufficient confidential reports as it is. The answer to the second is less obvious. At first sight a standardized report with national validity would appear to be desirable. The headteachers who initiated the 'Pupils in profile' project seem to have had this in mind:

> We believe that all pupils should be offered a documentary record at the completion of their secondary schooling. This record should be a balanced account of the pupils' attainments, interests and aspirations. The document should be externally validated ... As head teachers we wish to make it clear that parents and others are at least getting their money's worth. (Scottish Council for Research in Education, 1977, p. 28)

The two pertinent phrases are 'getting their money's worth' and 'externally validated'. It is understandable that those working in educational institutions should wish to render an account of their stewardship in coin other than examination results. Even if one takes the narrow view that the prime function of education is to advance vocational prospects, it has to be recognized that the ability to do well in examinations is only one among many which contribute to that end. It follows that in terms of vocational training alone, a wider account of personal achievement is necessary. The problem lies not so much in the desirability of such an account, but in the consequences if the reports are adverse. There is already a tendency to judge a school bad if the examination results of its pupils are bad. Suppose the nationally validated reports of personal achievement are equally bad, what then? 'Getting their money's worth' in parents' eyes may mean the production of paragons of all the skills and virtues; in effect they may have to settle for a school saying that we have tried to achieve those things but your child does not meet the 'standards' in any of them. (They could sometimes add, 'and it's your fault, not ours'.)

The concept of national validation is, in the strict sense of standards, utopian. The point has been made in earlier chapters that the more an assessment system is divided, the more difficult it is to attain comparability between the parts. Records of personal achievement constitute a further division right down to the individual. The idea that a formally constituted national or even regional body could validate the records, in the same sense that examinations are validated, is not worth pursuing. It could be argued that validation should amount to no more than agreement to use a common design for the reports. That implies agreement not on standards of assessment, but what should be assessed, how it should be assessed and in what form it should be reported. That has already been attempted and several of the projects in this field have reported the difficulty in reaching agreement on these elements of design even within a school, let alone nationally (Goacher, 1983a). A national system of records of personal achievement could be imposed if consensus proves impossible; but to pretend that the standards of achievement could be effectively moderated to give them national currency would be no more than self-deception.

Whether reports of personal achievement are adopted by agreement or imposition is not my immediate concern. What is important is whether the assessment of young people should move beyond the narrow range of examination skills to much wider attributes. The question is fundamental because it is a question directed not so much to the purposes of examinations, but to the purposes of formal education. The latter is not a question to which I can presume to provide an answer; but one comment is perhaps allowed.

The formative influence of examinations on the curriculum of educational institutions has been assumed rather than proved. It has to be admitted that in their early years examinations were deliberately used to change and control the curriculum. More recently, however, the teaching profession has not wholeheartedly accepted opportunities to break free from this formative influence (see Chapter 2). Could it be that the academic study of subjects is what most teachers and most educational institutions are best fitted to do. Let us forget for a moment the chicken-and-egg question as to which came first. The fact is that the curriculum and examinations are closely matched and the ties which bind them have proved difficult to loosen. This being so, cause and effect are not easily determined. It seems that the two perpetually reinforce each other.

If, then, teachers and the curriculum aim at so narrow a target, it is small wonder that they find difficulty when the target shifts and widens to records of personal achievement. Goacher makes the point:

> It was clear that in many schools the curriculum did not pay attention to the development and practice of a whole range of skills – cognitive, practical, individual and social – about which the record was intended to offer evidence. (ibid., p. 55)

This is perhaps a little hard; schools *do* have wider aims than examination results. But the message is clear: if records of personal achievement are to encompass the many human attributes which the present examination system does not, the curriculum – and those who operate it – must be directed more firmly to non-academic outcomes.[7] There is nothing new in this. Reference has already been made in this chapter to one school in the Scottish project which took such aims and reports as a matter of course; and in earlier chapters there is reference to the non-academic avenues to success in the nineteenth-century public schools.

There appears to be a simple way forward: reinforce a change in curriculum direction by instituting a formal system of assessing and reporting personal and social attributes. It was in this way that the curriculum in schools was redirected in the nineteenth century and nepotism and patronage weakened as a consequence. Thus it may be argued that the reinforcing bond between the academic, subject-based curriculum and examinations could be weakened if not broken.

It is a dangerous remedy. By and large there is agreement as to what should constitute an education in, say, French and physics and most other subjects. Examinations can reinforce that agreement. Lack of total agreement does not matter greatly, there may be marginal differences between one physics course and another but they will make little difference to a student's subsequent career. It is not so with personal and social attributes. There are acute differences of view on such matters as leadership, independence and persistence not only in the value to be placed on the concepts themselves, but in the context in which they should be exercised. It is not difficult to decide appropriate standards in mathematics; it is a different matter to determine standards of the more personal qualities which may be assessed in records of personal achievement. Such a prospect behoves the enthusiasts to display caution.

Notes: Chapter 11

1 Balogh, 1982, refers back to the Norwood Report (1943) and the Beloe Report (1960).

2 At the time of writing the Oxford Delegacy has established a research and development project in conjunction with some local education authorities with a view to establishing the Oxford Certificate of Educational Achievement (OCEA). Three components of the certificate are contemplated: P-component, pupil record or report; E-component, external examinations; and G-component, graded assessment: OCEA *Newsletter*, no. 2, July 1983.

3 Goacher, 1983a, p. 15, puts the issue starkly: 'Technically, these two approaches represent the divide between the formative mode of assessment, where the collection and collation of information is directed towards pupil self-knowledge and reorientation, and the summative mode, where accuracy and precision dominate and "no change" in pupil performance is implicit.'

4 It may be more difficult to maintain this kind of confidentiality in the years to come. The Data Protection Bill at present (1984) under discussion has some profound implications for access to personal information, particularly if it is to be electronically stored and retrieved.

5 The City and Guilds Profile Record for the 365 vocational course – Further Education Curriculum Review and Development Unit, 1982, pp. 35–9 – reports in twenty categories, the SCRE profile – Scottish Council for Research in Education, 1977, pp. 53–5 – in twenty-four and the ILEA Report Form Set A – ILEA, 1982, pp. 4–7 – in many more.

6 For a critical analysis, more detailed than is possible here, see Stevenson, 1983.

7 Raven, 1980, p. 109, refers to these non-academic attributes as 'competency': 'The key shift which is required in education – and in educational assessment – is, therefore, from a focus on content to a focus on competency.'

12

New Ventures: II Profiles, Graded Tests, Credit Accumulation

Chapter 11 explored the possibility of including personal and social attributes as a part of a record of personal achievement, thus contributing to a more comprehensive account of the outcomes of formal education. The record of personal achievement is seen as being more detailed, more specific and more wide-ranging than the record of scholastic attainment provided by subject-based examinations. The record of personal achievement could include examination results, but they normally consist of a single grade awarded at the end of a course of study and often at the end of formal education itself. As such, examination grades conceal far more of an individual's achievement than they reveal.

The purpose of this chapter is to comment on those new ventures which seek to make reports of *academic* achievement more informative. The term 'academic' is used in its widest sense to include all aspects of formal learning other than the more personal attributes mentioned in Chapter 11. There are some areas such as physical, artistic, moral and religious education which sit rather uneasily between the academic and the personal. But these too could be included; indeed, anything which is to be found in examination syllabuses could be called academic and classified in terms of the conventional pattern of subjects. Other forms of classification have been tried; for example, in terms of 'basic skills' which may be thought to operate across the whole curriculum: 'A series of tools which a pupil carries from activity to activity, more or less equally' (Scottish Council for Research in Education, 1977, p. 53).

The recent attempts to make records of academic achievement more informative have at least one and usually more of the following characteristics:

(1) They are much more fragmented than the customary examination results.
(2) The *modules* or subdivisions of the subject-matter as well as being more finely divided are to some extent self-contained.
(3) The modules are more homogeneous; that is, the difference between the activities *within* them is less than the difference *between* them.

(4) Because each module is smaller and more homogeneous, more precise statements about the nature of the attainment can be made in each than can be made in a single terminal examination grade.

(5) The modules may be taught sequentially, so that achievement can be reported during the course of study, not only at the end.

There is considerable confusion of nomenclature in the many assessment projects in this area. Nevertheless, three kinds of assessment, although not totally distinct, can be perceived: profile reporting of examination results; graded tests; and credit accumulation. And running through them all is the common trend towards criterion referencing.

Profile Reporting of Examination Results

Harrison (1983, p. 11) has surveyed and commented on recent work and summarizes its aims thus: 'How the results of public examinations ... might be presented in greater detail than they are at present so as to provide more information about different kinds of achievement within a subject.' It has already been noted (Chapter 10) that since examination grades are determined from a total mark which is the sum of the marks on the various parts, a particular grade can be achieved in many different ways. This is one of the main reasons why it is so difficult to describe what performance an examination grade actually represents. The purpose of profiling, therefore, is to identify the main performances within an examination and report each separately.

The logic appears to be unassailable; the practice is more dubious. The problems rest in:

(1) The identification of desirable performances; that is, the difficulty of criterion referencing.

(2) The isolation of each performance to an identifiable part of the examination; that is, the difficulty of making each part homogeneous.

(3) The confidence that can be placed in the mark or grade awarded to each part; that is, their reliability.

(4) The relation between the marks or grades in the various parts and a statement of a single total grade.

(5) The more practical difficulties which arise from the increased complexity of processing and reporting.

The making of finer divisions within subjects is certainly possible and has been practised both in teaching and examining. Heat, light and electricity have long been familiar divisions in physics; reading, writing, speaking and listening in second languages; language and literature in first languages; and physical, organic and inorganic chemistry. Such divisions appear to be part of the natural structure of the subjects. Many practitioners, however, would oppose this fragmentation on the grounds that the interdependence of the parts is essential to each subject's coherent identity. Against which could be argued that a system of single-grade reporting allows neglect of one or more essential elements.

If the separate assessment and reporting of the kind of elements listed above were required, there would be little difficulty in devising divisions in the examination to match them; indeed, this is still common practice. In the minds of students and teachers, and often in the textbooks, the differences between the elements are usually clear-cut, and this may well be reflected in the organization of the teaching of each subject. Traditional divisions are not sacrosanct, of course, and many recent curriculum projects have promoted other analyses of the various subjects with at least partial success. In short, if teachers can clearly identify parts of their subjects and teach them separately, and if examiners can equally well identify them and assess them separately, profile reporting of examination results is technically feasible.

Profiling becomes more difficult as the component parts become more abstract, generalized skills such as 'comprehension', 'evaluation' and 'looking for patterns' have become familiar as one dimension of examination specifications (see Chapter 4). Individual questions may be classified according to the kind of skill which they demand as well as their subject content. The point has already been made (Chapter 4) that agreement on classification by general skill is much more difficult to attain than agreement of content classification, and there are very few examinations in which classification of general skills is reflected by allocating each to a separate part of the examination.[1]

There remains the further doubt that these classifications of separate general skills may be more figments of our imagination than distinct entities. Factor analysis, searching for evidence of clearly identifiable skills, points more to a single general ability common to all parts of a subject (Leece, 1974), and even across subjects, as being the determining factor of performance. Harrison (1983, p. 25) goes further: 'Even more unsettling is the suspicion that part of this general factor (sometimes labelled "intelligence") is the ability to tackle tests and examinations successfully.' If this general factor predominates, profiling by specific skills is a dead duck.

It is an unfortunate fact of statistical life that the more a test is divided and consequently the fewer the questions in each part, the less is the confidence one can place on the mark or grade awarded to each part. In short, the reliability of each part is less than that of all the parts combined.[2] While acknowledging that too much emphasis can be placed on the search for reliability, it is debatable whether the public will accept examination grades in a profile which are even less reliable than those already published for whole subjects.

A good deal depends, of course, on the consequences of each test. If it is to be used diagnostically to reveal strengths and weaknesses in a student's work within the normal teaching process, then a finely detailed profile could be used effectively. This is exactly what short classroom tests do; any lack of reliability can be compensated in subsequent tests. In these circumstances the consequences of an untypical low mark in one component of a profile would not be calamitous. On the other hand, if the low mark were typical, the student might profit since the weakness could be remedied. This would not be so if a job or admission to further education hung on prespecified scores in nominated parts of a fine profile. One of the advantages of arriving at a single grade for a whole subject is that it allows *compensation*; a high mark in one part can compensate for a low mark in another. This is especially important if the low mark arises not from a weakness in the candidate, but from the approximate nature of the measure.

The apparently obvious solution would be to report both the grades in each part of the profile and a single grade for the whole subject. This may seem attractive but it brings with it other problems. The contribution of each part score to the order of merit depends not only on the part score itself, but on the distribution of the scores in each part (see Chapter 10). It follows that the overall grade would not necessarily correspond to the simple sum of the parts. One can imagine the flood of complaints with which the examination boards would be inundated when that proved to be so. Alternatives to the simple addition of component marks to determine an overall grade are discussed later in this chapter.

The award and publication of grades in profile form for parts of examination subjects would involve the examination boards in greatly increased work in designing and constructing examinations and at the awarding meetings and in processing results. This is the one time of the year at which the capacity of the boards is fully stretched; the doubling or trebling of the amount of work at that time is not feasible at present, nor is it likely to be feasible unless the timescale and cost were to be greatly increased.

Even if the examination boards could produce reliable profiles, it is by no means certain that the users would use them. The work reported by Harrison (1983) to ascertain employers' opinions points firmly to the view that they were not interested in details of achievement and that global grades were sufficient for their selection procedures. There is no evidence to show that further educators substantially differ in their requirements.

One is forced to the conclusion that the profiling of examination subjects as they stand at present in order to provide a more detailed report of an individual's achievement would be wasted effort. There are two qualifications to be made to that rather abrupt rejection. The present difficulty of identifying the appropriate parts within an examination could be partly overcome if the curriculum and examination were deliberately designed to separate those parts. The second is that if profiles were to be seen as a service to *teachers* rather than employers, the problems of reliability could be largely overcome because the reports would be on groups of students rather than on individuals. This brings us to a discussion on the use of examination profiles as an evaluative instrument for monitoring the curriculum.

Examination Profiles and Curriculum Monitoring

It has always struck me as rather odd that although one of their original purposes was to exercise some influence on the curriculum, examinations have never been used in any objective way to *monitor* and *evaluate* the curriculum or any part of it. Whatever we may think of the subject- and examination-based curriculum which dominates our secondary and tertiary education systems, it has to be recognized as a fact; and its main tangible outcome lies in what the students produce in examinations. Tons of scripts accumulate at examination boards' offices every year, the product of hundreds of thousands of young people at the end of two or more years' work. To what use is the mass of material put? To one use only: to assess, grade and package the same young people for dispatch to various activities or inactivities. After a short interval, the scripts are pulped. It does seem a limited use of such an output. Why cannot the material be used to evaluate not only the candidates, but their curriculum, their examination and – dare one say it – the quality of their teaching?

The idea was put to the test between 1970 and 1973 using the Nuffield A-level chemistry examination as a case study (Leece and Mathews, 1976). This examination was a suitable object for research because the structure of the course and the structure of the examination were closely matched at the design stage in a specification of subject-matter, objectives and teaching–learning activities. Each question could be described in terms of these three dimensions. It proved possible, therefore, to measure the average performance of all candidates in each part of the specification. The result was a profile of performance. It differed from the profiles discussed earlier in this chapter only in the fact that it was a profile of the average performance of *all* candidates, not of specific performance of *individual* candidates.

It would have been possible to have reported a profile for each candidate, but Leece (1974, p. 370) reported: 'the much lower reliabilities of the profile scores is alone sufficient to rule out the accurate reporting of a profile on individual students.' When it comes to an average performance of a large number of candidates, however, the problem of reliability diminishes. If, therefore, the average performance of all candidates on a particular part of the profile is lower than that in other parts, the difference is likely to be significant. When this occurs, one is justified in looking for *causes* of the difference. If this happened in one candidate, it might be assumed that it was caused by lack of ability of the individual in that area. But when it happens in all candidates (on average), then the cause may lie in a poorly designed part of the course or a poorly designed part of the examination or in poor teaching.

The production of a total population profile is largely a statistical process; as such, it will not reveal causes. But it would at least indicate where problems may lie; it could be the first step in the evaluation and improvement of the curriculum, the examination, or the teaching. The average profile performance of all candidates in a subject could be a powerful tool in curriculum monitoring and subsequent development.[3]

A further refinement lies in the possibility of reporting the profile of attainment of subgroups of candidates in various parts of a subject. The division into subgroups could be made by gender, type of school, other subjects taken, and so on. Of more immediate interest is the possibility of producing profiles for *teaching sets*, that is, the average profile performance of all the candidates who have been taught together. This kind of feedback could be valuable to teachers provided that the number of students in the set was large enough to give sufficient reliability to the average marks. It could reveal strengths and weaknesses in the performance of a teacher's *own set of students*. As it stands all that a teacher gets is a general examiner's report aimed at all candidates and usually based on general impressions rather than an objective evaluation such as that described above. Teachers have no means of deducing from a general report whether or not the judgements apply to their own candidates.

It is at this point that the suspicions of teachers may be roused. It is all very well to suggest that a profile of performance by teaching sets could be used by teachers to monitor and possibly modify their own teaching. But they are bound to be apprehensive lest such information be used by others to make judgements on their *teaching* performance. Such fears are understandable but surely not justified. It is already apparent that the overall examination grades of students of particular teachers are significantly higher or lower than those of others; performance is a function of teaching ability as well as learning. This might well be a source of pleasure or anxiety. But surely no teacher should feel unduly threatened or elated if it is revealed that his students on average do well or badly on one *part* of an examination? And let it not be forgotten that profiles of average performance on a national scale could equally well expose examiners to criticism; a bad general performance may arise from bad examining. The matter is too important to go by default solely out of sensitivity to criticism.

In order to be feasible the profile reporting of examination results requires a deliberate restructuring of examinations in each subject into distinct parts, each assessing something of significance (Francis, 1981), together with a matching structure for the teaching of the subject. Neither will be possible without a major reorganization of educational and examination systems. These are necessary requirements for both individual and group profiling and criterion-referenced grades, and the conditions do not hold at present in British secondary education. This is not to say that they could not, and there are developments in train which point in that direction. This brings us to a consideration of graded tests.

Graded Tests

Most examinations report in the form of a single grade at the end of a course of study, they are *terminal*. As a means of producing an order of merit from which various strata of candidates can be selected these terminal, single-grade examinations serve the purpose somewhat crudely but well enough, provided that the users of the results do not wish to know what individual candidates can actually do. If, on the other hand, the selectors do want to know what the candidates can do, the single terminal grade will not tell them. Not only does the single grade conceal actual performance, it allows no statement to be made about the qualities of students who reach a temporary limit of ability or ambition before that terminal point. Such students will have been steered into other channels before the examination, or if allowed to continue to the examination, will fail. Either way they have nothing to show for years of work. Traditional examinations are like a lift going only to the top floor; the movement is continuous, once you are on it, there are no intermediate stops. Graded tests are more like flights of stairs, designed to provide those stops.

In many subjects – although perhaps not all – teaching and learning is also stepwise, sequential and hierarchical, not continuous; it proceeds in quantum leaps from one unit to the next, each subsequent unit building on what has gone before. (It is not my concern to defend this stepwise course structure, simply to note the fact.) When such a system is linked to a single terminal examination, it requires a group of students of fairly uniform ability all capable of reaching the upper levels of terminal performance. Anyone who has taught will know that such uniformity is rare. Either through lack of ability or motivation some students fail to get a final grade of any value; to outward appearances they have learned little or nothing in their previous years' work.

If the appearance of failure is also real, it is a sad commentary on our teaching methods and curriculum organization; years of futile unacknowledged effort by young people is not something in which we should readily acquiesce. Until recently the conventional solution to this problem has been to extend downwards the level of terminal performance for which grade awards are made. In English schools this took the form of providing a lower-level terminal examination, CSE, to provide for those who could not attain the notional passing grade of GCE. But the grades are still single and terminal; the performances for which they are awarded cannot be described; and 'certificate inflation' has ensured that the value of the lower grades approaches zero.

Despite the notional criterion that CSE grade 4 represented the performance of an 'average' pupil, anything below CSE grade 1 or GCE grade C was never highly regarded and is increasingly disregarded. The advent of a single 16+ examination (GCSE) will do nothing to raise the value of these lower grades and the proportion of the school population obtaining the higher grades will remain low. It is not a state of affairs likely to encourage those of modest ability.

The search for alternatives at school level has been vigorously led by teachers of second languages, mainly in French and German. This movement has been more than simply a way of giving some credit to those who cannot or will not attain a worthwhile grade in a school-leaving certificate. Like many other curriculum development projects in the past, one of its mainsprings has been a dissatisfaction not only with the way in which second languages have been examined, but with the kind of teaching which the examinations have encouraged. It is no surprise that this dissatisfaction is intense among modern linguists. In no other subject is the gap between examination competence and real-life competence so evident as it is in the use of a second language – or even a first language for that matter. It is small wonder that many teachers of modern languages have united to develop radically different methods of teaching and assessment. These developments are generally referred to as graded objectives in modern languages (GOML), a survey of which has been published by the Schools Council (Harrison, 1982). They serve as a good example of the general principles of graded tests.

The three main tenets of this development in modern language learning have been set out by Harding *et al.* (1980):

(1) the traditional five-year course to CSE O level should be broken up into a set of shorter-term objectives each one leading to the next and building directly on its predecessor;
(2) objectives should be behavioural, that is, they should be defined in terms of what tasks a candidate would be able to perform;
(3) the graded objectives would not be aimed at a particular age or level of ability.

These principles of graded tests are not the invention of linguists, nor is theirs the sole province. The Associated Board of the Royal School of Music has experience of them going back to the last century, so have several other institutions which have assessed and awarded certificates for artistic, vocational and athletic skills. In the school curriculum, however, the proposals amount to a radical departure from traditional examinations to such a degree that it may be difficult to reconcile the two systems. It is not surprising that Harrison (1982, p. 30) reports: 'The more purist view (among GOML groups) is that the nature of graded tests is such that there can never be any compatibility with the public examination system.' There are other, more pragmatic advocates of graded tests who recognize the entrenched strength of traditional examinations and are prepared to seek a *modus vivendi* with the established system, even at the cost of some compromise of their principles. (In this they follow the practice of predecessors in other curriculum innovations.)

The publicity given to GOML has to some extent obscured the fact that it is only a part of a more general movement which brings into question the traditional view that an examination should be the culmination of a continuous course over a long period of time. Graded objectives and tests are only one way in which teaching and learning can be subdivided into discrete components each tested as if it were a self-contained course of study. 'Credit accumulation' is a related concept because it too implies a modular rather than a continuous growth in attainment. It is possible that the idea of credit accumulation is more generally applicable across the curriculum than the more closely defined graded tests. A more detailed study of credit accumulation, therefore, might serve to raise some more general issues, particularly those of curriculum organization and criterion referencing.

Credit Accumulation

The idea of accumulation of credits in discrete modules rather than a single terminal assessment stems, in part, from the first principle of GOML. The obvious limitation of its application is that the nature of some subjects is not in the form of a hierarchical sequence of modules each dependent on the mastery of its predecessor. Some teachers of language may find such a structure is best for their purpose; but it is still not generally accepted by all teachers of language, nor is there anything like general agreement on the substance of each module even among the converted (Harrison, 1982, ch. 5). This is simply a reflection of the particularized, independent and local development of the various schemes which allow small groups of teachers to follow what they have found to be good practice.

It should be recognized, however, that graded objectives linked to graded tests are simply one form of modular curriculum organization. At its simplest this means that a course of study is divided into pieces which, although not totally independent one from another, may be taught largely as self-contained units. It follows that attainment in each module may be assessed by equally self-contained tests.

The graded objective projects, with their associated graded tests, are a special case of the wider concept of modular curriculum. They are special by virtue of the relationship between the elements of modules. The principal feature of their relationship is hierarchical: a prescribed attainment in one is necessary before going on to the next. This relationship necessarily requires a fixed sequence of modules, both for testing and teaching. It could also be described in terms of increasing difficulty or complexity. This gives the award of grades a special logic: the successful completion of a module will indicate a higher attainment than those preceding it, hence the grade attached to it will have greater value. Equally logical would be the award of a still higher grade to the attainment of a subsequent module.

It is not difficult to perceive a workable relation between this ladder-like award of grades with the present examination system. If, for example, there were seven steps in the graded tests and seven grades in the terminal examination system, the highest-graded test achieved could be taken to correspond to the corresponding grade in the terminal examination results.[4]

A similar hierarchical relationship could be devised in other areas, mathematics, science and music, for example, in which an ascending sequence of teaching and testing modules would be feasible. Whether such a relationship would be generally acceptable is another matter. It would, for example, be at variance with much of the work in integrated science in which the links between the units are more like a net than a ladder. The same could be said for much project- and problem-based curriculum designs. But it does not follow that simply because the teaching and learning of other subjects is not as clearly ladder-like as it is in languages, a cumulative, modular form of testing is not possible. There can be few, if any, educational activities which are not subdivided into reasonably self-contained units taught in sequence. No subject is so coherent and integrated that it is impossible to distinguish different elements within it each of which could constitute a module with a discernible beginning and end and studied over an appreciable period of time. The relation between the elements may not be strictly hierarchical; nevertheless, there may be a degree of accumulation and increasing complexity or depth of work. A module successfully studied in, say, English literature or religious studies in year 5 of a course is likely to demonstrate greater perception and knowledge than one studied in year 3; it follows that it should carry greater weight.

Are not, it may be argued, many traditional examinations modular in the sense that they comprise several discrete parts? In Chapter 5 there is a discussion of the various ways in which the whole may be divided into its constituent parts both in design and in operation. There are, however, essential differences between this kind of division and that which operates in systems of credit accumulation. For instance, credit accumulation presupposes that the credits for performance in the various modules can be held accumulating over a period of time, perhaps for two or more years, before they are put together to award a composite grade and certificate; whereas in traditional examinations performance in the various parts is usually assessed at the same time at the end of the course of study. Even when one of the components consists of coursework marked earlier, it is usually regarded as a terminal mark and considered at the end of the course as if it denoted a terminal performance.

There is another difference. The marks awarded to parts of a traditional examination are usually added together and the decision on the final grade to be awarded is made on the aggregate marks. When this is done, the relative marks in each part lose whatever significance of performance they may have had: the attainment of a very high or a very low mark in any part is not reported separately and the final grade may hide an outstandingly good or bad performance in one or more of them; whereas in a credit accumulation system the grade or mark in each module may be reported separately and the overall grade, if one is to be awarded, may be determined by other processes than the simple aggregation of marks. It is common practice in credit accumulation to report both the overall grade and the grades in the contributing modules.

There are some credit accumulation systems in operation, although not usually in school examinations. The Open University operates credit accumulation for the award of degrees. Many universities determine the class of their first degrees by methods other than the simple aggregation of marks. Most first-degree awards, however, do not exhibit the other necessary characteristics of credit accumulation, the longer period of time over which the credits can be acquired and the separate publication of grades in the separate modules. There are an increasing number of 'open colleges' which use credit accumulation.[5] These colleges provide an alternative qualification to the GCE for entry to higher education.

The introduction of a system of credit accumulation into schools is likely to prove more difficult. Both the Open University and open college systems require a good deal of independent study and the sequence and organization between modules are not subject to the severe constraints of timetabling within a school. Also the modular system within both is coarse, that is, the number of modules to be organized is small, no more than the number of subjects normally taken in school examinations at the age of 16. In this sense it is not significantly different from the old grouped School Certificate. The main difference rests, therefore, on independent study and credit accumulation over time rather than on the modular aspect. Any attempt to subdivide school subjects into finer modules, and to allow the accumulation of credits at the sub-subject level, will require a much more complex organization of both the curriculum and the examinations. An example may help to reinforce this point.

It is conceivable that students of each subject at GCE A level could study six modules spread over the normal two years of study between the ages of 16 and 18. A subject could offer more than six modules. There could be, for example, a core of three or four basic modules accompanied by an array of optional modules from which two or three are chosen.[6]

Each module could span one term because the present terminal examination at the end of the second year would not be necessary, thus allowing six full terms of study rather than the present five. There are several ways in which these modules could be assessed; the following hypothetical plan is only one among many.

Each module would be taught over one term. (The actual number of teaching hours would depend on the nature of the subject.)

Year 2 modules would be at a higher level than those in year 1 ('higher level' is a vague concept, in this context it could be taken to mean more difficult than year 1 and closer to work in higher education). Performance in each module would be graded as pass or fail. (Grading could be finer, on a five-point scale, for example; this, however, would greatly increase the complexity of the assessment within each module and overall.)

Successful completion of a module would be more closely criterion-referenced, so a pass could be equated with competence in a specified performance. It follows that the pass mark would be near to the top of whatever scale was used. For example, if assessment were by objective test, the pass score is likely to be nearer 80 than 40 per cent.

The results could be reported both as a single grade (as required at present) or as a profile of performance in each module separately or both.

Overall performance would not be assessed from the aggregate of the marks for each module.

Given those assumptions, rules for the award of an overall grade could be set out as follows (other sets of rules could be formulated equally well, these serve as only one example):

Grade A – pass in at least five modules, including all three at level 2.
Grade B – *either* pass in four modules including all three at level 2 *or* pass in five modules including all three at level 1.
Grade C – pass in four modules.
Grade D – pass in three modules including at least one at level 2.
Grade E – pass in two modules including at least one at level 2.
Grade O – (corresponding to O level) pass in two modules at level 1.

The rules may be set out as diagrams (see Figure 12.1).

The required performances could be more closely specified by nominating particular modules as essential. In the example given in the figure the two asterisks could denote a common core of modules, comprising necessary elements of a subject, without the successful completion of which an overall passing grade would not be awarded.[7] The apparent neatness of the diagrams should not be allowed to conceal the

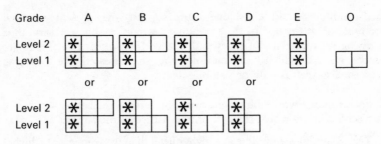

Figure 12.1

complexity of this example of a modular system and the radical changes which it would require in the procedures of schools and examining boards.

Some Problems

Perhaps the most obvious problem is the need to reorganize the curriculum into six self-contained packages each of the same duration. This is likely to require a complete restructuring of teaching schemes; and it may (but not necessarily) require changes in substance as well. To match the new teaching structure examination material would have to be similarly restructured.

If all the modules were to contain an element of external assessment, examinations would have to be organized three times a year. It is inconceivable that this could be done on the same scale as our present annual examinations. (It would, however, eliminate the need for 'mock' examinations and special 'resit' examinations.) The sum of the previous points is that the relation between examination and curriculum will be more rigid than it is at present.

If the judgement of performance in each module were to be pass or fail, the criteria would need to be generally agreed and more clearly identified than they are at present. On the other hand, a normative system of finer grading would add greatly to the complexity of reporting.

It is difficult to see how the accumulation of credits could be allowed over an indefinite timespan within the closely constrained organization of a school timetable. In this sense one of the principal advantages of credit accumulation is lost. A related difficulty arises in the question: 'would six credits acquired over four years be equivalent to the same six acquired over two years?'

Some Advantages

While some teachers may regard with disfavour the closer links between curriculum and examination, others may welcome the opportunity to reconsider the essential structure of their subjects and the nature of the outcomes they wish to achieve. By so doing they may predetermine both the structure of the examination and the criteria for assessment of performance.

The structure and criteria could also form the basis for an examination profile. As well as providing an overall grade, strengths and weaknesses between the modules would be apparent to those who wish to look for finer distinctions between attainments. It does contain some of the characteristics of graded tests, even in this example which envisages only two levels of performance. Students who reached their limits of performance or interest could stop their studies at the end of level 1. In this sense the modular system could be used for guiding students at the end of year 1 in their choice of subsequent courses.

The system would permit greater flexibility in the choice of courses. Students who now take three A-level subjects would study eighteen of these modules. In theory they could pick among the modules to build up a total course of any mixture which suited their interests or needs. Organizationally this is most unlikely. Nevertheless, one can foresee the possibility of building a more varied combination of subjects than at present. Any scheme similar to this one would allow a broadening of the curriculum for individual students while not losing some specialisms.

Various forms of independent study, including the growing number of computer-linked units, would ease the organizational constraints which arise from conventionally taught modules, in which groups of students have to be matched with particular teachers at particular times.

So there is evidence for and against modular systems whether they be in the form of a flexible credit accumulation or in the more rigid and hierarchical form of graded tests. Whatever the system is called, it would involve greater explicit fragmentation of the curriculum and examinations, a more complex system of entry to each part and assessment by criteria of performance in each part rather than by position in an array of total scores. These two aspects, organization and criterion referencing, require a more detailed discussion.

Organizational Problems

One of the features of the organization of the secondary school curriculum is that movement from one part of the curriculum to another is determined by *age*. By and large all students move together each year and the curriculum is organized in steps of one year's duration. One of the effects of the further fragmentation which necessarily follows from any of the schemes discussed in this chapter is that movement from one curriculum stage to the next would be more frequent and would not be dependent on the age of the student. It would be determined by *readiness* as demonstrated by performance in a module of curriculum.

It matters not whether the next step is vertically up a graded test ladder or horizontally on the same level to a module in a different curriculum area; the result would be a great increase in movement. At present the main movement is once a year, possibly followed by allocation to options or sets on the basis of ability or choice. Once the allocation has taken place, it is likely to be fixed for a year. The elements in the organization are teachers, groups of students, modules of curriculum and non-personal resources. The reallocation of those elements on an annual basis manifests itself as a school timetable.

Those who have had to manage this organization and produce an annual timetable will know how complex a business it is, but it is feasible and is now supported by an effective theory of organization.[8] The effect of the introduction of a finer structure of modules and grades, together with the introduction of readiness as the principle for movement, would be to increase the number of organizational dimensions.

Frequency of Movement
Movement would take place at intervals shorter than a year. In the simple example given above the movement would be each term. If the same teacher were involved and the same physical resources, and all the students moved in the same group at the same time to the same subsequent module, there might be little difficulty. But the constancy of none of these factors could be certain in credit accumulation or graded curriculum schemes without undermining the principles on which they are based.

Movement at shorter intervals is only one of the problems; the principle of readiness requires movement of individuals from one age cohort to another. This could take place either up or down and at intervals other than the annual upward movement of each age cohort. The criterion of performance rather than of age to determine movement of students within the curriculum organization of a school is now uncommon in British secondary schools. It *might* be possible to reintroduce it on the ground that educational needs should outweigh organizational simplicity. One cannot imagine it happening as a general principle, however; and to try to mix both performance and age as criteria for movement is likely to result in even greater confusion.

Frequency of Testing
We have grown accustomed to examinations as an annual event, the termination of the academic year when the harvest of certificated students is gathered in. This is not only an administrative convenience; there is the argument that examinations should measure what students know *now*, not what they knew in the earlier parts of a course. There is more to it than that; Chapters 5–7 give some indication of the refinement of organization and scale of administration required to produce our present array of school examinations. To increase the frequency of testing on the same

scale and in the same form would demand an increase in resources for the examination system beyond any possibility of realization.

Access to Tests
Examinations are not available on demand. Schools are *informed* of the annual examination timetable well in advance. The examination boards avoid school and public holidays and some of the greater religious festivals, but the timing is not negotiable; to differ by anything more than one half-hour requires formal approval from the board. To say 'Some of my students are not yet ready to take the examination; may we postpone it by three months?' would be regarded as absurd. The whole system of confidentiality, marking, standardization and awarding would be thrown out of phase, and chaos could ensue. Yet that is what the principle of readiness requires.

Despite the reservations, it would be unduly pessimistic to dismiss these new ventures as organizationally impossible. They *could* be organized given the resources. The use of new forms of computerized testing and processing could help to refine and speed up the examining system. The problem of organizing the modules within the school curriculum is likely to be much more difficult; and there remains the difficulty of managing the flow of individuals or groups of students from one module to another on the principle not of age, but of readiness in terms of a prescribed level of performance. So we are brought back to the idea of performance- or criterion-referenced testing first discussed in Chapter 10.

Criterion-Referenced Examinations

Chapter 10 was concerned with distinguishing between tests which are norm-referenced, primarily intended to put candidates in an order of merit, and criterion-referenced, primarily intended to determine whether candidates have reached a prespecified level of performance. The conclusion reached there was that public examinations (as they are now) do not attach meaningful statements of performance to the grades by which they report the results for the following reasons:

(1) The various performances are not identified with sufficient precision.
(2) Each examination covers a wide range of kinds of performance and hence is not sufficiently homogeneous.
(3) Candidates can achieve the same mark through different performances.
(4) If the examination allows choice, then candidates in effect take different examinations, unless all questions are equivalent which is rarely the case.
(5) Even if the *parts* of an examination are more homogeneous and

exactly specified, the procedure by which all the marks of all the parts are added together to determine a single final grade obscures the more exact statements of performance in each part.

(6)   The marks awarded are not exactly related to levels of performance, thus a candidate who gets 100 per cent does not necessarily perform twice as well as one who gets 50 per cent.

This is not to say that present examinations provide no description of what the candidates can do. Clearly the fact that a candidate has achieved a grade A in French, coupled with a knowledge of the syllabus and examination design in French, is some indication of what the candidate can do; and it is different from what a candidate with a grade A in, say, physics can do. There is also crude quantitative information in the sense that it can be assumed, although not with absolute confidence, that someone with a grade C performs at a lower level or knows less than someone with a grade A in the same subject. Of course, that information may be sufficient for the external users of the results. If that is so, the search for a more precise statement of performance serves little purpose except within the educational institution itself. If, on the other hand, a more precise statement *is* required, the new ventures described in this chapter, and to some extent in Chapter 11, may make statements of performance the more feasible. In other words, they may allow a shift towards criterion referencing and away from the present norm-referenced bias. This arises from the following characteristics which the new ventures have in common.

They all involve a division into several parts each to some extent discrete and assessed separately. The curriculum of each part, in terms of subject-matter and skills, can then be made more homogeneous than that normally associated with a single traditional examination. This, in turn, should make it easier to confine and describe the domain of performances to be assessed in each part. Given a relatively simple set of performances, correspondingly it will be easier to define what level of performance constitutes satisfactory completion.

The foregoing suggests conditions which would favour a move towards more strongly criterion-referenced assessment. The smaller the task, the less complex it is; and the greater the agreement on what constitutes success, the greater will be the reliance which can be placed on statements of competence in that task. And if those statements are separately reported, which is usually the case, they do not suffer the disadvantage of being hidden in the aggregation of scores which occurs in traditional examining.

A conversion to modular, more exactly criterion-referenced examinations may appear tempting in the face of the undoubted shortcomings of traditional examinations. Before the bandwagon gathers too much momentum, however, it would be as well to consider some of the consequences. Perhaps foremost among these is the necessary restructuring of the curriculum into modules which match the intervals of assessment. If the examination system were linked to graded tests, this would involve not only the study of the same modules, they would have to be in the same sequence. Furthermore, the substance and objectives in each module would have to be more exactly prescribed than at present. All the tests would have to be common to all candidates and the degree of choice (if any) within them would need to be severely limited. All of this would bring about a much closer correspondence between assessment and curriculum than at present exists. Whether these conditions are imposed nationally or locally, or even within a single institution, matters not; once they have been prescribed, the room for divergence by individual teachers or students would be considerably constrained.

These consequences of more exactly criterion-referenced tests may be welcome in some areas of the curriculum. Subjects which can be neatly divided, in which skills and subject-matter can be generally agreed and in which competence can be more readily identified might well be suitable for such treatment. Mathematics, foreign languages and some of the sciences come immediately to mind. Basic tests for numeracy and literacy are even more likely targets. Even there the problems of organization mentioned earlier in this chapter would still apply. But there will be many other areas in which the resulting uniformity, rigidity and lack of spontaneity would be much less acceptable and even more controversial.

The viability of criterion-referenced public examinations can only be proved one way or the other by a feasibility study. This would need to be both long and costly. It would necessarily involve the dismantling of an existing syllabus and restructuring into distinct, criterion-referenced parts. It would require the redesign and reorganization of the tests, together with the system of awarding and reporting grades of performance. If comparability of standards were to be maintained, the experimental curriculum and examination would have to be run in parallel with a matched control group studying for the traditional examination. It is a daunting (but not inconceivable) prospect.

Notes: Chapter 12

1 The Schools Council Integrated Science Project went a considerable way towards this.
2 Harrison, 1983, pp. 25–6, quotes as an extreme example the School Leaver's Attainment Profile of Numerical Skills (SLAPONS) which consists of eighteen topics with only five questions attached to each; he writes: 'Comparing a pupil's attainments and an employer's demands topic by topic expects too much accuracy of both the test and the job template.'
3 The research on Nuffield A-level chemistry is reported in *School Science Review*, vol. 57, no. 198–9, and vol. 58, no. 203–4. It revealed areas of the curriculum in which the candidates consistently underperformed and subsequent work on the project took note of the fact. To be effective, however, the production of profiles of average performance

would need to be routine and periodical, if not annual; and some of the processes for recording marks would have to be changed.

4   There is an apparently trivial, but potentially difficult, problem in this relationship. Public examination grades are often reported on a scale in which 1 is the highest. The relationship would then be:

published examination grades	1	2	3	4	5	6	7
grade test attained	7	6	5	4	3	2	1

If this state of affairs remained, it carries inherent confusion with it: see Harrison, 1982, pp. 33–4.

5   The open college system of the University of Lancaster – Open College Federation of the North West, 1982 – shows some of the characteristics of credit accumulation at a lower level. Although it is intended for mature students, it provides a qualification for access to higher education; as such, it may be related to the more usual qualifications which lead from school to higher education. Matriculation requires the successful completion of six units: four at the lower-level stage A and two at the higher-level stage B. Stage A units are internally assessed, and stage B units are externally assessed. The accumulation of the necessary credits can take place over a period of five years.

6   It is interesting to note that the inter-board working parties set up in 1980 to identify common-core material in eleven subjects at A level may make a step in this direction. The proposed core syllabus in physics, for example, consists of four sections, with which could be offered a set of options.

7   Of current interest would be the application of such a system to the award of an 'intermediate'-level pass. This could require the successful completion of all three level 1 grades. More recent is the suggestion for an 'advanced supplementary' (AS) level: DES, 1984. Perhaps this could be met by taking three modules specified as grade D in Figure 12.1.

8   The first theoretical work, useful to secondary schools in England and Wales, is contained in Davies, 1969. This has subsequently been modified and improved by the Inspectorate.

13

What of the Future?

In a perfect world, where everyone was self-motivated, where there was no competition, and where it could always be assumed that what was taught was also learned, examinations would probably be superfluous. (Schools Council, 1972, p. 74)

The debate on public examinations in British schools has reached a critical point. The decisions made now and during the next decade will profoundly affect formal education for a long time to come, even if the outcome were to leave things more or less as they are. In this concluding chapter I project the main themes of the preceding chapters in an attempt to perceive a possible state of affairs in the future. I limit the discussion to the compulsory years of secondary schooling since it is this period which has the most formative effect on the majority of young people. It might clarify the discussion briefly to rehearse these main themes.

The two main functions of public examinations, although subject to changes of emphasis and detail, have remained essentially the same since the middle of the nineteenth century: they determine the greater part of the curriculum of secondary schools and the levels of attainment and motivation within it; and they are used to select young people for places of work or other educational institutions. In other words, they maintain or change what goes on in secondary schools and they influence the position of individuals in society: they are prime agents in curriculum and social engineering. The seat of control may be difficult to identify, but the effect is evident. Consequently consideration of the future of the examination system cannot be divorced from wider educational issues in a rapidly changing social context; it ought not to be regarded as self-contained and self-justifying. Tinkering with it will not adequately serve the needs of education in the twenty-first century; radical change is needed and I hope that the suggestions which follow will contribute to a debate in that direction.

Examinations and the Curriculum

Mass public examining is most effective in both its functions when it is associated with a high level of uniformity within schools: uniformity of syllabuses, uniformity of examination technique, uniformity of teaching and uniformity of organization. A fairly constant pattern was maintained until about the middle of this century. Since then there has been a great decline in uniformity. Syllabuses and examinations and examining agencies have multiplied; we have experienced an increase in diversification and fragmentation, a strong move towards the individualization of curricula and examinations, and an increase in the number of occasions and levels at which assessment takes place. From large, unchanging structures of curriculum and examinations we have moved to a dispersion of much smaller, rapidly changing and largely unrelated entities; it has been as if a solid has changed to vapour; or to borrow yet another term from the physical sciences we have experienced a big rise in the level of entropy.

The new ventures described in Chapters 11 and 12 tend to extend this process of diversification still further. If records of personal achievement become biographical, comparability between them of the kinds discussed in Chapter 9 will become impossible; it is difficult enough even under the present system. This leads me to suggest a first law of public examinations:

> For given resources, the common currency of certificates of attainment is inversely proportional to their diversity.

In other words, the price to be paid for personal, individualized assessment is a decline in their usefulness as a *general* standard of qualification for access to employment or education. This is not to say that they could not have a useful *local* standard and serve particular, individual purposes.

It is curious that while this diversification continues a contrary movement is taking place, a movement towards consolidation and uniformity, in which it is suggested that in some areas of the curriculum a common assessment should be applied to as big a proportion of the school population as possible. This contrary movement would involve common syllabuses, common techniques of assessment and common criteria of performance applied nationwide (DES, 1982). 'Back to basics' is perhaps too crude a term to apply to it; nevertheless, it has the clear purpose of encouraging the attainment of a common standard in a basic education by as many young people as possible and the reflection of that standard in the curriculum of schools. The similarity to the use of a grouped school certificate to achieve a similar end is obvious, so is the intention to impose a counterbalance to the potential chaos which could arise from an extremely individualized assessment.

In my view it is the tension between these two apparently opposing movements which should dominate discussion on public examinations. It epitomizes the tension between the so-called 'subject-centred' and 'child-centred' views of education and between uniformity and divergence in the curriculum. Indeed, it is not too fanciful to see it as a microcosm of the political tension between the corporate state and freedom of the individual. As in all such situations, the position of equilibrium between the two shifts according to the prevailing values of those in a position to change it; and the values can be as much political as educational. What is of interest in the field of public examinations in England and Wales at present is that central government appears to be inclined to exercise more authority than hitherto and, somewhat perversely, to pull in both directions at the same time.[1]

So the main thrust of this final chapter is to explore the implications of this tension and the nature of a compromise which would bring these two apparently opposing movements into an equilibrium that is best both for individuals and formal education as a whole. In formal education the issue lies between what should be *prescribed* for all and what should be left to the *choice* of individual students, teachers and educational institutions. In public examinations the issue lies between what should be assessed by *common* criteria determined nationally and what should be assessed by *particular* criteria determined by individuals.

The problem is one of our own making. First, we have come to rely unduly on public examinations to form the curriculum; and secondly, we have tried to bestow status by taking into the field of public examination areas of education which are manifestly unsuited for such treatment. There are many such areas: the arts, religion, morals, and social, environmental and political issues, to which it is improper to apply national standards of performance, except possibly at a very elementary level of basic knowledge. Examination boards have tried to embrace individual curriculum designs, extravagant aims and objectives, expensive and only partially effective moderating procedures, and the assessment of skills self-evidently inappropriate to the inscriptive medium on which public examinations strongly rely. They are even venturing, with some caution it must be admitted, into records of personal achievement. It is surely time to stop the pretence that examination boards can effectively assess everything and to identify those things for which they are best suited.

What Do Examinations Do Best?
The tenor of my argument is that public examination boards have already ventured into unsuitable territory and that they should be wary of further advances; they should get out of the quicksand and back on to rock. I hasten to add that this is in no way a criticism of the new ventures in individualized assessment, nor of the more traditional examinations; still less am I saying that certain heavily examined subjects should dominate the school curriculum. I simply assert that public examination boards as we know them will find it extremely difficult to promote both national standards in the curriculum *and* an individualization of the curriculum; the two functions are distinct and opposing and it is better to keep them

so. The question now arises what is the proper sphere of activity of examination boards; what *do* they do best?

> They operate best under *uniform* conditions rather than *diverse* conditions. It follows that they are more suited to large-scale, standardized assessment than to small-scale, particular assessment.
>
> They are more suited to assess *conforming* responses than *non-conforming* responses. In other words, they are better designed to give credit to predictable behaviour, prescribed by examiners, than to divergent, irregular behaviour on which there is considerable room for difference of opinion.
>
> They assess the *product* of learning rather than the *process* of learning.
>
> They are more suited to the assessment and recording of *intellectual* performance than attributes of *personality*.
>
> They rely mainly on the *inscriptive* medium of communication rather than the oral and the substantive or practical.

These characteristics limit the appropriate use of public examinations, allowing their legitimate function within a national education system to be more clearly defined. They point to a more distinct separation of those parts of the curriculum which are *dependent* on the examination system from those which are *independent*.

The Dependent Curriculum
This brings us back to the question of control, first raised in Chapter 3. To what extent should examinations be controlled at a national level, and to what extent should the school curriculum be determined by externally imposed examinations? This raises the still bigger question of whether central government should exercise any control over the curriculum. It appears to me self-evident that in a democratic society it *should*. It is unreasonable for government to compel all its young people to eleven years of compulsory schooling and, at the same time, reject responsibility for the curriculum to which those citizens are exposed. The question is not whether government *should* exercise control, but to what extent and by what means; in particular, whether some part of the curriculum in the years of compulsory schooling could and should be made dependent on national public examinations. I suggest that such a position can be justified given certain conditions, which would in one way limit the operation of examinations and in another widen their scope.

(1)   The first condition would be adherence to the five characteristics already given which are necessary for the most effective functioning of public examinations. A stricter regard to those characteristics would inevitably restrict the scope of public examinations at the statutory

school-leaving age. It would decrease the number of subjects submitted to examination and the amount of subject-matter within each; it would end the pretence that national standards can be applied to internal and individualized assessment; and it would restrict externally imposed oral and practical examinations to a few essential areas.

(2) The second condition would be the requirement for more definite statements about the actual performances to be attached to examination grades: a move towards a more strongly criterion-referenced awarding process. Given the near impossibility of performance-based grading in certificates which report only single terminal grades, such a move would require fundamental changes to the examining process, involving an expansion of activities which might more than compensate for the loss incurred in the contraction of syllabuses. (This point is taken up later.)

(3) As a consequence of condition 2, examination boards would have to divide their assessment of each subject into discrete parts and operate largely within a modular structure; but not necessarily in a sequential system of graded tests, although such tests would almost certainly be used in some areas. It follows that a further condition would be a profile system of reporting results, and the decline in importance of single terminal grades. Such a change would have far-reaching effects on the way the teaching of some subjects is organized.

(4) Also arising from a move to stronger criterion referencing would be the need for increased access to tests. This is likely to operate in two ways. First, and most certain, is that tests should be available in the years preceding the statutory school-leaving age, linked to some form of credit accumulation. How far back these should go is an open question: for tests of literacy and numeracy, they could well operate four years before the school-leaving age, but in other examined subjects two years might be sufficient. Secondly, if the criterion of performance rather than age is to determine movement from one module to another, it might be necessary to have access to tests at more times during the school year than solely at the end of it.

(5) An increased bias towards a criterion-referenced modular system, with a consequent increase in access to tests, has organizational and financial implications. The two-dimensional expansion within the school year and across the age range would by itself demand an increase in resources beyond the capacity of the present examining boards operating individually in England and Wales for which even a severe curtailment of syllabuses might not compensate.

This raises a contentious organizational issue. Partly by design and partly by historical accident, we have operated our public examining system through many autonomous organizations. If that part of the curriculum dependent on public examinations is to operate more uniformly and subject to national criteria, it is difficult to see how a case can be made for continuing such diversity. Already moves have been made to group CSE and GCE boards into large regional associations, stopping short of outright amalgamation; should not this process go still further *up to the statutory leaving age*? The spectre of state control will be raised (1984 is perhaps not the most propitious year to air this view). But is this such a bogy? Does it not depend on how a democratic government operates? It does not follow that the examinations will be actually designed and operated by government; indeed, that would not be possible – the limitations of operational control by government have already been set out in Chapter 3. There is no reason why a national professional body, operating under very general government guidelines, could not control acceptable national examinations in the limited area of the dependent curriculum. This being so, the pooling of some of the resources and expertise of the existing examination boards could go a long way towards meeting the consequences of the more rigorous performance testing suggested above.

The Entitlement Curriculum
I suspect that already in this chapter I have raised the blood-pressure of many readers strongly committed to the autonomy of teachers and schools. It is time to redress the balance.

There has been much said and written in recent years on what children should be offered in common in their curriculum during the compulsory years of schooling. The idea is growing that if children are compelled to undergo many years of compulsory schooling, they are entitled (DES, 1983a) to experience a common, minimum provision of curriculum. White (1973) and others make a case that some aspects of curriculum are essential if children are not to be placed at a disadvantage in their growth to autonomous adults. Becher and Maclure (1978, p. 16) suggest the 'public curriculum': 'those aspects of the curriculum which embody an education system's shared assumptions, however formulated, about the main things which pupils should do and learn in school.'

There is, of course, much discussion on what the entitlement to curriculum should be. One thing is certain, that it should not be exactly equated with the concept of the examination-dependent curriculum outlined above. Nevertheless, it is insufficient simply to require that children be entitled to experience a common curriculum as part of their total school experience. There are several areas of the curriculum in which participation alone is not enough. In literacy, numeracy and micro-electronic communication at the very least the intention to ensure that the great majority of children reach a minimum level of performance must surely be part of the entitlement.

The relationship between total curriculum, the entitlement curriculum and the examination-dependent curriculum is not clear-cut. But the implication is that within the total educational experience during the compulsory years of schooling there is a part to which everyone is entitled and experiences in common – as far as that is possible; and within that entitlement there is a still smaller part which ought to be subject to, and to a large extent determined by, a public examination system. It would be rash to attach quantities to these three related aspects of schooling. I have already indicated that the examined curriculum should be limited to a core within subjects which themselves would be a core within all subjects. So the expectation would be that the examined curriculum would form no more than one-half the total curriculum (in terms of time) even in the two or three years immediately preceding the statutory school-leaving age.

Diversity or Conformity?
It is likely that the specification of the examination-dependent curriculum would be determined at national level and that it would be set out in terms of actual levels of performance not in generalities. It does not follow that the tests themselves would all be of the objective type. Nevertheless, they are likely to involve a large measure of uniformity in design and conformity in response. It could also be anticipated that even if the teaching profession as a whole dominates the national examining authorities, the degree of prescription would be such as to constrain freedom of choice of both students and teachers even more than the present examination system does. It has already been pointed out that performance-based assessment would determine what was taught and how it was taught much more precisely than do the present examinations.

At first sight such a prospect of a uniform, conforming, examination-dependent element in the secondary school curriculum may displease many in the teaching profession. On reflection, however, they may come to see within the proposal the possibility of greater not less freedom for teachers and students to mould the *total* period of compulsory schooling more closely to their needs and interests. Complete autonomy for both teachers and students is not a realistic goal; freedom is finite. The problem in secondary education at present is that freedom is thinly spread. The public examination system, while allowing some degree of choice, pervades by far the greater part of the secondary school curriculum; and as I have indicated in preceding chapters, it has recently penetrated to parts not previously reached. Furthermore, the influence of higher education permeates downwards through the 16–18-year-old group well into the years of compulsory schooling (Eggleston, 1980). It is not good enough just to allow teachers to have choice between options within an examination system. That sort of freedom is fraudulent.

What I am suggesting is that the degrees of freedom within the school curriculum be more clearly defined; that the line between the examination-dependent curriculum and the independent curriculum be more clearly drawn both within and between subjects; and that the former should be greatly diminished in the time allowed to it. In this way freedom, while constrained in the dependent curriculum, could be greatly enhanced in everything which lies outside it. In some respects this kind of polarization is analogous to that which has occurred within examinations themselves, in which conforming objective tests are clearly separated from free-response questions.

Over the years I have experienced one consistent and powerful argument against this point of view: that the examination-dependent curriculum, though notionally smaller, would soon encroach on and ultimately dominate the whole curriculum. While acknowledging the force of that argument, I cannot accept its despairing implications because it rests on three unjustified assumptions:

(1) that the whole assessment and selection system at the end of compulsory schooling must continue to be dominated by public examinations;

(2) that society is satisfied with secondary schooling as it is;

(3) that there is no other way that the account due from teachers and schools to society can be paid than in the currency of traditional examination results.

The last point now has to be faced: is there any way in which a substantial part of the school curriculum can shake off the chains of terminal examinations yet still be subject to public scrutiny?

The Independent Curriculum

It would be presumptuous for any one person to lay down a detailed prescription for the secondary school curriculum, whether dependent or independent of public examinations, and I do not intend to do so. Presumably the general framework and criteria for an 'entitlement' curriculum, and the examination-dependent element within it, will be set out by some national body; and the use to which the remaining time is put will rest with individual schools. Whatever arrangements are made, there are still some important questions to be asked about that considerable area, whether it be an entitlement or not, which would be independent of the control exerted by a public examination system.

How can the independent curriculum achieve at least equal status with the dependent curriculum; and how can it be prevented from becoming the playground for every fanciful educational whim? Exhortation alone will not be sufficient. Ironically it may be through the increasing concern shown by central and local government that a happy coexistence of an examination-dependent and an examination-free curriculum might be obtained without domination by either. If private curricular enterprise is to flourish, it will need to do so within limits, no matter how loosely set if it is not to degenerate into licence. Above all the bounds of the examination-dependent curriculum will have to be clearly set if sufficient ground is to be reserved for the independent sector to take root and flourish.

The independent curriculum will require systems and agencies of validation and control other than that at present exercised by public examinations. Other agencies already exist, though some are no more than nominal and others still embryonic. There are the inspecting and advisory agencies both national and local; there are the governing and parental bodies; and there are the professional organizations of teachers. Despite much complaining, none of these bodies has been powerful enough to cage the examination machine and keep it within its proper limits. Only concentrated effort, supported by central government, could do so with sufficient authority to allow individual teachers and students profitably to employ more of their time unfettered by examinations.

But even if public examinations were excluded from a substantial part of the period of compulsory schooling, that in itself would not solve the problem of making the independent curriculum publicly respectable and accountable. This matter is somewhat beyond my brief; but having taken it so far, it is not inappropriate to make a few general suggestions rather than leave a void. The essential structure of an accounting system would need to involve three stages of the curriculum process: *design, operation* and *outcome.*

Design and Validation

At present the opportunities for imaginative curriculum design, independent of examinations, by secondary school teachers are insignificant. This is not to say that imaginative teaching techniques are not exercised; that is another matter, but they are exercised within a curriculum framework largely determined by the prospect of the great majority of students having to sit terminal examinations. Teachers can vary the interpretation, but the score has been written for them.

What about Mode III examinations? Do they not allow sufficient independence? No, they do not – at least not as they stand at present. They will have to conform to national criteria. They are assessed very largely on the basis of written products, not on the learning experiences which they provide. A modicum of national currency is purchased at great expense through external moderating systems which attempt to equate them with Mode I examinations. And above all they are confined to students of lower general ability. They have seduced more teachers and more students than ever before into liaison with the public examination system (Lello, 1979, p. 151). In doing so they have decreased the time available in schools for the development of those activities and those non-examinable attributes which society seems to want in its young people, but for which it manifestly fails to provide.

Teachers in higher education have one advantage in this respect. Most courses in higher education are initiated and designed by those who are going to teach them. More than that, those who teach them examine them, and they also have a say in who should be appointed as an external examiner (Williams, 1979). That, however, does not constitute freedom to do as they wish; their course design has to be *validated* and that can be a formidable experience. Validation means the submission of one's design to the scrutiny and criticism of various bodies, ranging from departmental committees through faculty boards to the ruling body of the institution. Not until all agree is the teacher authorized to start the course. It can be a painful process to witness one's efforts taken apart and referred back to be redesigned and resubmitted.

That is what secondary schools lack. They do not possess the kind of validating system which would allow them greater autonomy in their own affairs and still give a stamp of public approval. They do not have the authority to determine the details of their curriculum except for the tiny fraction which at present lies outside the influence of public examinations. (This does not necessarily apply to boarding schools, not because the curriculum of boarding schools is independent of public examinations – far from it; it is simply that they have more available hours in the day.)

I see no reason why the school teaching profession should not be allowed to devise a substantial part of the secondary school curriculum, free from the constraints of examination syllabuses, but subject to a thorough validating procedure. It does seem odd that schoolteachers should receive training in curriculum design and are then largely denied the opportunity to exercise it, while teachers in higher education, with no training in curriculum design, are then required to do so.

I hasten to add that I am suggesting that it is the *process* of validation within schools which should move in the direction of the higher education model, not the substance of the courses or the form of the assessment. By and large the substance of courses in higher education is academic and the assessment techniques old-fashioned. I will return to the substance of the independent curriculum in a moment; meanwhile some thought, at a general level, must be given to the kind of validation process which could work in schools.

A formal submission of the design of parts of the curriculum could be done in three stages: first, to like-minded colleagues (department or faculty); then to a body responsible for operating the curriculum of the school (hence representing all teaching staff); and finally, to a body which has the ultimate responsibility for authorizing the whole curriculum of the school, including teachers, governors, parents and officers of the local education authority. A similar point is made by Burgess and Adams (1980, ch. 13).

I anticipate many objections: 'time-consuming' and 'bureaucratic' come immediately to mind. Such a screening process would certainly not be a soft option to validation by public examination boards. On the contrary, the public defence of one's intentions demands real professionalism; it is only too easy to follow the requirements of an examination syllabus and past papers, and to do so is to diminish the function of teachers to that of mere executives. As an exercise in accountability this alternative system of validation could be rigorous and fruitful.

It is no good secondary school teachers complaining that examinations are stultifying the curriculum and, at the same time, decline to justify their curriculum intentions when some measure of freedom is offered. One thing is certain: the profession cannot reasonably expect to be handed a large slice of the time spent in compulsory schooling, freed from examinations, on the basis of do-with-it-as-you-please.[2]

The Substance of the Independent Sector

A recurring theme in this commentary has been the bias of the secondary school curriculum to *academic* studies supported by the written tests of public examinations. Formal education has become largely concerned with abstractions; the experiences and problems and social interactions in schools are in the main remote from those of the real world. In advocating a more precise definition of the examination-dependent curriculum and a substantial decrease of its demands on schooltime I do not deprecate the importance of intellectual activity in the years of compulsory schooling; indeed, the concentration and confining of examined studies may well enhance it. But nothing would be served if the independent curriculum were filled with a spate of courses similar to those already being examined, and I fear that it might well turn out to be so. It may be that academic work is what schools and schoolteachers do best; certainly it is largely for academic work that teachers are trained and schools are equipped. If that is the case, it is small wonder that children leave ill-equipped for life at work, or on the streets.

This train of thought leads me to suggest that the term 'courses' is not entirely appropriate when applied to the independent curriculum. It may be that the validating bodies of a school should be more concerned with giving approval to *activities* and *experiences* rather than to courses. I refer readers to the writings of Eisner, who draws a distinction between educational objectives formulated in terms of prescribed, measurable outcomes and educational objectives formulated in terms of activities and experiences. My suggestion for a clearer separation of the examination-dependent curriculum from the independent curriculum reflects the distinction made by Eisner.

I claim no originality for the view that a substantial part of the curriculum should be liberated from the behavioural/examination objectives type of specification. There have been many attempts to construct parts of the curriculum in other terms; but their success has not been significant. One of the more imaginative was the Stenhouse Humanities Project, which was based on the view that the process and substance of the curriculum were more important than prescribed outcomes. There were many reasons for its limited success: it tended to be reserved for those considered unsuitable for public examinations; it dealt with contentious issues; and the 'neutral chairman' was in reality still a schoolteacher and the participants still pupils in a classroom; but one must applaud the attempt.

I take it as axiomatic that many – possibly most – educational activities should not be subject to prescribed outcomes, therefore, they should not be subjected to standardized tests or examinations. Such activities ought to include all community, moral, political and religious experience; and most of physical and artistic activities.[3] There are others such as safety, health, nutrition and vocational education in which an element of basic knowledge may be necessary but are still not appropriately assessed within the same examination system as the traditional academic disciplines.

The acceptance of such a view would require a fundamental change from the curriculum design traditionally required by a validating body since it would be concerned not with the specification of behavioural objectives and assessment techniques, but with a specification of kinds of experience and activity. How, for example, would a validating body view a proposal to make a school self-sufficient in vegetables? – a common and substantial part of the school curriculum in many parts of Africa. Surely they would not insist that it should constitute a Mode III 16+ examination! (Incidentally its success, or lack of it, would be readily assessable and apparent.)

I accept the implications of my argument. Schools, schoolteachers and teacher educators would need radically to change their activities. While maintaining a diminished (in terms of time) scholastic function, they would have to adopt activities of a very different kind to meet educational needs in the less academic areas which I have listed above. Failing this, they would have to accept a diminished role and a complementary system of education organized separately and operated by people other than the traditional classroom teacher.

Of course, many complementary organizations already exist, often supported within schools. There are the various athletics and games organizations; and there are the churches. Scouting is one of the older ones and Outward Bound one of the newer, and there are many locally organized spheres for community service. But they are voluntary. Young people in schools are not required to engage in activities other than in the classroom – save for a little compulsory physical education; and the rejection of purely classroom education is becoming evident. But looming above all these is the difficult issue of *work experience*.

Work experience during the years of compulsory schooling has been out of favour in English schools in this century. In the nineteenth century it was an inevitable, often necessary, experience for most pupils in the elementary schools. Now even relatively trivial activities such as newspaper delivery and potato-picking weeks are often viewed with disfavour. There are, however, signs of a change. There is the Technical and Vocational Education Initiative (TVEI), which falls within the years of compulsory schooling, and there are the recent proposals for pre-employment education immediately after the statutory school-leaving age (DES, 1982).

The significance of the TVEI is not so much its advent as its origins. It sprang from the Manpower Services Commission, concerned primarily with recruitment to industry and commerce, not from those institutions normally responsible for education in schools. It could be seen as an interjection in an attempt to reduce the linguistic, academic bias of present-day schooling in favour of a more technological and vocational curriculum.

It will be interesting to see whether TVEI can maintain momentum after the initial flush of enthusiasm has faded. It could well be assimilated into an already bloated comprehensive examination system by the introduction of some new technological and commercial syllabuses, a step which inevitably would turn it into an abstraction rather than a contact with the real world of work. At worst it could become the province of the lower- and middle-ability groups, leaving those of higher ability to fill their time with academic examinations as they have always done – better that the TVEI should die than that.

But a still more serious criticism of a strictly vocational curriculum is its obsolescence and its narrowness. There is little point in training 14 year-olds in vocational techniques which may be obsolete by the time they are old enough to use them in earnest. And given the seemingly inevitable decline in paid employment, a vocationally biased curriculum ought not to make more than a partial contribution to the independent curriculum as a whole. A curriculum dominated by the acquisition of vocational skills could prove to be just as big a disillusion for young people as that dominated by academic skills. The independent curriculum will have to be a good deal broader and more imaginative than this if it is to lead to worthwhile living as well as efficient machine minding.

There is another view of vocational education. It is to put young people into places of work, so that they can experience it at first hand rather than vicariously in the classroom. Hard, physical work certainly could be thought to be one of the suitable – indeed essential – experiences within the independent curriculum. At the very least, days of physical labour would make the lot of most of the world's population more real to young people than reading about it in books or seeing it on film. However, the problems of integrating work experience within the curriculum of schools are formidable and the precedents are not encouraging.[4]

The case is somewhat different for those who have just passed the statutory school-leaving age and have no aspirations or academic ability for higher education, nor a job to go to. For them, if they continue in formal education, the issue of a strong vocational element in the curriculum is much more acute. In a sense they are still within the period of compulsory education, since there is nothing else open to them. They have a record of low academic attainment, so further striving for examination success is unlikely to be rewarding. It is significant that government seems to have concluded that academic schooling and its attendant examination system have failed these young people and that their future education should be placed in other hands. This is demonstrated in the government proposals for a new qualification at 17 plus, the Certificate of Pre-vocational Education (CPVE).

The courses leading to the CPVE are intended to have radically different aims from most secondary school courses:

> they should: offer a broad programme of general education with emphasis on its various types of employment;
> develop personal attributes such [as] self motivation, adaptability, self reliance, a sense of responsibility and an ability to work constructively with others;
> help each student to discover what kind of job he or she might expect to tackle with success. (ibid., para. 14)

It is difficult to see how these aims could be fostered in school classrooms and assessed by the public examination system as they now stand. This change in direction could well influence the earlier years of secondary schooling, at least for the less academic children; indeed, this is specially proposed in the White Paper (see ibid.).

It does seem that secondary schools in England and Wales are approaching a critical period. If they do not confine their academic curriculum and examinations within appropriate areas, and if they do not initiate suitable educational activities for the independent curriculum, they may well find their functions considerably reduced and a good part of the education of the young placed in other hands.

However, let us assume that the greater part of the period of compulsory education will remain with schools as at present instituted. How can a substantial part of the outcome of their curriculum be monitored and reported, after the design stage, without the intervention of a public examination system?

Monitoring the Action and Reporting the Product of the Independent Curriculum
Crude though it may be, the use of examination results to judge the performance of teachers and schools has the merit of being quantifiable and easily recognizable. No doubt this will continue for that part of schooling for which it is appropriate, although possibly in a changed form. But what of the part which is independent of examinations? The validation

of course design is not enough in itself; the most impressive design is useless if it is badly or improperly implemented, and examination results would no longer serve as a monitor of the effectiveness of teaching. What could replace examination results? Should anything replace them?

The issue comes more clearly into focus when it is brought to bear on some of the more sensitive topics which might form part of the independent curriculum: peace studies, moral education and race relations, for example. None of these could be properly monitored by using a public examination to measure the performance of the students. Even if they were subject to examination, the activities themselves, the *process* of the curriculum, would remain hidden. We might prefer it to be so; that having authorized the validating bodies to approve course designs, we are content to draw a veil over what actually happens. If that were to be the attitude, I can only comment that it is not one which we apply to many other activities in society. Engineering, building, food production, energy production and commerce are all subject to systems of inspection, auditing and accountability. Think of the monitoring and public scrutiny to which the atomic energy industry is subject. Why should the activities of compulsory schooling be largely exempt, particularly if there is to be no measure of its product?

One of the difficulties is that schooling has been regarded mainly as a private activity: one man or woman closeted in one room with a score or so of children. Rarely does a headteacher or head of department 'sit in'; the visits of inspectors and advisers are infrequent and the circumstances contrived; and inviting the public to observe has been unthinkable. There are some professions which have enjoyed similar privacy, doctors and lawyers, for example, but their successes and failures are rather more obvious than those of a teaching profession freed from public examinations.

So I suggest that it is not good enough to rely solely on the 'professionalism' of teachers for the proper conduct of the independent curriculum. If the yoke of examinations is to be lifted from a substantial part of the curriculum, it seems only reasonable that activities in that part should be a good deal more open than hitherto. I am not for one moment suggesting constant inspection, but could not reasonable access to school activities be afforded to those who have a legitimate concern in them? Teachers in training accept observers – why should this practice stop as soon as they are established in their work?

There remains the need for some form of report on the participation of the students in that part of the curriculum for which examination certificates are not appropriate. Surely it is to this area that records of personal achievement best could be applied. But if these records are to be free from all the constraints which confine examination certificates, there should be no attempt to apply national criteria and normative grades to them. To subject young people to continuous competition for grades in *all* areas of their schooling would be intolerable. Some sort of nationally agreed format may be possible; after that, the more descriptive and individualized they are the better. Variety and lack of standardization should be seen as virtues. A national system of standardized examinations cannot be expected to cater for the infinite variety of each individual's education; on the other hand, a totally individualized assessment cannot expect credible national standardization. But what will employers and further educators make of individual records of personal achievement? This brings us to a consideration of the future of examinations in their second function: as instruments for selecting young people.

Examinations and Social Engineering

Whether we like it or not, at the end of the period of compulsory schooling decisions are made about the next destination of young people which are likely to determine the course of the whole of their subsequent lives, not just their immediate future. It is a critical time of choice and selection, and at present the decisions are made on inadequate evidence. All that the selectors openly receive from the school and examination systems is a certificate of grades (or in many cases no grades at all) in a bewildering array of subjects from a bewildering array of sources. The grades provide no information about what the recipients can actually do; there is no certainty of equivalence of standards (see Chapter 9); and their quality depends on family background, type of schooling and other social factors as well as the natural ability of the young people themselves.

Selectors may also get confidential references: subjective, unchecked and unseen by those to whom they refer, and concerned mainly with *teacher's* impressions of children's personalities under classroom conditions. Interviews may be sterile because there is no starting-point for the conversation; there is little that the interviewers can read in advance which would tell them what the young people have done during the previous years in school other than a list of subjects. It all amounts to woefully meagre criteria on which to make a judgement that may affect the whole of a subsequent life.

It has to be admitted that any system of selection will be fallible. Wrong choices and wrong judgements are bound to be made. These can only be alleviated by allowing opportunities later in life to retrain and re-educate and to change occupation. It is encouraging to see this kind of flexibility happening to an increasing extent. But the initial judgement at the statutory school-leaving age is still the crucial one. No matter how much remedial action is subsequently possible, it may be at the price of many wasted years. Surely we can find a better system of judgement than the one we use now.

In their present form public examinations can add no more to this selection procedure. For all their limitations they have made a greater contribution to social equity and mobility during the past 100 years and more than any other aspect of national life, except the growth of democracy itself. For this we should be grateful both as individuals and as a community. At the same time, we should recognize the dangers inherent in excessive reliance on examinations as the sole criterion for selection (see Ingenkamp, 1977, p. 13). I do not wish to labour the weaknesses of the present system of selection through public examinations; these I trust have become evident in some of the preceding chapters. Nevertheless, I must now consider the extent to which the changes suggested in this chapter would assist in the initial process of setting young people on that path in life most suited to them.

Performance-Based Examinations

The first thing to be said is that I see not a diminished but increased use of public examinations, but in a much restricted area. I accept the need for a purge of the multifarious examined subjects which threaten to embrace the whole of the later years of compulsory secondary education. And I accept the need for a similar purge *within* those subjects still to be examined of all the accretion and clutter which have threatened to obscure the distinctive contribution each can make to the understanding of our human condition. Nevertheless, I foresee an increase in public examinations in other directions, all stemming from one dominant shift in principle. That shift would be towards a system of *awarding grades for actual performance*; in technical terms a move away from norm referencing towards criterion referencing. The implications of this are discussed earlier, but it may be helpful to summarize them again.

A move towards performance-based examinations would require a redesign of courses and examinations to provide a modular structure. This structure would allow a distinction between different parts of a subject and a distinction between different levels of attainment in each part.

It follows that a performance-based system could include some aspects of graded tests and credit accumulation, allowing candidates to take the tests *when they were ready* rather than solely at the end of compulsory schooling.

Any modular system greatly increases the number and variety of separate tests which candidates would take. For example, five subjects each divided into five modules, and each available at five levels, would give rise to $5 \times 5 \times 5$ tests all of which would have to be separately assessed. Hence radical changes would be required in the organization of examination boards. They would have to design and operate a greater variety of tests in each subject and at levels of age and ability of which they have little experience. Given limited resources, this could only be achieved by a drastic curtailment of the number of syllabuses, and the use of common tests across the country.

The reporting of results would also have to be a good deal more complex than at present. The practice of reporting a single grade for each subject could become redundant and be replaced by credit accumulation.

Perhaps the most important consequences of performance-based grading would be that every young person, capable of normal schooling, would arrive at the statutory school-leaving age with some achievement in examinations to show. No longer, then, could the accusation be made that 'The examination system is designed to deny success to many' (Joseph, 1984b). And while the modules could be extended downwards to accommodate the less able, they could also be extended upwards to stretch the more able.

The implications for selectors, accustomed to the present system, are considerable. No longer could they make their judgements on such crude specifications as 'five O levels, including mathematics and English'; they would have to be more discriminating and take a closer look at the evidence presented to them. Some will no doubt grumble about the increased detail, but considering the importance of the judgement to the applicants, it is surely not too much to ask employers and educators to spend a little more time and care on the scrutiny of qualifications. After all, there will be compensations: the variety of syllabuses would be greatly reduced; the grades would be more closely related to particular skills; and a more detailed profile of performance would be available for each candidate. Furthermore, the personal characteristics and individual activities and attainment of each candidate would be included in a record of personal achievement, together with the examination certificates.

A good deal will rest on the willingness of employers and further educators to stand by the assertion, often made, that they look for many more qualities than the ability to achieve high grades in examinations. They claim that they want to apply additional criteria; my suggestions would give them opportunity to do so. Indeed, they may have to do so because there would be a much greater number of young people leaving school with almost identical qualifications in examined subjects.

What these additional criteria are, and how they can be applied, is a matter of great importance. Records of personal achievement can do no more than point to past interests and activities; they cannot confirm that their holders will be subsequently suitable for whatever occupation they have chosen. Employers, educators and the candidates will have to accept some risk and wrong selections; but no more (perhaps less) than the reliance on examination certificates produces now. However, they will not be faced as they often are at the moment with a large number of candidates with *nothing* to show for all their years of schooling.

The General Certificate of Secondary Education (GCSE)

The statement of the Secretary of State for Education to the House of Commons on 20 June 1984 was timely since it allows me to comment on its general implications. It announced a 'reform' of public examinations in England and Wales at the statutory school-leaving age (16+). The main provisions are:

(1)   The existing twenty examination boards to be brought together into five groups.
(2)   All syllabuses are to be governed by national criteria.
(3)   Differentiated papers or questions (see Chapter 5) are to be used in every subject to reflect the differing abilities of candidates.
(4)   Grade-related criteria will be applied.
(5)   The higher grades (A–C) will be the responsibility of the GCE boards. The final proposal is perhaps better quoted in full:

> We propose an additional step to encourage the ablest pupils to pursue broad and balanced courses in the fourth and fifth years of secondary education. We shall invite the Secondary Examinations Council and the Examination Boards to co-operate in the introduction of Distinction Certificates for candidates achieving good grades in a broad range of key subjects. (Joseph, 1984a, para. 4)

In some respects the announcement epitomizes much that I have written. It proposes a greater degree of commonality in examination syllabuses, linked with a more integrated organization. It proposes a move from a norm-referenced bias to grades which are more closely related to performance (criterion-referenced). It recognizes the need to allow the most able and the least able the opportunity to achieve something by way of examination certificates. And it assumes the need to maintain a 'broad range of key subjects'.

At first sight the proposals constitute a fundamental change in the examination system of England and Wales. In *effect* they may not be as radical as they appear.

The combination of GCE and CSE is a logical consequence of the policy to bring together grammar and secondary modern schools into comprehensives. Like the reorganization of the schools, the reorganization of examinations is intended to obviate the divisiveness of the binary system; at least to delay the decision about which candidates should attempt the higher grades and which the lower.

But the comprehensive systems of schools and examinations can both be cosmetic to a large extent. An analysis of the curriculum of comprehensive schools, particularly in the two years preceding the school-leaving age, reveals that many of them are in effect organized as grammar and secondary modern schools within the single institution. A distinction is made between the academic and the non-academic and this is reflected at present as a distinction between those who enter for GCE and those who enter for CSE.

The proposed system of examinations is closely parallel. The two names and the two kinds of examining authority will associate. (I use the word 'associate' deliberately since a total integration of the GCE and CSE boards seems to be unlikely under the present proposals; the outcome is more likely to be akin to the split-site comprehensive schools.) There will be a greater degree of commonality between syllabuses which will allow decisions about examination entry to be taken later than they are at present. But the discrimination between the able and less able, the academic and the non-academic, will be only delayed, not renounced.

It is also clear from the national criteria already approved that most of the examinations are likely to be similar to what we now have: assessment at the end of compulsory schooling published as single grades. Working parties are to be set up to prepare 'grade-related criteria'. In Chapters 10 and 12 I have pointed to the incompatibility of the design of our present examinations with meaningful statements about performance and capability. If grade-related criteria are to be no more than the abstract, bland statements such as those I have quoted earlier, then working parties to that end are not worth the money they will require. On the other hand, if performance criteria are related to a modular, credit-accumulation structure, much of the work already done on the subjects of the single system will have to be restructured and so will the whole process of public examining.

Perhaps the most interesting proposal is the 'distinction certificate for candidates achieving good grades in a broad range of key subjects'. The link to the grouped certificate is clear. Indeed, its origins can be traced back to the Oxford and Cambridge locals. It reinforces my recurring themes: that the main function of schools is academic; and that competition for higher education and employment is based largely on academic criteria.

It is not my intention to express a personal judgement on the proposals. It may well be that they reflect the proper functions of schools and the examining bodies. However, although the proposals may to some extent be reforming, they should not be thought to be revolutionary. *Plus ça change, plus c'est la même chose!*

In Conclusion

Writing comments and suggestions in a book is all too easy. They may be the culmination of many years' experience in all aspects of the examination industry; but I am under no illusion about the difficulties involved in putting them into practice, even if they were acceptable and the will and resources existed. Fundamental change is difficult within a pluralist form of control because a dominant, single seat of power cannot be identified.

I would point, however, to the consequences of doing nothing or just tinkering with the examination system. At no time in recent history has secondary schooling, and the public examinations on which it depends, come under such adverse criticism, linked as they are to a curriculum which stems directly from a nineteenth-century model of education. The advent of secondary schooling for all, whether it be selective or comprehensive, has not caused the problems, it has simply served to highlight them. Not only do most young people fail to achieve anything of note in school-leaving examinations, they are required to attempt tests which bear little relation to the tests they will face immediately afterwards and throughout life. There is no record of *what they can do and have done*.

It should not be thought that I am against the traditional subjects, academic work and intellectual pursuits. Not a bit of it. What I have had the temerity to suggest in this chapter could serve to enhance activities of the mind, not to diminish them. What I do assert is that many of the claims for intellectual merit based on public examination certificates are at present spurious. By more clearly defining the area within which schools might properly pursue tests of intellectual attainment, and by more clearly defining the criteria by which intellectual attainment can be judged, examinations might regain the justified esteem they once had and do much to bring about that rise in standards of which much is being said and written.

Nor should it be assumed that outside the examined curriculum the activities would be necessarily non-intellectual. Just because an educational activity is not examined does not cause it to be mindless. Indeed, the opposite could be the case. If a child chooses to spend a large part of the independent curriculum in reading or writing or computing, why not? Better that than the blood sports and obsessive, compulsory athleticism which occupied much of the non-examined part of nineteenth-century schooling. Conversely, if a child wishes to indulge more practical or sporting or vocational pursuits, why not? Provided that the schools are prepared to expose these activities to the open scrutiny of a validating procedure advocated earlier in this chapter, there could be available a great variety of academic and non-academic pursuits free from the constraint of traditional examinations.

Where would all this leave the examining boards? Certainly not abolished; only they could command the necessary expertise and authority to give credibility to a changed system. Pruned, yes, but all the more vigorous for it. And let me say again: all that I have written in this chapter relates to the years of compulsory secondary schooling. The examinations after the statutory school-leaving age would continue to support the academic excellence of sixth forms. They may be changed, but there is every reason to expect that they would be able to increase in number and variety given some rationalization of the function of the boards in the years of compulsory schooling. The boards would certainly not be able to achieve academic excellence if they get entangled with assessments which properly rest with teachers and schools.

I see no good reason for the abolition of examinations for the period of compulsory education; but there is a good case for radical change in their scope, how they operate, and the way in which the results will be published and used. They remain a sure shield against the abuses of patronage and political,[5] racial and sexual bias. They assist in the defence of academic standards and intellectual values in formal education at all levels. They can ensure that essential knowledge and skills can be attained by the great majority of young people during the years in which they are required to be at school. I ask only that the strengths and limitations of examinations, in traditional and revised forms, be more fully understood and I hope that this book has made some contribution to that end.

Notes: Chapter 13

1   The ambivalence is evident in DES, 1981, *The School Curriculum*, which should be read together with the critique in the Bedford Way Paper, No. 4, *No, Minister*, of the Institute of Education, 1981. More recently, DES, 1983b, *Records of Achievement at* 16+, encourages individualized assessment, while DES, 1983a, *Curriculum* 11-16: *Towards a Statement of Entitlement*, reports on the feasibility of a common curriculum in eight key areas, to comprise 70–80 per cent of the time available. This problem is not confined to the United Kingdom, see Elley and Livingstone, 1972.

2   The secretary of state, Sir Keith Joseph, in his address to the North of England Education Conference in January 1984 also seems to agree in principle: 'There is now no serious dispute that the school curriculum is a proper concern not only of the teachers, but also of parents, governing bodies, LEAs, and the Government' (para. 30).

3   Ross, 1978, p. 263, voices the views of many teachers of the creative arts: 'The notion that an assessment of an individual pupil can be rendered as a mark, and that this mark can then have general significance among all other such similar marks, is idiotic in the area of education we are responsible for.'

4   Price, 1977, and 1979, p. 26, refers to short-lived attempts in the Soviet Union and China (in the Mao era) to put into effect the Marxist dictum, 'the education of the future will ... combine productive labour with instruction and gymnastics'; see also Grant, 1979. Handy, 1979, p. 138, writes: 'One enclosed environment [schools] is a bad preparation for multiple open environments in later life ... I am arguing for devices such as work experience schemes etc. ... for qualification systems that allow other forms of competence recognition besides examinations.'

5   Other countries have been less fortunate. Castles and Wüstenberg, 1979, p. 122, refer to the period of the Cultural Revolution in China: 'The criteria for selection [to higher education] were a high level of political consciousness and involvement, successful participation in practical work, and good health.' For an account of the return to examinations as the determining criterion for selection in China see Kerr, 1978. Grant, 1979, makes similar references to selection in the Soviet Union.

Bibliography

Acton, T. A., and Rutter, M. (1980), 'Educational criteria of success', *Educational Research*, vol. 22, no. 3, pp. 163–9.

Agazzi, A. (1967), *The Educational Aspects of Examinations* (Strasbourg: Council of Europe).

Assessment of Performance Unit (APU) (1982), *Summary Report No. 8: Third Primary Mathematics Survey* (London: Department of Education and Science).

Associated Lancashire School Examining Board (1979), *Regulations for Moderators* (Manchester: ALSEB).

Association for Science Education (1976, 1977), *School Science Review* (London: ASE), Vols 57 and 58.

Bailey, P. (1978), *Leisure and Class in Victorian England* (London: Routledge & Kegan Paul).

Baldwin, P. (1983), 'The competitive ethos in Victorian and Edwardian education as manifested in examinations and athleticism', MA dissertation, University of Lancaster.

Balogh, J. (1982), *Profile Reports for School Leavers*, Schools Council Programme No. 5 (London: Longman).

Bardell, C. S., Forrest, G. M., and Shoesmith, D. J. (1978), *Comparability in GCE: A Review of the Boards' Studies 1964–1977* (Manchester: Joint Matriculation Board).

Becher, T., and Maclure, S. (1978), *The Politics of Curriculum Change* (London: Hutchinson).

Becher, T., Eraut, M., and Knight, J. (1981), *Policies for Educational Accountability* (London: Heinemann).

Bell, R., and Prescott, W. (eds) (1975), *The Schools Council: A Second Look* (London: Ward Lock).

Bennett, S. N., and Rutter, M. (1980), 'Review dialogue', *British Educational Research Journal*, vol. 6, no. 1, pp. 97–102.

Blackstone, T., and Mortimore, J. (1982), *Disadvantage and Education* (London: Heinemann).

Bloom, B. S. (1956), *Taxonomy of Educational Objectives: Handbook I* (London: Longman).

Bloom, B. S., Hastings, J. T., and Madaus, G. F. (1971), *Handbook of Formative and Summative Evaluation of Student Learning* (New York: McGraw-Hill).

Bloomfield, B., Dobby, J., and Kendall, L. (1976), *Mode Comparability in the CSE*, Schools Council Examinations Bulletin No. 36 (London: Evans/Methuen).

Boyson, R. (1969), 'The essential conditions for the success of a comprehensive school', in C. B. Cox and A. E. Dyson (eds), Black Paper Two: The Crisis in Education (Manchester: Critical Quarterly), pp. 57–62.

Brereton, J. L. (1944), The Case for Examinations (Cambridge: Cambridge University Press).

Briggs, D. (1980), 'A study of the influence of handwriting upon grades using examination scripts', Educational Review, vol. 32, no. 2, pp. 185–94.

Brimer, M. A., Madaus, G. F., Chapman, T. K., and Wood, R. (1978), Sources of Difference in School Achievement (London: National Foundation for Educational Research).

Broadfoot, P. S. (1979), Assessment, Schools and Society (London: Methuen).

Brown, G., and Desforges, C. (1977), 'Piagetian psychology: time for revision', British Journal of Educational Psychology, vol. 47, pp. 7–17.

Brown, S. (1981), What Do They Know? A Review of Criterion-Referenced Assessment (London: HMSO).

Bruce, G. (1969), Secondary Schools Examinations (Oxford: Pergamon).

Bruner, J. S. (1966), Towards a Theory of Instruction (Cambridge, Mass.: Harvard University Press).

Burgess, T. (1979), 'New ways to learn' (Cantor Lecture), Journal of Royal Society of Arts, vol. 127, no. 5271, pp. 7–17.

Burgess, T., and Adams, E. (eds) (1980), Outcomes of Education (London: Macmillan).

Burstyn, J. W. (1980), Victorian Education and the Ideal of Womanhood (London: Croom Helm).

Castles, S., and Wüstenberg, W. (1979), The Education of the Future: An Introduction to the Theory and Practice of Socialist Education (London: Pluto Press).

Central Policy Review Staff (1980), Education, Training and Industrial Performance (London: HMSO), May.

Christie, T., and Forrest, G. M. (1980), Standards at GCE A Level, 1963 and 1973 (London: Macmillan).

Christie, T., and Forrest, G. M. (1981), Defining Public Examination Standards (London: Macmillan).

Christopher, R. (1969), The Work of the Joint Matriculation Board (Manchester: JMB).

Cox, C. B., and Dyson, A. E. (1969), Black Paper Two: The Crisis in Education (Manchester: Critical Quarterly).

Davies, T. I. (1969), School Organisation (Oxford: Pergamon).

Deale, R. N. (1975), Assessment and Testing in the Secondary School, Schools Council Examinations Bulletin No. 22 (London: Evans/ Methuen).

Department of Education and Science (DES) (1977a), Curriculum 11–16 (London: HMSO).

DES (1977b), Ten Good Schools (London: HMSO).

DES (1979), Statistics of Education. Vol. 2, School Leavers' CSE and GCE (London: HMSO).

DES (1981), The School Curriculum (London: HMSO).

DES (1982), 17+: A New Qualification (London: HMSO).

DES (1983a), Curriculum 11–16: Towards a Statement of Entitlement (London: HMSO).

DES (1983b), Records of Achievement at 16+: Some Examples of Current Practice (London: DES).

DES (1983c), *School Standards and Spending: Statistical Analysis* (London: HMSO).

DES (1984), *Advanced Supplementary Examination* (London: HMSO).

DES/Welsh Office (1982), *Examinations at 16+: A Statement of Policy* (London: HMSO).

Dore, R. (1976), *The Diploma Disease* (London: Allen & Unwin).

Education Department of South Australia (1981), *Into the 1980s* (Adelaide: Department of Education, South Australia).

Eggleston, J. F. (1980), 'Interrelations between assessment and curriculum', in R. W. Fairbrother (ed.), *Assessment and the Curriculum* (London: Chelsea College, University of London), pp. 158–74.

Eisner, E. W. (1969), *Instructional and Expressive Objectives*, Monograph No. 3 (Washington, DC: American Educational Research Association).

Eisner, E. W. (ed.) (1971), *Confronting Curriculum Reform* (Boston, Mass.: Little, Brown).

Eisner, E. W., and Vallance, E. (1974), *Conflicting Concepts of Curriculum* (Berkeley, Calif.: McCutchan).

Elley, W. B., and Livingstone, I. D. (1972), *External Examinations and Internal Assessments* (Wellington, NZ: New Zealand Council for Educational Research).

Entwistle, H. (1978), *Class Culture and Education* (London: Methuen).

European String Teachers' Association (1984), *Music Competitions: A Report* (London: ESTA).

Fairbrother, R. W. (ed.) (1980), *Assessment and the Curriculum* (London: Chelsea College, University of London).

Fleming, P. R. (1976), *Examinations in Medicine* (Edinburgh: Churchill Livingstone).

Fletcher, S. (1980), *Feminists and Bureaucrats* (Cambridge: Cambridge University Press).

Forrest, G. M. (1971), *Standards in Subjects at Ordinary Level of GCE, June 1970* (Manchester: Joint Matriculation Board).

Forrest, G. M., and Shoesmith, D. J. (1978), *Comparability in GCE* (Manchester: Joint Matriculation Board).

Forrest, G. M., and Smith, G. A. (1972), *Standards in Subjects at the Ordinary Level of the GCE, June 1971* (Manchester: Joint Matriculation Board).

Forrest, G. M., and Vickerman, C. (1982), *Standards in GCE: Subject Pairs Comparisons, 1972–80* (Manchester: Joint Matriculation Board).

Forrest, G. M., and Williams, C. A. (1983), *Inter Board Study in GCE Physics (Ordinary) 1980* (Manchester: Joint Matriculation Board).

Francis, J. C. (1981), 'Profile reporting in external examinations', *Educational Research*, vol. 24, no. 1, pp. 55–61.

Fulton, O. (ed.) (1981), *Access to Higher Education* (London: Society for Research in Higher Education).

Further Education Curriculum Review and Development Unit (1982), *Profiles* (London: FEU).

Gagné, R. M. (1970), *The Conditions of Learning* (London: Holt, Rinehart & Winston).

Gaskell, E. (1975), *The Life of Charlotte Brontë* (Harmondsworth: Penguin Books); originally published 1857.

Gaudry, E., and Speilburger, C. (1971), *Anxiety and Educational Achievement* (New York and London: Wiley).

GCE and CSE Boards' Joint Council for 16+ (1981), *Glossary of Terms for a Single System of Examining at 16+*.

GCE and CSE Boards' Joint Council for 16+ (1982), *Report of Subject Working Party in History*.

GCE and CSE Boards' Joint Council for 16+ (1983a), *Report of the Working Party for English*.

GCE and CSE Boards' Joint Council for 16+ (1983b), *Recommended Statement of 16+ National Criteria for English*.

Goacher, B. (1983a), *Recording Achievement at 16+*, Schools Council Programme No. 5 (London: Longman).

Goacher, B. (1983b), *Research into Secondary School Reports* (London: National Foundation for Educational Research).

Goacher, B. (1984), *Selection Post-16*, Schools Council Examination Bulletin No. 45 (London: Evans/Methuen).

Goacher, B., and Reid, M. I. (1983), *School Reports to Parents* (London: National Foundation for Educational Research).

Gordon, P., and Lawton, D. (1978), *Curriculum Change in the 19th and 20th Centuries* (London: Hodder & Stoughton).

Grant, N. (1979), *Soviet Education* (Harmondsworth: Penguin Books).

Halsey, A. H., Heath, A. F., and Ridge, J. M. (1980), *Origins and Destinations: Family, Class and Education* (Oxford: Clarendon Press).

Handy, C. B. (1979), 'The challenge of industrial society' (Cantor Lecture), *Journal of Royal Society of Arts*, vol. 127, no. 5271, pp. 137–43.

Harding, A., Page, B., and Rowell, S. (1980), *Graded Objectives in Modern Languages* (London: Centre for Language Teaching and Research).

Hargreaves, D. H. (1982), *The Challenge of the Comprehensive School, Curriculum and Community* (London: Routledge & Kegan Paul).

Harrison, A. (1982), *Review of Graded Tests*, Schools Council Examinations Bulletin No. 41 (London: Evans/Methuen).

Harrison, A. (1983), *Profile Reporting of Examination Results*, Schools Council Examinations Bulletin No. 43 (London: Methuen).

Harrow, A. (1972), *A Taxonomy of the Psychomotor Domain* (New York: McKay).

Headmasters' Conference (1982), *Curriculum 8–16: A Curriculum for Independent Schools* (London: HMC).

Her Majesty's Inspectorate (HMI) (1975), *Survey 12* (London: Department of Education and Science).

Heywood, J. (1977), *Assessment in Higher Education* (London: Wiley).

Hofmann, B. (1964), *The Tyranny of Testing* (London: Collier-Macmillan).

Honey, J. R. (1977), *Tom Brown's Universe* (London: Millington).

House of Commons (1981), *The Secondary School Curriculum and Examinations*, Second Report from the Education, Science and Art Committee, HC 116-1, Vol. 1, December.

House of Commons Expenditure Committee (1977), *The Attainment of the School Leaver* (London: HMSO).

Humber, R. D. (1968), *Heversham – the Story of a Westmorland School and Village* (Kendal: Titus Wilson).

Illich, I. D. (1971), *Deschooling Society* (New York: Harper & Row).

Ingenkamp, K. (1977), *Educational Assessment* (London: National Foundation for Educational Research).

Inner London Education Authority (ILEA) (1982), *Record Keeping and Profiles. Guidance for Schools* (London: ILEA).

Institute of Education (London University) (1981), *No, Minister*, Bedford Way Paper No. 4 (London: London University Institute of Education).

James, A., and Jeffcoate, R. (eds) (1981), *The School in the Multicultural Society* (New York: Harper & Row).

Joint Matriculation Board (1981), *Annual Report 1980* (Manchester: JMB).

JMB (1982a), *Annual Report 1980–81* (Manchester: JMB).

JMB (1982b), *Marking A-level Physics* (Manchester: JMB).

JMB (1982c), *Marking A-level History* (Manchester: JMB).

JMB (1982d), *GCE Regulations and Syllabuses 1984* (Manchester: JMB).

JMB (1983a), *Problems of the GCE Advanced Level Grading System* (Manchester: JMB).

JMB (1983b), *Annual Report 1981–82* (Manchester: JMB).

JMB (1983c), *Marking A-level English Literature* (Manchester: JMB).

Joseph, Sir K. (1984a), Statement to House of Commons, 20 June.

Joseph, Sir K. (1984b), Address to North of England Education Conference.

Kaunda, K. A. (1973), *Letters to my Children* (London: Longman).

Keatinge, M. W. (1896), *The Great Didactic of John Amos Comenius* (London: A. & C. Black).

Keeves, J. P. (1981), *Education and Change in South Australia* (Adelaide: Department of Education, South Australia).

Kelly, A. (ed.) (1981), *The Missing Half* (Manchester: Manchester University Press).

Kelly, P. J. (1971), 'A reappraisal of examinations', *Journal of Curriculum Studies*, vol. 3, no. 2, pp. 119–27.

Kerr, C. (1978), *Observations on the Relations between Education and Work in the People's Republic of China* (Berkeley, Calif.: Carnegie Council on Policy Studies in Higher Education).

Krathwohl, D. R., Bloom, B. S., and Masia, B. B. (1964), *Taxonomy of Educational Objectives. Handbook II* (London: Longman).

Lawson, J., and Silver, H. (1973), *A Social History of Education in England* (London: Methuen).

Leece, J. R. (1974), 'An analysis of Nuffield A Level chemistry', PhD thesis, University of Lancaster.

Leece, J. R., and Mathews, J. C. (1976), *Examinations: Their Use in Curriculum Evaluation and Development*, Schools Council Examinations Bulletin No. 33 (London: Evans/Methuen).

Lello, J. (ed.) (1979), *Accountability in Education* (London: Ward Lock).

Little, A., and Westergaard, J. (1964), 'The trend in class differentials in educational opportunity in England', *British Journal of Sociology*, vol. XV, no. 4, pp. 301–16.

MacIntosh, H. G. (ed.) (1974), *Techniques and Problems of Assessment* (London: Edward Arnold).

MacIntosh, H. (1982), 'The prospects for public examinations in England and Wales', *Educational Analysis*, vol. 4, no. 3.

MacIntosh, H. G., and Smith, L. A. (1974), *Towards a Freer Curriculum* (London: University of London Press).

Maclure, J. S. (1975), *Educational Documents: England and Wales 1816–1968* (London: Methuen).

Maccoby, E. E., and Jacklin, C. N. (1974), *The Psychology of Sex Differences* (Stanford, Calif.: Stanford University Press).

Madeley, K. (1979), 'Examinations in physical education', MA dissertation, University of Lancaster.

Mangan, J. A. (1981), *Athleticism in the Victorian and Edwardian Public School* (Cambridge: Cambridge University Press).

Mansell, J. (1982), 'Intellectual apartheid', *Times Educational Supplement*, 28 May.

Mansell Report (1979), *A Basis for Choice* (London: HMSO).

Marks, J., Cox, C., and Pomian-Sreednicki, M. (1983), *Standards in English Schools* (London: National Council for Educational Standards).

Mathews, J. C. (1974), 'Structured questions', in H. G. MacIntosh (ed.), *Techniques and Problems of Assessment* (London: Edward Arnold), pp. 7–18.

Mathews, J. C. (1977), *The Use of Objective Tests*, Teaching in Higher Education series No. 9 (Lancaster: University of Lancaster).

Montgomery, R. J. (1965), *Examinations: An Account of their Evolution as Administrative Devices in England* (London: Longman).

Montgomery, R. J. (1978), *A New Examination of Examinations* (London: Routledge & Kegan Paul).

Mortimore, J., and Mortimore, P. (1984), *Secondary School Examinations: The Helpful Servants, Not the Dominating Master*, Bedford Way Paper No. 18 (London: London University Institute of Education).

Mukhopadhyay, A. (1984), *Assessment in a Multicultural Society: Social Sciences at 16+*, Schools Council Programme No. 5, Improving the Examinations System (London: Longman).

Murphy, R. J. L. (1980), 'Sex differences in GCE examination statistics and success rates', *Educational Studies*, vol. 6, no. 2, pp. 169–78.

Newbould, C. A., and Massey, A. J. (1979), *Comparability Using a Common Element* (Cambridge: University of Cambridge Local Examinations Syndicate).

Norwood Report (1943), *Curriculum and Examinations in Secondary Schools* (London: HMSO).

Novosiltseva, Z. (1980), 'The conduct of examinations' (abstract), USSR Academy of Pedagogical Sciences.

Nuffield Foundation (1975), *Revised Nuffield Chemistry Teachers' Guide I* (London: Longman).

Nuttall, D. L. (1973), *Mode Comparability* (Sheffield: West Yorkshire and Lindsey Regional Examining Board).

Nuttall, D. L., and Willmott, A. (1972), *British Examinations: Techniques of* Lindsey Regional Examining Board).

Nuttall, D. L., and Willmot, A. (1972), *British Examinations: Techniques of Analysis* (London: National Foundation for Educational Research).

Nuttall, D. L., Backhouse, J. K., and Willmott, A. S. (1974), *Comparability of Standards between Subjects*, Schools Council Examinations Bulletin No. 12 (London: Evans/Methuen).

Open College Federation of the North West (1982), *A Handbook of Procedures and Syllabuses* (Lancaster: University of Lancaster), November.

Orr, L., and Nuttall, D. L. (1983), *Determining Standards in the Proposed Single System of Examinations at 16+*, Comparability in Examinations Occasional Paper No. 2 (London: Schools Council).

Oxford Delegacy (1983), *OCEA Newsletters* (Oxford: Oxford Delegacy), July.

Oxford Local Examinations (1978), *Information on Marking Modern Language at Ordinary Level* (Oxford: Oxford Delegacy).

Packenham. T. (1979), *The Boer War* (London: Weidenfeld & Nicolson).

Perkin, H. (1969), *The Origins of English Society* (London: Routledge & Kegan Paul).

Petch, J. A. (1953), *50 Years of Examining* (London: Harrap).

Peterson, A. D. C. (1982), 'A bitter taste of the Polish diet', *Times Educational Supplement*, 21 May.

Plewis, I., and others (1981), *Publishing School Examination Results*, Bedford Way Paper No. 5 (London: University of London Institute of Education).

Popham, W. J. (1978), *Criterion-Referenced Measurement* (Englewood Cliffs, NJ: Prentice-Hall).

Price, J. J. (1981), 'Gender differences in the examination statistics of the JMB, 1963-1980', MA dissertation, University of Lancaster.

Price, R. F. (1977), *Marx and Education in Russia and China* (London: Croom Helm).

Price, R. F. (1979), *Education in Modern China* (London: Routledge & Kegan Paul).

Pring, R. (1975), 'Integration: official policy or official fashion', in R. Bell and W. Prescott (eds), *The Schools Council, a Second Look* (London: Ward Lock), pp. 116-41.

Rampton Report (1981), *West Indian Children in our Schools* (Interim Report) (London: HMSO), June.

Raven, J. (1980), 'Bringing education back into schools', in T. Burgess and E. Adams (eds), *Outcomes of Education* (London: Macmillan), pp. 105-18.

Roach, J. (1971), *Public Examinations in England 1850-1900* (Cambridge: Cambridge University Press).

Robbins Report (1963), *Report on Higher Education* (London: HMSO).

Ross, M. (1978), *The Creative Arts* (London: Heinemann).

Rowntree, D. (1977), *Assessing Students: How Shall We Know Them?* (London and New York: Harper & Row).

Royal Society (1982), *Science Education 11-18 in England and Wales* (London: Royal Society).

Rutter, M., Maughan, B., Mortimore, P., Ouston, J., and Smith, A. (1979), *Fifteen Thousand Hours, Secondary Schools and their Effects on Children* (London: Open Books).

Ryle, A. (1969), *Student Casualties* (Harmondsworth: Penguin Books).

Satterley, P. (1981), *Assessment in Schools* (Oxford: Blackwell).

Schools Council (1964), *CSE: An Introduction to Objective Type Examinations* (London: HMSO).

Schools Council (1968), *Enquiry I: Young School Leavers* (London: HMSO).

Schools Council (1971a), *A Common System of Examinations at 16+* (London: Schools Council).

Schools Council (1971b), *CSE: An Experiment in the Oral Examining of Chemistry*, Examinations Bulletin No. 21 (London: Evans/Methuen).

Schools Council (1972), *16-19 Growth and Response*, Working Paper No. 45 (London: Evans/Methuen).

Schools Council (1973), *Assessment of Attainment in Sixth Form Science*, Examinations Bulletin No. 27 (London: Evans/Methuen).

Schools Council (1976), *Question Banking*, Examinations Bulletin No. 35 (London: Evans/Methuen).

Schools Council (1979), *Standards in Public Examinations: Problems and Possibilities*, Occasional Paper No. 1 (London: Schools Council).

Schools Council (1980a), *Focus on Examinations No. 2: Essentials or Choice* (London: Schools Council).

Schools Council (1980b), *Focus on Examinations 6: Standards in School Examinations* (London: Schools Council).

Schools Council (1981), *Examining in a Multicultural Society* (London: Schools Council).

Schools Council (1982), *Multicultural Education* (London: Schools Council).

Scottish Council for Research in Education (1977), *Pupils in Profile* (London: Hodder & Stoughton).

Secondary Schools Examinations Council (1963), *The Certificate of Secondary Education*, Examinations Bulletin No. 1 (London: HMSO).

Sheridan, W. (1974), 'Open-ended questions', in H. G. MacIntosh (ed.), *Techniques and Problems of Assessment* (London: Edward Arnold), pp. 1–6.

Simon, B. (1974), *The Two Nations and Educational Structure 1780–1870* (London: Lawrence & Wishart).

Skurnik, L. S., and Connaughton, I. (1970), *The 1967 Monitoring Experiment*, Schools Council Working Paper No. 30 (London: Evans/Methuen).

Smith, C. H . (1976), *Mode III Examinations in the CSE and GCE*, Schools Council Examinations Bulletin No. 34 (London: Evans/Methuen).

Stevens, A. (1980), *Clever Children in Comprehensive Schools* (Harmondsworth: Penguin Books).

Stevenson, M. (1983), 'Pupil profiles', *British Journal of Educational Studies*, vol. 21, no. 2, pp. 102–16.

Sutherland, M. B. (1981), *Sex Bias in Education* (Oxford: Blackwell).

Swales, T. (1980), *Record of Personal Achievement*, Schools Council Pamphlet No. 16 (London: Schools Council).

Tattersall, K. (1983), *Differentiated Examinations*, Schools Council Examinations Bulletin No. 42 (London: Methuen).

Thyne, J. M. (1974), *Principles of Examining* (London: University of London Press).

Tomlinson, S. (1981), 'The educational performance of ethnic minority children', in A. James and R. Jeffcoate (eds), *The School in Multicultural Society* (London and New York: Harper & Row), pp. 119–46.

Tomlinson, S. (1983), *Ethnic Minorities in British Schools* (London: Heinemann).

Trenaman Report (1981), *Review of the Schools Council* (London: DES).

Tumin, M. M. (1970), 'Evaluation of the effectiveness of education', *Interchange*, vol. 1, no. 3, pp. 96–109.

Van Praagh, G. (1973), *H. E. Armstrong and Science Education* (London: John Murray).

Vellins, S. (1982), 'South Asian students at British universities', *New Community*, vol. 10, no. 2, pp. 206–12.

Verma, G. K. and Bagley, C. (eds) (1982), *Self Concept, Achievement and Multicultural Education* (London: Macmillan).

Wardle, D. (1974), *The Rise of the Schooled Society* (London: Routledge & Kegan Paul).

Waring, M. (1979), *Social Pressures and Curriculum Innovation* (London: Methuen).

White, J. C. (1973), *Towards a Compulsory Curriculum* (London: Routledge & Kegan Paul).

White Paper (1978), *Government Observations on Tenth Report*, Cmnd 7124 (London: HMSO).

Williams, G. L. (1978), 'In defence of diplomas', *Higher Education*, vol. 7, no. 3, pp. 163–71.

Williams, W. F. (1979), 'The role of external examiners in first degrees', *Studies in Higher Education*, vol. 4, no. 2, pp. 161–8.

Willmott, A. S. (1977), *CSE and GCE Grading Standards: The 1973 Comparability Study* (London: Macmillan).

Wood, R. (1976), 'Sex differences in mathematics attainment at GCE Ordinary level', *Educational Studies*, vol. 2, no. 2, pp. 141–60.

Wood R. (1978), 'Sex differences in answers to English language comprehension items', *Educational Studies*, vol. 4, no. 2, pp. 157–66.

Wyatt, T. S. (1973), *The GCE Boards and Curriculum Development* (Oxford: Oxford and Cambridge Schools Examination Board).

Young, M. F. A. (1975), 'On the politics of educational knowledge', in R. Bell and W. Prescott (eds), *The Schools Council, a Second Look* (London: Ward Lock), pp. 33–52.

Index

ability, general and specific 146–62, 167
Abitur 4
abolition of examinations 123, 242
academic achievement 8, 11–13, 27, 31, 54–5, 63, 99, 121, 186, 200, 202–17, 240–2
accountability 43, 229, 231, 235
achievement and attainment 165–7
advisers 229–30, 235
affective domain 13, 54–5, 116, 121–2, 187
aggregation of marks 174–5, 179, 183, 211
  alternatives to 212–5
Amateur Athletic Club 15
answers, types of 102–8
apprenticeship 7
aptitude
  and attainment 165–6
  tests 140–2, 146, 160–1
art examinations 152–3, 209
Assessment of Performance Unit (APU) 38
Associated Examining Board (AEB) 49
Australia (see also South Australia) 24, 62–5
awarding process 93–8, 143–4

Baccalaureate 4
basic skills 192, 202, 222
Bayesian theory 137
behavioural objectives 37, 209, 231–2
bias in examinations 120–37
bias in reference tests 140
Bloom (see also taxonomies) 52–3, 57–60
boarding schools 195
Board of Education 8
borderlines 96, 143, 167, 178
Bryce Commission 44
Business Education Council 46

calculators, see electronic devices
capability (see also competence) 8, 22–3
certificate(s)
  currency of 222
  inflation 25, 126
  grouped 27, 61–5, 165, 186, 222
  single subject 61–3
Certificate of Prevocational Education (CPVE) 234
Certificate of Secondary Education (CSE) 23, 48–50, 61–2, 75, 79, 98, 135, 139–63, 208–9, 226, 239–40

cheating (see also invigilation)
  electronic forms of 114
China 4, 34, 41, 115
City and Guilds of London Institute (GCLI) 7, 49
chief examiners
  in examination construction 81–4
  in marking 91–3, 106
  in awarding 93–8
  in comparability research 142–5
  as repositories of "standards" 92–3, 96, 182
choice in examinations
  between boards 138–45
  between options 76–81
  between questions 77, 182
  between sections 79–80
Clarendon Commission 14
class bias in examinations 120–3
cognitive domain 116, 121–2, 153
College of Preceptors 9
common core and common element 76, 80, 213, 226–8, 239
commonality and individuality in examinations 72, 80, 118, 136, 222–3
community education 232
comparability of examinations 70, 138–64
  between boards 94–5, 138–45
  between modes 72, 157–62
  between questions 79
  between subjects 94–5, 145–54
  between syllabuses 81, 153
  over time 95, 155–7
  by cross moderation 142–4
  by reference tests 140–2, 146, 152, 160
compensation 205
competence (see also capability) 21, 116, 177, 179
competition, other forms of 12–16, 59, 180–2
competitive function of examinations 4–6, 8–9, 12–13, 19–26, 126, 166–7, 180
comprehensive schools 122–7, 239–40
concurrent assessment 75
Confederation of British Industry (CBI) 43, 46
confidential reports 187, 192, 195, 198
content of examinations 59–65
control of examinations 36–51

governmental 37–41, 224, 226
examination boards 48–50, 224–6
market forces 46–8
teacher 29, 41–6
core plus options 76–81, 213
correlation 152–3, 175
cost of examinations 20–2, 81, 105, 113, 135, 143, 160
course work 112
credit accumulation 75, 210–5, 237, 240
criteria
for marking 102–8, 142–4
for grade boundaries 96–8, 142–4
national 30, 39–40, 71
performance 38
criterion referencing and criterion-referenced (*see also* performance referencing) 122, 151, 167, 176–83, 196–7, 208–19, 225, 227, 237, 239
cross moderation 142–4
cultural bias in examinations 132–6
curriculum
core 32, 62,141, 159, 213, 226–8
dependent on examinations 224–6
engineering 11, 26–33, 60–3, 189–90, 221
entitlement 226–8
evaluation 206–8
and examination design 67–72
hidden 34
independent of examinations 228–32
modular 210–19, 237
public 226
sequential 211
validity 67–72, 105, 112, 116–7, 158, 182
vocational 233–4
curriculum vitae 191, 197

Darwinism 12–14
dependent curriculum 224–6
depth in examinations 166
"deschooling" 118
descriptive function of examinations 165–7, 180
design of examinations 67–81
diagnostic functions of examinations 190, 192, 197, 205, 215
"diploma disease" 24–5
differentiated papers 76–7
difficulty, level of (*see also* facility index and test analysis) 75–7, 108
disadvantage in examinations 64, 120–37, 197–8
discrimination between candidates 170–6

distinction certificate 239–40
distribution of marks and grades 93–4, 146, 151, 170–6
diversification and uniformity 222, 227–8
domain referencing 182
domestic and technical subjects 152–3

easy subjects, *see* hard and easy
effective domain 20–2, 116
egalitarianism and examinations, 10, 20, 120–37
Eisner 231
electronic devices in examinations
as aids to cheating 111
for clerical assistance 195
as data sources 111, 114
for marking 89, 104, 107
for communication 114, 226
elementary schools 11–12
employers and examinations 22, 46–8, 99–100, 205, 236–8
Endowed School Act 14
entitlement curriculum 226–8
entrance to higher and further education 123, 154, 186, 236–8
entry, patterns of 128–32, 140
equivalence, *see* comparability
errors in examinations 87, 91–8
essays 74, 102, 105–6, 174
ethnic minorities 132–5
evaluation of schools 99, 123–7
examination boards
constitution of 42–6
control of examinations 48–50, 224–6
curriculum influence of 33
efficiency of 87–8, 93, 98
function of 67–85, 87–100, 165–7, 223–4
future of 223–6, 237, 241
gossip about 138–9
comparability between 138–45
and records of personal achievement 189, 223
limitations of 224
examinations and the curriculum (*See also* curriculum) 9–11, 26–34, 38, 61–5, 67–72, 189, 199, 221–8
examinations, diversity and conformity 227–8
examinations, external and internal 157–62
examinations, the tension between generality and particularity 221–4
examiners
assistant 90–3
chief 81–4, 90–8, 106, 142–5, 182

external 47, 74, 94, 157–62, 230
internal 70–2, 74, 94, 157–62
meetings of 91–3
reports of 90
training of 83
Exeter Committee 11

facility index 75
fairness and examinations (*see also* comparability) 120–137, 138–64
fixed response questions (*see also* objective tests) 104–5
Football Association 16
fragmentation of examinations 210–15
free-response questions 105–6, 228
Further Education Curriculum Review and Development Unit (FEU) 188, 196

games competitions 12–16, 180–1
general ability (*see* ability)
General Certificate of Education (GCE) 48–50, 60–2, 75, 79, 129, 135, 139–63, 208–9, 212–4, 239–40
General Certificate of Secondary Education (GCSE) 30, 39, 48–50, 76, 80, 183, 209, 226, 238–40
General Medical Council 6
generality and individuality in examinations 221–3
grade(s) (*see also* norm referencing and criterion referencing)
awarding 93–8
boundaries 93–6
criteria 96–8, 142–4, 240
descriptions 97–8
literal and numerical 163
graded objectives and tests 122, 166, 208–10, 237
graded objectives in modern languages 209–10
grammar schools 14, 121, 239
grouped certificate 27, 61–5, 165, 186, 222

handwriting, effect of 113–4
hard and soft
boards 138–45
subjects 145–54
hay fever 129
heterogeneous and homogeneous tests 179, 203, 217–8
higher education
access to 10, 99–100, 121, 154, 186
examinations 5, 6, 47, 115
external examiners 47, 159, 230
influence on school examinations 9–11, 13
validating function 229–30
history examinations 97
homogeneous tests 179
humanities project 231–2

impression marking 105–6
independent curriculum 228–36, 241
independent schools 126, 195
independent study 212, 215
Indian Civil Service 4, 5
individualization 72, 118, 186–7
of curricula 80, 186, 222–3
of examinations 80, 222–3
of personal records 236
industry (*see also* work experience and vocational examinations) 43, 46
inscriptive medium in examinations 112–5, 117, 224
inspection 11, 37–41, 127, 229–30, 235
integration of subjects 60
internal examiners and examining 70–2, 74–5, 85, 115, 157–62, 175
interviews 236
invigilation 88–9, 111
item analysis 93, 105
item banks 113

Joint Matriculation Board 10, 39, 44, 147–54

Keeve's Report 62–4
knowledge *see* recall

leaks of examination papers 87
language examinations
English 116, 131, 135, 147, 161, 171–3, 211
second language 116, 209–10
and graded tests 209–10
and oral examinations 115–6
learning, types of 68–72
leniency/severity
between boards 138–45
in marking 91–3, 143, 152
in Mode III 157–62
level of performance 166
literacy 219, 225, 226
Local Examinations 9–11, 16, 60–2, 128, 240

Manpower Services Commission 233
mark schemes 56, 90–3, 106–8, 143, 178
marking 89–91, 102–8
criteria for 102–8

double 90, 106
electronic 89, 104, 107, 114
by impression 105–6
positive and negative 90, 104, 197
reliability of 90, 138
standardization of 91–3, 107
tough and tender 91
marks, value of 167–71
mastery learning *see* performance referencing
mathematics examinations 107, 112–7, 130–1, 134, 155–6, 171–3, 211
Mechanics Institutes 7
mean score 171
media of communication in examinations 112–8
electronic and keyboard 114
inscriptive/written 112–3, 117, 224
oral 115–6
substantive/practical 116–8
median score 167
medical examinations 89, 118
memory (*see also* recall) 53, 58
menstruation, effect on examination performance 129
middle class schools 10
minority languages 135
moderation and moderators 142–4, 154, 159–60, 199, 229
Modes 74, 135, 157–62, 229
modules and modular structure 75, 202–19, 225, 237, 240
monitor tests 140–2, 146–7
moral education 232
motivation 23–4, 121–2, 152, 161, 189
motor domain 116, 121–2
multicultural examinations 134–5
multiple choice questions *see* objective tests
music examinations 166, 209, 211

national criteria 30, 39–40, 71, 118, 135, 144, 222–3
nepotism 4, 34, 200
norm referencing 151, 167–83, 196, 237
Norwood Report 23
Nuffield Science projects 28, 42, 47, 69–70, 110
numeracy 219, 225, 226

objectives
behavioural 37, 231–2
expressive 231–2
taxonomies of 52–59, 116
and examination specifications 55–7, 65–6

objective tests 75–6, 89, 93, 98, 104–5, 107, 132, 227, 228
open-book examinations 10
Open Colleges 212
open-ended questions 105–6, 109–12
Open University 75, 186, 212
options (*see also* core plus options) 76–81, 87
oral examinations 16, 55, 57, 71, 115–6
orders of merit 166–71, 180–1, 205
organisation of curriculum and examinations 75, 81, 87, 210–7, 237
outcomes of examinations 28–31
Oxford and Cambridge 9–11, 16, 29, 60–2, 129
Oxford Certificate of Educational Achievement (OCEA) 189

parents
associations of 43–46
choice of schools 100, 125
influence of 5, 121–2
validation by 229–30
patronage 8
payment by results 7
performance referencing (*see also* criterion referencing) 97, 151, 153, 156–7, 162, 166, 177, 215, 227, 237–9
percentiles 168
personal attributes of students (*see also* records of personal achievement) 12–14, 99, 186–201
physical education 13, 16, 232
physics examinations 97
Piaget 56
political education 232
positive discrimination 181
practical work, assessment of 70–1, 74, 93, 111, 116–8, 175
preparatory committees 83–5
primary schools 79, 122
profiles, personal (*see also* records of personal achievement) 187–201
City and Guilds 196
profiling of examination results 203–8
professional institutions and examinations 6–8, 21, 229
prognostic function of examinations 20–2, 165
projects, assessment of 93
psychomotor domain, *see* motor domain
public schools 8, 14
publication of results 98–100, 205
and evaluation of schools 99, 123–7
Pupils in Profile 192, 195–6, 198
purpose of examinations 18–35, 167, 180

quartiles 168
qualification(s) 166, 169
question(s)
    choice of 77–9
    classification of 73–4, 109–12
    fixed response 104–5, 110
    free response 73, 105–6, 110
    information demanding/providing 109–12, 114
    objective 73–4, 81–3
    reviewing 84
    revising 84
    spotting 79
    stem of 108, 110
    structured 73, 81–3, 108, 110
    "take-away" 110
    writing 81–3

racial bias 132–5
Rampton Report 132–5
range of marks 170–6
ranking 175
readiness, concept of 215–7
recall (*see also* memory) 58
records of personal achievement 185–201, 238
reference tests (*see also* subject pairs analysis) 140–2, 146–7, 154, 160
references (confidential) 188, 236
regression analysis 141–2
regression to the mean 174
Regulations for Secondary Schools 39
reliability 21, 75, 90, 106, 116, 138, 142, 167, 203–4, 206
reports (*see also* records of personal achievement) 187, 192, 195, 198, 207
Revised Code 11–12, 37–8, 52
revisers of examination papers 84
revision for examinations 58, 88
Royal Institute of Chemistry 6
Royal Society of Arts 7
Royal Institute of Civil Engineers 6
Royal Society 188

scholarships 121
school(s)
    ethos/processes 124–7
    examination results 123–7
    choice of 125–7
    evaluation of 99, 123–7, 199
    reports 187
    selective and non-selective 123–7
    single sex and mixed sex 128–32
school bias in examinations 123–7

School Certificate (*see also* grouped certificate) 49, 60–1, 63, 165, 212
Schools Council 39, 42–3, 47, 70, 134, 154, 188
science examinations 28, 42, 47, 69–70, 103, 107, 110, 117, 129, 134, 147, 211
Science and Art Department 7
Scottish Council for Research in Education 188
scripts
    allocation to examiners 101
    marking of 89–91
    retention of 113, 155
    use in curriculum evaluation 206–8
Secondary Schools Examination Council 39, 49
selection for employment and further and higher education 19–26, 99–100, 154, 156, 186–9, 236–40
self-perception 19, 190
sex bias in examinations 127–132
skills 54-7, 177, 204
    basic 192, 202, 222
    communication 113
social attributes 187–201
social bias in examinations 120–37
social engineering 11, 221, 236–40
social mobility 10, 26, 121, 189
South Australia, examinations in 62–5, 154, 189
specification for examinations 55–7, 65–6
spelling 113
standard(s) 91–8, 123–4
    of performance 162, 182–3
    of aptitude or attainment 165–6
    chief examiners as repository of 91–8, 182
    comparability of (*see* comparability)
standardization
    of marking 91–3, 106
    between subjects 145–54
    between examination boards 138–45
stress in examinations 23, 88, 99, 129
structured questions 73, 81-3, 108
subject(s) 59-65
    choice of 122
    comparability between 94–5, 145–54
    criteria, *see* national criteria
    hard/easy 132, 145–54
    recognized 60–3
    status of 60-5
subject committees 68, 151, 154
subject pairs analysis 147–54
subjective marking 174
suicide and examinations 88
syllabus(es) 59–65, 78, 144–5

taxonomies of educational objectives 52–9, 116
teacher(s)
  autonomy 29, 230
  control by 29, 41–6
  control of 234–6
  function of 232–6
  future of 230–6
  marking by 89–91
  performance of 206–8, 234
  workload of 191, 195
teacher representation 41–6
teaching styles 68–72
team writing of examination questions 82–3
Technical Education Council 46
Technical and Vocational Education Initiative (TVEI) 47, 233
techniques of examining 102–19
technology examinations 31–2, 117
terminal assessment 75
"things aren't what they used to be" 155–7
timetables for examinations and schools 74, 216
trade unions 8, 43, 46
typing 114

uniformity in examinations 221–8

Union of Cheshire and Lancashire Institutes 7
university examinations (*see* higher education)
USSR 29, 115

validation
  of mode III examinations 158–9
  of non-examined curriculum 198, 229–36
validity 140, 167, 194
  curriculum 67–72, 105, 112, 116–7
  face 141
viva voce examinations 16, 57
vocational education 11, 209, 232–4

weighting within examinations 55–7, 65–6, 176, 205
working class
  bias in examinations 120–137
  competitions 15–16
  social mobility through examinations 15–16
work experience 232–4
written medium of examining 112–5, 117, 224